Praise for *Riches Among the Ruins:*

"Robert Smith has charted the deepest and darkest waters of the global financial system. His book is a great adventure story about finding opportunities in developing countries before Wall Street created the term *emerging markets*."—**David Hale, Chairman, David Hale Global Economics**

"A timely and prophetic excursion to the wilder shores of finance by one who's been there and back."—**Laurence Bergreen, author of *Over the Edge of the World: Magellan's Terrifying Circumnavigation of the Globe***

"Hopscotching the world throughout his career to find opaque financial discontinuities, Bob shares a fascinating tale of intrigue and courage. And unlike most folks in the financial markets, he was always risking his own money!"—**Peter A. Derow, Company Director and former Chairman, Institutional Investor, Inc.**

"Bob Smith, the pioneer in emerging market debt investing, shares his incredible adventures with the lucky readers who can learn so much about risk and life from this book."—**John D. Spooner, investment adviser and author of *Do You Want to Make Money or Would You Rather Fool Around?***

"Robert Smith is a true expert and pioneer in the art of investing in the emerging and submerging markets. In *Riches Among the Ruins* he takes us through a tour of fascinating cases. The lessons learned reach the worlds of finance, politics, economics and much more. Pick up a copy and enjoy!"—**Arminio Fraga, Gavea Investimentos Ltda.**

"This is one rollercoaster ride of a story. Robert Smith has bought low and sold high all over the world. He has confronted financial crises, as when he invested in Russia just before its default in 1998.

And he has given sage advice about the potential pitfalls of buying bonds in Central America, Africa, and Asia. But mostly, his country-by-country tale offer insights into the potential for all markets, and the adventures that face anyone who invests in debt-laden countries, including the United States."—**Frank Partnoy, author** *F.I.A.S.C.O. Blood in the Water on Wall Street* **and** *Infectious Greed: How Deceit and Risk Corrupted the Financial Markets*.

"Bob Smith has lived and worked in many corners of the developing world, some obscure and little known, others beautiful but nasty. He has been both a fairly conventional U.S. government official and a risk-taking entrepreneur. The book offers a taste of Bob's life, sometimes harrowing, sometimes profitable, but never boring. A great read!"—**Stephen Bosworth, Dean of the Fletcher School at Tufts University and former U.S. Ambassador**

RICHES AMONG THE RUINS
Adventures in the Dark Corners of the Global Economy

ROBERT P. SMITH
with Peter Zheutlin

WITHDRAWN
UTSA Libraries

AMACOM

AMERICAN MANAGEMENT ASSOCIATION

New York • Atlanta • Brussels • Chicago • Mexico City • San Francisco
Shanghai • Tokyo • Toronto • Washington, D.C.

Special discounts on bulk quantities of AMACOM books are available to corporations, professional associations, and other organizations. For details, contact Special Sales Department, AMACOM, a division of American Management Association, 1601 Broadway, New York, NY 10019.
Tel: 212–903–8316. Fax: 212–903–8083.
E-mail: specialsls@amanet.org
Website: www.amacombooks.org/go/specialsales
To view all AMACOM titles go to: www.amacombooks.org

Library of Congress Cataloging-in-Publication Data

Smith, Robert P., 1940–
Riches among the ruins : adventures in the dark corners of the global economy / Robert P. Smith with Peter Zheutlin.
    p.   cm.
Includes index.
ISBN-13: 978-0-8144-1060-8
ISBN-10: 0-8144-1060-X
1. Investments, Foreign—Developing countries.   2. Debts, External—Developing countries.   I. Zheutlin, Peter.   II. Title.
HG5993.S65   2009
332.67'3091724—dc22

                                                    2008035289

Printing number

10   9   8   7   6   5   4

In memory of my parents, DAVID SAUL and FRIEDA M. SMITH,
and my uncle, HORATIO MIKELS,
whose gift of his stamp collection when I was eleven years old
inspired my thirst for adventure.

CONTENTS

AUTHOR'S NOTE

MANY OF THE NAMES of individuals and institutions in this book have been changed, but all the individuals and institutions described are real. Where a pseudonym was used, it is in quotes the first time it appears in the text.

RICHES AMONG THE RUINS

INTRODUCTION

ON A SINGLE DAY in 1998, I lost $15 million in the ruins of the Russian economy. A short time before I had been a guest on a tour of Russia sponsored by MFK Renaissance, a Russian investment empire headed by Boris Jordan. He is an American-born investment banker of Russian descent. Among the country's new class of power brokers—known as the oligarchs—he is the only one born outside of Russia. The tour was by invitation only, organized for movers and shakers in the international investment community who had been invited to come see the vast potential of the new Russia and, not incidentally, it was hoped, to invest there.

I was deeply impressed, and when I returned home I added to my Russia holdings, which were already quite significant. Russia has vast natural resources and a large, well-educated population. With its powerful nuclear arsenal, a landmass that stretches across ten time zones, and its geopolitical importance, Russia was too big to fail, I thought. The international community and its financial institutions, the International Monetary Fund (IMF) and the World Bank among them, would never let the Russian economy collapse. The stakes were simply too high. Global stability and security would demand that the financial cavalry ride to the rescue on white stallions if worse ever came to worse. The IMF and the World Bank did try to ride to Russia's rescue, but I was mistaken about the possibility of the Russian economy failing.

For more than thirty years, I have made my living by creating a market for the sovereign debts of governments in what are often called, sometimes euphemistically, emerging markets or, sometimes, third-world countries. I've made and lost tens of millions of dollars by investing in the world's most derelict and downtrodden economies: economies racked by war or revolution, where inflation has run amok or corruption and greed sap the economic lifeblood out of an entire nation; economies battered by bullets and bandits. I like to think I know what I am doing.

I certainly thought so when, giddy with the potential I saw in Russia, I bought $9 million in Russian government bonds for Turan Corporation, the company I founded in the 1970s to trade in emerging market debt. I was so swept away by Russia's promise that I invested several million of my own money in Russian bonds and other debt instruments as well. But when the Russian government defaulted on its foreign debt obligations on August 17, 1998, the value of Russian paper in my accounts plummeted instantaneously by nearly 80 percent. Never has money disappeared so fast.

In retrospect, it was all foreseeable. Throughout my career I have thrived on making instinctive decisions, but in this case my instincts were wrong—temporarily, at least. I didn't panic. I held on and even bought more Russian paper, which was now selling for next to nothing. By 2001, I had not only recouped my losses, but made a nice sum, though not before losing a lot of sleep.

A headline in *Forbes* magazine once declared, "Indiana Jones, Meet Bob Smith." Some called me the King of Jungle Bonds, and others credited me with contributing significantly to the birth of the debt market and "possibly even to the entire emerging market investment community, well ahead of Wall Street's more prominent houses."* I rather like the Indiana Jones image, though I am not as

---

*Peter Marber, *From Third World to World Class: The Future of Emerging Markets in the Global Economy* (New York: Perseus Books, 1998), 231.

prepossessing a presence as Harrison Ford in his fedora and Territory Ahead wardrobe. Indeed, if you passed me on the street, you might mistake me for the small-time collections lawyer I was in my youth. Indiana Jones searched for riches among ancient ruins. I search for riches among modern-day economic ruins. Along the way, the adventures have been many and Hollywood couldn't begin to invent some of the characters I have thrown my lot in with. It's been a unique education in human nature and the nature of the global economy we live in today.

In the opening of his insightful book *The Lexus and the Olive Tree*, *New York Times* columnist Thomas L. Friedman describes how the sudden devaluation of the *baht*, Thailand's currency, in December 1997, set off a global economic panic sometimes referred to as the Asian flu. Russia's default was indirectly related to the Asian flu, which triggered a dramatic loss of confidence in emerging markets. Friedman's point was that today's highly integrated global economy is like a single ecosystem in which a small change in one seemingly remote place can trigger a series of unexpected changes in all parts of the global economic ecosystem. Or, as some described it, Thailand sneezed and the world caught a cold. The devaluation of the baht was akin to the proverbial butterfly that flaps its wings somewhere in western Africa, triggering a tiny perturbation in the environment that eventually leads to a massive hurricane that strikes the United States.

Yet, what happened to the global economy following the devaluation of the Thai baht was more of a psychological phenomenon than an economic one. Markets are supposed to be extremely efficient processors of vast amounts of information that result, ultimately, in rational economic outcomes. But people, the millions of us who every day make large and small financial decisions, are not rational. We are creatures prone to excesses of both pessimism and optimism. We are emotional. And emotions, especially contagious emotions like excessive pessimism and excessive optimism ("irrational exuberance," as Alan Greenspan once famously called it), move markets all the time.

In *The Lexus and the Olive Tree*, Friedman, while often explaining the global economy at street level, also takes a bird's-eye view, especially as he describes the huge amounts of capital that rush across international boundaries daily like huge tsunamis. I surf those perilous tsunamis, and the view in this book is sometimes from the crest of a tsunami. But because I, too, am human and prone to irrational exuberance from time to time (as happened with my investments in Russia), sometimes my perspective is from the beach, after the wave has crashed ashore, leaving me bedraggled, alone, and a good deal poorer.

Economic bottom feeder? I've been called that and worse. I call it opportunism, and while my motives were and are financial, what I've done has sometimes provided bankrupt governments with a light at the end of the tunnel. As for me personally, I have used the riches I have found among the ruins to build a theater and arts center at my high school alma mater, the Roxbury Latin School in West Roxbury, Massachusetts; to build a new student center at my college alma mater, Bowdoin College in Maine; to renovate a synagogue in Bath, Maine, my mother's hometown; and to set up a foundation to support research in mental illness, specifically schizophrenia. This isn't an excuse or a rationalization for wealth. At the end of the day, it's about doing well and doing good, and in my view everyone who has done well has an obligation to do good.

In this book, I will take you to some of the most dangerous countries on earth: dangerous economically and, quite often, dangerous physically. In my search for riches among the ruins I often have taken great personal risks, traveling to places where violence is always at your elbow and Americans are not always welcome. Debt traders like me do business where you have to hold on to your wallet and your life. It's not for the faint of heart.

What is a debt trader? The young Turks, the "Masters of the Universe" as Tom Wolfe called them in *The Bonfire of the Vanities*, the "Big Swinging Dicks" as Michael Lewis called them in *Liar's Poker*, who sit at bond-trading desks on Wall Street. They are one species of debt trader because bonds, simply put, are debt obligations of corporations and governments.

I am a rarer subspecies of debt trader than those who spend their days on the telephone in a New York office tower. I specialize in trading the debts of governments in the darkest corners of the global economy, the so-called second and third tier credit countries on the borderline of default or in urgent need of rescheduling their debt. In my heyday, to do my job, whether in Guatemala, Russia, Nigeria, or other developing countries, I had to be "boots on the ground," as they say in the military. I had to pound the pavement and ingratiate myself with the people, many unsavory, who mattered when it comes to doing the business I do. I had to make connections. I often had to risk flights on substandard airlines, stay in no-star hotels, and eat strange food. I sometimes had to dodge bullets and shake down artists. It's hard work compared to sitting at a trading desk in New York, but I don't have the attention span to sit long at a desk. In Yiddish parlance, I have *shpilkes*, which, roughly translated, means "ants in the pants." I'm restless and I love to travel. I have craved adventure in exotic places ever since I was eleven and my uncle gave me an album filled with colorful stamps from countries in all corners of the world. In my small room in my parents' home in Brookline, Massachusetts, I would look up those countries in the *World Book Encyclopedia* and dream of seeing the world someday.

Before I get too far along in my story, let's have a crash course in some basic economics. Much of what I do is esoteric, understood by only a handful of financiers. I traded in obscure economic instruments such as Turkish nonguaranteed trade arrears. Few people have even heard of them. And every year, clever people think up new and ever more complicated financial instruments. You can even trade global warming futures today.

To appreciate this book, however, you don't need to be a Nobel economist or a Harvard MBA, because no matter how obscure the financial instrument, to be successful in the global economy you need, first and foremost, to understand people. And primarily this is a book about people, not Turkish nonguaranteed trade arrears. But it will help to understand some basics.

When a corporation, whether it's a garage-based start-up or a powerhouse such as Google, wants to raise capital (money), it basically has two choices. First, it can sell shares. There's no guarantee the shares will go up, of course, and when you buy a share you agree to go along for the ride, for better or for worse, until you sell the share or the company goes bankrupt. (This is a vast oversimplification, but there's a method to the madness here.) The company owes you nothing. There is no promise to pay you anything in return for your investment.

The second choice when a company needs money is to borrow it. There are many ways to borrow money—bank loans and lines of credit, for example. But the company can also go out into the marketplace and borrow money from anyone who wants to be a lender. When you buy, say, a General Motors corporate bond, you and every other purchaser of GM bonds is, essentially, a lender. (Never mind the admonition "neither a borrower nor a lender be"; most of us are both.) The bond represents a debt that GM owes to you and everyone else who holds a GM bond. And, just like a bank, you aren't going to lend your money to GM for nothing. You buy a bond because GM promises to pay you back the original loan amount plus a stream of interest along the way. You see, any Tom, Dick, or Harry can become GM's bank, or more precisely, one of GM's banks, just by buying one of its bonds. A bond, simply put, is a debt obligation, a promise, of the issuer, in this case GM. You are the lender and GM is the borrower.

Governments, too, need money to operate and they, too, for our simplified purposes, have two ways to raise money. One is very different from the way corporations raise money. It's taxes. Whether on income, estates, sales of goods, imports, cigarettes, or profits, taxes are one way governments raise money to pay their soldiers, pave the roads, provide social security for the elderly, and perform the countless functions we depend on governments to perform. (Governments can also just print money, and when they print money willy-nilly to cover their costs, the risk of inflation increases.)

The other way governments raise capital is the same way corporations do: Governments issue bonds, or borrow. They borrow money just like corporations: from you and me and, often, from huge buyers such as pension funds, insurance companies, and college endowment funds that buy their bonds. And they borrow from other countries. The government of China, for example, has purchased billions of dollars in U.S. government bonds, in essence lending the United States operating capital. China thinks it's a good bet. The Chinese government is confident it will get back both its principal and a tidy sum of interest because it is confident the United States can, and will, pay its debts. Historically, that's been a good bet. The implications of the United States of America being so deeply in debt to China are enormous. If China and other large holders of U.S. debt, such as Japan, suddenly decided that betting on the United States government to make good on its debts was a bad idea, we'd be in very, very deep trouble.

Governments may also issue bonds, payable in dollars, to encourage foreign investment or to settle trade supplier debt. If Ford Motor Company is going to build a plant and sell cars in Mexico, for example, it wants to be sure there will be a way to convert its peso profits into dollars. Dollar-denominated bonds give foreigners a way to take profits made in local currencies and turn them into dollars. Whether the government issuing the bonds can make good on its promise to pay its bondholders in dollars is where the risk lies.

The debts of corporations and governments take countless forms, but the principle is the same. Debts, or more precisely, debt instruments such as bonds, promissory notes, and commercial trade claims, are promises to pay money at a future date. How good that promise is—how reliable the borrower is—determines the level of risk. You can pretty much be assured that the U.S. government is going to repay its debts (it has the power to print dollars and levy taxes to get the money to pay those debts and is relatively efficient at doing so, despite billions of dollars of tax fraud every year). That the government of, say, war-ravaged Iraq or politically unstable Afghanistan will be able to repay its debts is less certain. And, typically, the higher the risk, the higher the promised rate of return.

Simply put, what I do, and what my company, Turan Corporation, does, is buy various forms of government debt (also called sovereign debt) in the world's battered economies. We buy promises. And we make money by holding those promises or reselling them at a markup to third parties who will assume the risk that those debts will someday be paid or, at the very least, think (as we did) that someone else will pay even a bit more for those debts at some point in the future. We buy from sellers who may have given up hope of being paid and are eager to recoup some of their losses—sellers who would rather have something than nothing. We either hold the debt until better times or sell immediately to buyers willing to assume the risk. We buy from the pessimists and sell to the optimists.

If the fortunes of the debt issuer take a turn for the better it's a good buy, because the chances are improved that the debt will be repaid with interest, making the debt more valuable to the person holding it. If the issuer's fortunes take a turn for the worse, the holder of the debt may lose all or part of his investment. Trading debt can be a bit like the childhood game of hot potato. You don't want to be the one holding the potato when the bottom falls out.

When I bought and sold my first Turkish trade arrears in the early

1980s—my initial foray into debt trading—the global trade in the sovereign debt of emerging market countries was probably less than $300 million a year. It was a niche business back then. Today, more than $1.7 *trillion* worth of such debt is traded annually.

My big trading days are over. The globalization of the market and the availability of information rapidly transmitted electronically has made the business much less lucrative than it used to be when no one had a clue what value to attach to a Nigerian promissory note or an El Salvador bond. But it was a hell of a run, filled with vibrant characters and cockamamy schemes that, even today, seem incredible, even though I thought up some of them myself.

In the early days, before computerization allowed the price of a bond to be posted worldwide within seconds of a trade, I thrived on the lack of transparency in the market, making a considerable fortune in the process. Unlike today's bond traders, who sit at desks in New York, London, and Hong Kong staring at computer screens and screaming into telephones, my business required that I travel into the darkest reaches of the world's fledgling global economy and pound the pavements.

In this book of financial adventure I will take you to the steamy streets of El Salvador as a violent proxy war, fueled by the superpower Cold War rivalry, claimed tens of thousands of lives and battered the economy. I will take you on a magical mystery tour of the new, democratic Russia, a country so rich in opportunity that I impulsively invested, then lost, then regained a small fortune. And I will take you into the Green Zone just after the fall of Saddam Hussein, as U.S. officials struggled to right Iraq's war-torn economy.

What do these stories—which span years of development of emerging markets as a major economic force—have to teach us about the highly integrated economic world we live in today? Why should we care?

At the micro level, if you have a pension plan, own mutual funds, or have money in a retirement account, chances are some of your money is now invested in emerging markets. The endowment fund of the college you attended likely has significant exposure to such markets, too, and over the past five years your return on investments in emerging markets has averaged an astonishing 24 percent annually. Money managers and fund managers, who live for better returns, are always scouring the globe for the next big boom, and many believe that India and China, hot investments for many years, may soon run out of steam. Attention now is shifting to high-risk/high-reward economies such as Vietnam, Georgia, and Ghana.

At the macro level, in our highly integrated global economy, financial catastrophe in an emerging market country far from our shores can, under some circumstances, ripple right through our own economy with far-reaching consequences for all of us, not just those with some stake, however small, in emerging markets. The aforementioned Thailand example is one case in point. Russia's default in 1998, which triggered the collapse of a giant hedge fund, Long-Term Capital Management (LTCM), is another example. In the LTCM case, the Federal Reserve intervened and pressured major Wall Street banks to bail out LTCMs to help prevent a complete meltdown in the U.S. bond market.

In addition, U.S. foreign policy is, more than ever, economic policy. Trade disputes with China, a country that is helping to keep the U.S. Treasury afloat with massive purchases of U.S. government bonds, dominate the often-testy relationship between the two countries. The rise of Hugo Chavez in oil-rich Venezuela, where major industries, many foreign-owned, are being nationalized, presents a serious challenge to U.S. interests in Latin America, especially as Chavez finds sympathetic ears in other Latin American countries. Gordon Brown, England's prime minister, is a staunch advocate of debt forgiveness so that poor countries, especially in Africa, can try and jump-start their derelict economies without the crushing financial burden of massive foreign debt. Brown understands that the ever-widening gap between rich and poor is a major threat to global stability and security.

In short, what happens in the emerging markets matters to your pocketbook as well as to the future of the country and the world.

My thinking about the developing world and its role in the international economy began to take shape when I was a foreign service officer in Vietnam in the 1960s and later in South and Central America. It continued to evolve when I was a lone, small-time operator in the 1980s, trying to earn a buck by making a market in developing-world bonds. I wanted adventure, I wanted to see the world, and I wanted to get rich doing it. And it has continued as the nascent global economy of the 1980s became the juggernaut of late-twentieth and early-twenty-first century globalization.

For example, I saw how Salvadoran-born maids, gardeners, and taxi drivers in the United States became the major source of El Salvador's modest foreign reserves, as the thousands of small checks and money orders they sent to relatives back home began to add up. Today, more than ever, there is massive movement of human beings (each a tiny economic engine) across borders. Their movement is both a reflection of economic realities and a profound force shaping them. Today's bitter and crucial debate over immigration policy has its roots in this phenomenon. Jobs, too, as Americans are acutely aware, are now far more exportable as well. To the detriment of the American worker, emerging market countries—India and China, most notably—have been a sponge for jobs that once existed here. In the global economy, the United States is squeezed on both sides of the labor equation: Migrant workers fill many low-skilled jobs even as other low-skilled and even blue- and white-collar jobs go overseas.

There have been other important changes since my early trading days that reflect the far-reaching impact of globalization. My business in Turkey, El Salvador, and Guatemala was sometimes based on the need for foreign companies doing business there to convert profits, earned in the local currency, into dollars; at other times the need was for governments to pay for imports in hard currency. Today, El Salvador has solved this problem for foreign businesses, and for itself, by adopting the U.S. dollar as the official currency, as Panama and Ecuador have done. As a result, those countries are far more attractive to foreign investors and there's a major positive impact on their economies.

In Turkey, I observed how the country tried to bolster its chronically struggling economy with elaborate debt/equity swaps that sought to convert the nation's trade debts owed to foreign firms into equity investments in domestic projects. Today, as was the case in the early 1980s when I did business there, the country's secular military is warily eyeing a more fundamentalist Muslim prime minister and Turkey's revolving door of civilian governments overthrown by military coup could continue. This is one factor that makes Turkey such a high-risk/high-reward emerging market play.

Little did I know when I was running around Guatemala City and San Salvador in my $99 suit and carrying a briefcase stuffed with millions of dollars of bonds, or trading Turkish debts, that I was an advance man for the forces of globalization. But those early dealings were, in fact, a harbinger of big changes to come.

For more than three decades—decades that just happened to be the most intensive period of globalization in human history—I've been an eyewitness to that process in places few others have ventured to go. I have a unique perspective on how the process of global economic integration has played out in the remote niches of the global economy. In each chapter of this book, there are lessons to be learned about human nature and about the complex new world in which we live. Those lessons are sometimes profound, sometimes not. But in each chapter, hopefully, you will deepen your knowledge about the world and the times in which we live. That may seem a grandiose claim, but every time I travel for business I learn something new, and I try to share it in this book. That way, the next time a baht falls in Thailand, you will not only hear about it, but understand why it could affect you.

CHAPTER 1

EL SALVADOR

Bullets, Bombs, and Bonds

ON MARCH 24, 1980, Oscar Romero, the popular archbishop of San Salvador, delivered a sermon in which he issued a desperate plea to the Salvadoran military. "In the name of God," said Romero, "stop the repression." Just a few moments later, Romero, an outspoken advocate for El Salvador's poor and dispossessed, stepped into the sunlight in San Salvador's main square and was assassinated by gunshot, a victim of the right-wing death squads that operated at the behest of El Salvador's U.S.-backed military. Three days later, the U.S. House Appropriations Committee approved $5.7 million in new military aid to El Salvador.

Romero's assassination was one of the most infamous acts of right-wing violence in El Salvador's brutal civil war, a war that raged from the late 1970s through the 1980s, but it was hardly the only one. In May 1980, 600 Salvadoran peasants trying to flee to Honduras were killed by Salvadoran and Honduran troops. In December of that same year, three American nuns and a Catholic lay social worker were raped, shot, and buried thirty miles from San Salvador. In early January 1981, two American land reform advisers were shot and killed at the San Salvador Sheraton Hotel. And countless Salvadorans disappeared as well.

The Marxist rebels that flourished amid El Salvador's poverty and social inequality waged a guerilla war from the countryside and inflicted pain of their own, often targeting symbols of American power and capitalism. Under the banner of the FMLN, or Farabundo Marti National Liberation Front, the guerillas staged a series of bombings of banks and businesses. In late March 1981, the San Salvador offices of Citibank were destroyed when a blast ripped through an eighteen-story office building across from the Camino Real Hotel. A few years later, in June 1985, FMLN gunmen opened fire at a restaurant in San Salvador's popular Zona Rosa district, killing four U.S. Marines and nine Salvadorans. The murder and the mayhem went on and on, which is why El Salvador in the mid-1980s was such a perfect place to do business.

I was already familiar with the country when I began creating a market for El Salvador government bonds during this period. In 1970, after an eighteen-month stint in Vietnam as a young financial officer stationed at the U.S. Embassy in Saigon by the U.S. Agency for International Development (USAID), I was sent by USAID to Washington, D.C., for intensive Spanish-language training, then briefly to the Dominican Republic where I made loans on behalf of the U.S. government to state and private enterprises. From there, I went to El Salvador to assist in the writing of agricultural loans to the Salvadoran government.

The two years I spent in Vietnam (the subject of Chapter 2) at the height of the Vietnam War satisfied an urge I had harbored since childhood: to escape from the narrow confines of my middle-class Jewish upbringing in Brookline, Massachusetts, and to see the world.

My parents both hailed from small towns in Maine; my father from Patten, an hour and a half north of Bangor, and my mother from Bath, a shipbuilding town on the Kennebec River. My grandfather, Aaron, moved his family to the Dorchester section of Boston when my father, David, was in high school. My father returned to Maine to attend Bowdoin College, then came back to Boston with my mother, Frieda, to attend Boston University Law School. My parents aspired to nothing more than middle-class Jewish respectability and achieved it through my father's work as a collections lawyer. For me, their only son, they had one goal: to turn me into a replica of my father. With their small-town Maine roots, they had achieved all they ever could have imagined, financially and socially. Life was good, indeed perfect, and they wanted the same for me. It was inconceivable to them that I could do any better than my father did, or that I should even want to try, or that there was much of interest in the world beyond the banks of the Charles River. They never traveled outside the United States. A picnic atop Mount Desert Island in Maine was their biggest adventure.

In 1958, during my senior year at the prestigious Roxbury Latin School, which sent an astonishing number of graduates to Harvard (and all ambitious, middle-class Jewish boys from Boston were supposed to aspire to Harvard), my father informed me that he would only pay for me to attend college on the condition that I attend either Harvard or Bowdoin. Roxbury Latin was called the "marine camp of the mind" by some, as rigorous and demanding as any high school in the country. I worked my tail off there, but despite my efforts I didn't distinguish myself as a scholar; I was wait-listed at Harvard (I'm still waiting) and had no choice but to pack my bags for Maine. An all-male college in the middle of frigid Maine wasn't exactly what I had hoped for, not only because the chances of having a sex life at an all-male college in Brunswick, Maine, were slim to none, but also because I could see myself headed already for life as a carbon copy of David Saul Smith. My parents were thrilled.

Once I had graduated from Bowdoin in 1962 and, like my father, from Boston University Law School, class of 1965, my first departure from the path my parents had in mind for me was enlisting for the tour of duty with USAID in Vietnam from 1968 to 1969. I was willing to do virtually anything to avoid going into law practice with my father. Why their son preferred to head for a war zone rather than join his father in a law office in Boston doing collections work for clients such as *The Boston Globe* was beyond my parents' comprehension. "What's a nice Jewish boy like you doing in a place like Vietnam?" they would ask. I doubt they ever realized that it was that stamp collection my uncle, my mother's brother, gave me when I was eleven that set me on a course to Southeast Asia. Night after night in our Brookline home I would close the door to my bedroom and pore over the stamps my uncle had collected from exotic places all over the world—tiny island nations in the South Pacific, the great powers of Europe, African kingdoms—and ache to see some world beyond the grasp of David and Frieda Smith.

I have traveled obsessively and extensively all my adult life, but it was Vietnam in the late 1960s that established what would become a lifelong pattern of looking for riches among the ruins. From the relative safety of sultry Saigon, my colleagues at USAID and I would study local currency valuations and venture out into the countryside, often hitching rides on military flights, to write obscure reports about the rice crop or the Vietnamese labor force, even though many of us had virtually no formal training in economics. We would smoke cigarettes, and not infrequently pot, while banging out our reports on Smith Corona typewriters by day, the humid air and nonstop noise of Saigon's busy streets wafting through the windows. At night, like moths to a flame, we hit Saigon's infamous nightspots on the Rue Catinat, drinking heavily and making nonsensical conversation with the Vietnamese girls who gave us the privilege of plying them with "Saigon tea," drinks that we were not supposed to know contained no alcohol. I had little money and was known to many of the girls as "Cheap Charlie No. 10," ten being at the bottom of the barrel. Life abroad was even better than the stamp collection had suggested, so when my tour ended in Vietnam, I was ready for more.

It was more than a decade before I traded my first El Salvador bond, in 1985. But it was a decade earlier that I first traveled to El Salvador. It was a small, peaceful, lush country where Americans could travel without fear. The revolutionary fervor that swept Cuba when Castro overthrew Batista in the late 1950s, and that soon spread to other Central American countries, had not yet touched Salvador. Unlike neighboring Guatemala, El Salvador was stable and its people struck me as gentle, if not docile, given the poverty in which most of them lived. Beneath the surface, however, trouble lurked. A handful of powerful families controlled the country with their vast wealth. It would only be a matter of time until this fundamental injustice would erupt, as it did, into civil war.

During my six months in El Salvador, I traveled nearly every mile of the country, which isn't difficult since Salvador is slightly smaller than Massachusetts. You could drive the length and breadth of the country in a matter of hours had the Massachusetts Turnpike been relocated there. I soaked up as much of the ethos of the place as I could, meeting as many people as I could, so when I returned to Salvador in the early 1980s, amid the murder and mayhem of the civil war, I was well equipped to do what I came to do—create a market where none existed for El Salvador bonds, the sovereign debt obligations of the government. I was on familiar ground.

When my USAID work in El Salvador ended in 1971, I went back to Washington, D.C., and studied Portuguese at the State Department's Foreign Language Institute. Then I moved to Brazil, still on assignment for USAID, and later, in 1973, went to work for Deltec Bank in Sao Paulo. Deltec at that time was a pioneer among international banks in making loans to Latin American governments, and it was at Deltec where I began to learn a thing or two about the complexities of emerging-market lending.

It was an eventful three years in Brazil. I met my Brazilian-Lebanese wife, Salua, there, in an elevator, in 1971, and received what I like to call my "Harvard Business School education" at the hands of an international fugitive I had fallen into business with (more on this experience in Chapter 7). When that business failed, I felt I had no choice but to return to Boston, where I succumbed to the pressure to join my father in his law practice. We lasted all of three months together in 1975. He was paying me $125 a week. I hated the work and my father was overbearing. I thought I would go insane. I'd come home to Salua and say, "I can't take this. Maybe we should go back to Brazil." I always thought Salua's mother was pushing for us to return to the States because I could make more money there. But, in Brazil, I would be far outside my parents' sphere of influence. Brazil was exotic, the beaches beautiful, and the women more so. I could have lived happily ever after in Brazil.

I quickly left my father's practice and started my own, still doing collections, in an office I rented from my father. It wasn't a big move, but any distance I could put between my father and me was a distance I was willing to travel.

As soon as I was able, I moved to offices of my own. I used several tricks to create the impression that my little collections practice was an empire so that I would attract ever larger and more prestigious clients. The name of the firm was on the door, Smith, Levenson & Smith (I still used the name of my father's firm, with his assent), but I also had nameplates made for a handful of real and bogus enterprises that were part of the Robert Smith empire—Katanga Mining Corporation of Zaire, Leme Trust (a trust I created to hold my flat on Beacon Street), and the Urca Trust, to name a few. I also scheduled all of my appointments for four o'clock in the afternoon so that when clients came to the office the waiting room was always filled with people, creating the impression I was in great demand. Sometimes you have to fake it in order to make it. My mother was unimpressed. "You're not half the man your father is," she would say.

By 1976, my collections practice was growing and I detested every minute of it. The collection agencies that hired the collection lawyers got rich as middlemen, a lesson that wasn't lost on me. They'd charge clients 35 percent of any debts they collected, but had schmucks like me do the real work for a cut of 20 percent. On a $1,000 debt, they'd make $150 just for passing the work along. When we collected, the collection agencies looked like geniuses to their clients who had no idea who was really doing the labor.

To get business, I joined the Commercial Law League of America and attended its convention in Chicago that year, a giant schmooze-fest of collection lawyers and agencies looking for love. It was mid-winter and freezing, and I decided to hustle the Chicago collection agencies directly by going to their offices, about fifteen of them, all congregated on a street near the Loop. To save money, which I had precious little of in those days, I walked the two or three miles from my hotel in a stiff icy wind, struggling to hang on to my briefcase with one hand and my toupee with the other (I ditched the toupee years ago), smoking a cigarette every five minutes. "This is what my life has come to?" I thought. "I should kill myself!"

Ironically, it was through my collections practice that I eventually found my talent for making money in derelict economies when I was hired by a collection agency to collect a debt owed by a Turkish firm. We'll come to how I started in the debt trading business in Turkey in Chapter 3, but for now, suffice it to say that buying and then selling foreign debt obligations—trade claims and bonds—was something I had already done successfully, first in Turkey and later in Guatemala, before returning to El Salvador in 1984.

El Salvador in the 1980s was ripe for the picking for a lone operator like me for two reasons. First, for the large institutions we normally associate with investment banking, bond trading, and the
like—the Citibanks, Chase Manhattans, and Merrill Lynches of the
world—the money to be made in the relatively modest amounts of
bonds issued by a country such as El Salvador is miniscule. When the
big boys saw me running around San Salvador trying to make a deal
they thought it was a joke. At first, I thought they might be right.
But I was happy to pick up the crumbs they wouldn't touch.

Second, your typical banker usually isn't keen to stay in hotels
where foreigners are shot, or to work in office buildings that are
blown up. Sitting behind a glass door that says Citibank on the front
and handing out business cards that identify you as a vice president of
Citibank in a country with a deadly leftist insurgency is like putting a
bull's-eye on your back. In short, for the big guys, El Salvador was
high risk, low return. For me, a solo practitioner in a $99 seersucker
suit from Filene's Basement and a bad toupee, the risk to life and limb
was lower and the returns, which looked like the five-cent deposits on
soda cans to Citibank, looked pretty good to me. Indeed, in the mid-
1980s, when I started traveling to El Salvador on business about twice
a month, I returned home each time with not less than $100,000
profit in my pocket. Those are pretty good crumbs.

One of the biggest challenges for foreign companies doing business in the developing world is how to convert profits made in local
currencies into dollars or another hard currency (for simplicity, we'll
speak of dollars). In El Salvador in the 1980s, every foreign company
operating there had this problem and by helping them solve it, I
made myself a very nice sum.

Today, El Salvador, like Panama and Ecuador, has a "dollarized"
economy; the U.S. dollar *is* the local currency.* But, before globaliza-

---

*In theory, adopting the U.S. dollar as the local currency, according to the Council
on Hemispheric Affairs, "provides a form of financial measurement for countries
prone to erratic economic policies. Dollarization affords them the discipline and

tion forced the liberalization of currency and capital controls in much of the world, countries such as El Salvador issued their own currency (the *colon* in El Salvador's case) and by law made that currency the only legal tender for settling debts and paying for goods and services. This meant that everyone who received payments from abroad had to sell his hard, or convertible, currency to the Central Bank in exchange for the local currency, and anyone who wanted hard currency had to buy it, again at the legally fixed rate, from the Central Bank. Commonly, as was the case in El Salvador, the exchange rate is artificially low.

Predictably, when an exchange rate is set by fiat and not by the market, people with hard currency try to hide it wherever they can— under mattresses, in the walls of their homes, or in overseas bank accounts. They don't want to be forced to sell at the government's clip-joint rates. Conversely, everyone who has large amounts of the local currency and wants dollars has to buy them, by law, from the Central Bank. In theory, this situation should be good for the buyer of dollars because the exchange rate is artificially low. But there's a catch. To prevent a run on the Central Bank's limited dollar reserves (and in countries like El Salvador, the reserves were almost always negligible), the bank set strict limits on how many dollars you could buy over a certain time period and for what purposes, such as travel abroad. The Central Bank of El Salvador's foreign reserves were tiny because there's only so much coffee and sugar to export to the United States, and when a country's imports far exceed its exports, its balance of payments is negative and it doesn't have large amounts of foreign currency to exchange. This might not be a problem if the local currency printed by the government was backed by hard cur-

---

financial credibility necessary to attract foreign investment and the stability to effectively be integrated into global markets. Dollarization also reduces the transaction costs associated with currency conversion for poor South American countries." But countries that dollarize their economies also give up part of their sovereignty.

rency reserves, but typically, governments in developing countries just print money haphazardly to pay their bills. So, in a place like El Salvador, you'd have huge amounts of colones, the local currency, chasing a very limited supply of dollars. That's why black currency markets spring up. People who can't get dollars from the Central Bank at the fixed rate start shopping elsewhere, even if it's going to cost them more in the local currency to buy a dollar. They go where the supply is. And that's what I did, too, as we will see.

It's not just Mom and Pop who are affected by currency and capital controls. Foreign companies doing business in El Salvador, such as British American Tobacco (BAT), had a problem as well. BAT sold cigarettes throughout El Salvador and ended up with huge sums in colones that were virtually worthless outside of the country. So what is BAT to do? It can reinvest some of its colones locally and pay its local suppliers and workers in colones, which it did. But BAT is not in business in El Salvador to get rich in colones. If it can't convert all those colones to dollars at the Central Bank—because the bank doesn't have sufficient foreign reserves—and the sums are too large to exchange on the black market (not to mention illegal), how can BAT get dollars for its colones and bring its profits home?

To give companies a way to get their money out, governments often issue bonds payable, with interest, in dollars (they are called "dollar-denominated" bonds). That's what the government of El Salvador did. In the case of El Salvador, five-year bonds (that is, bonds that mature and are fully paid in five years) were paying 12 percent interest and, unlike many foreign bonds, regular principal and interest payments were being made. Companies like BAT buy the bonds from the government using colones (at the legal, or fixed, exchange rate) as payment and in return get a piece of paper that says the government will pay, over time, a certain sum in dollars with interest along the way.

The $64,000 question, of course, is whether that promise to pay is worth the paper it's printed on. Therein lies the risk and, thus, the potential market for the fiscal promises of the government of El

Salvador. After all, where is the government of El Salvador going to get the dollars to pay the bondholders? And since the government of El Salvador can't issue bonds endlessly without undermining faith that those bonds will be paid as promised, there's only a certain amount of them to go around. That's where I came in.

Simply put, I found companies that had purchased dollar-denominated El Salvador bonds with their profits and now, because they needed or wanted cash ("to monetize their profits," as we say in the business), or because the home office in London or New York wanted to improve its balance sheet, wanted to sell them. And I found buyers willing to buy them. Buyers would buy because they, too, needed to covert colones into dollars and believed the government of El Salvador would eventually make good on its promises or, at the very least, because they thought this was their best shot at some day getting dollars for their colones. (Some of the corporate finance strategies behind the decision to buy and sell were more complex than this, but for our purposes, this example will suffice.)

I was the classic middleman. I made my money on the spread: the difference between the price that the seller was willing to sell his bonds to me and the price a buyer was willing to pay. But how does one guy from Boston create a market for an instrument where none exists? The key is *chutzpah*.

Today, with the Internet connecting markets all over the world in real time, you could never do what I did in El Salvador in the 1980s. Services such as Reuters and Bloomberg track virtually every offer to buy or sell virtually every financial instrument in the world. If you wanted to buy an El Salvador bond today, you'd call your broker and get a quote based on the latest buy and sell orders listed on the Bloomberg screen. You'd know exactly what the market deems the value of an El Salvador bond to be at any given point in time. Your broker may not have the bond in his inventory, but she can access the inventory of every brokerage firm in the world and procure it for you.

In the mid-1980s, no one had any idea what an El Salvador bond was worth—which is to say, they had no idea what value others might attach to it. This ignorance, this information vacuum, was my bliss. The seller's price was simply a measure of how desperately he wanted to dispose of a paper promise of the government of El Salvador and the buyer's measure of how eager he was to convert his local currency into a glimmer of hope of seeing dollars down the road. The spread, my profit, was the difference between the two. In a fledgling market, with no reporting mechanisms and precious little information floating around, the spread can be enormous, and there were no regulatory or legal restrictions on how much you could make on such a transaction. Though my sellers and buyers, usually the representatives of foreign companies doing business in El Salvador, often knew each other, played golf together, or broke bread together at American Chamber of Commerce breakfasts, I knew it would take some time before they eventually started to compare notes. At the beginning, I doubt any of them even mentioned they were trying to sell or buy El Salvador bonds because the market didn't exist yet. But until the market matured it was a gold rush, and I developed a monopoly on that most precious of all commodities in any market: information. I found out who wanted to sell, who wanted to buy, and their price, and I held that information very tight to the vest.

When I returned to El Salvador in 1984, more than a decade since my stint there as a USAID loan officer, the country had changed dramatically. San Salvador had a new, modern airport, but the strong military and security presence there was the first visible evidence that the country was no longer the peaceable backwater that had charmed me in 1970. I knew, of course, that the country was in the grips of a vicious civil war—it was one reason I saw such great opportunity there—but it was sad to see. At the time, I was apolitical; the politics of the war, and of the U.S. role in it, were of no interest to me. I was an economic mercenary happy to live off of El Salvador's woes. Today, though I have made millions of dollars as a capitalist, philosophically and politically I believe that the great concentration of wealth in the hands of a few, and the widening gap between rich and poor, is unjust and breeds precisely the kind of violence that ravaged El Salvador in the 1980s.

The country was nearly devoid of tourists, rich Salvadorans were waiting out the conflict from the comfort of Miami condominiums, leaving their business interests in the hands of hired help, and fear was everywhere. In 1970, an American had nothing to fear in El Salvador. In 1984, every American had to fear for his life. Those who came to work with Salvador's poor were at the mercy of right-wing death squads, and those representing U.S. government or business interests were at the mercy of left-wing rebels. I did everything I could to be innocuous. I wore my cheap suits, I took taxis, never a hired car, and when asked, I usually told people I was from Canada. I tried to be the invisible man.

My first task was to try to locate or create a list of the holders of El Salvador's dollar-denominated bonds. In a tiny country like El Salvador, government institutions are less formidable than, say, the United States Treasury Department with its legions of employees and endless layers of bureaucracy, so it was not as difficult as you might think to walk into the Central Bank and ask for an appointment with its president. I spoke decent Spanish. A little Spanish and a little charm can go a long way, and I never had to ask for that appointment because I got what I wanted from a male secretary guarding the bank president's office.

San Salvador was and is, in many ways, a small town with a handful of business centers. Early one morning I was shaken out of bed in the wee hours by an explosion at the Sheraton Hotel, a short distance away from the Camino Real Hotel where I was staying. I put on my rumpled suit, stepped out into the steamy heat of the capital, and congratulated myself on having had the good sense not to have booked a room at the Sheraton. As I stepped out of the air-conditioned hotel, my glasses fogged up immediately and I hailed a cab. I looked like Mr. Magoo.

Every taxicab in El Salvador was a parody of itself. The driver invariably had photographs of his wife and children plastered everywhere except the front mirror, from which hangs a likeness of the Madonna. A plastic Jesus adorned the dashboard. (Salvador is a predominantly Catholic country.) The exhaust system, if it were still attached to the car, would be nonfunctional. And the radio either didn't work or was turned up to excruciating volume, which never stopped the driver from kibitzing endlessly. "Big baseball fan." "My sister lives in California. Do you know her?" "How do you like El Salvador?" However, in four decades of doing business, I have always learned something of value from cab drivers about the local economy. They are on the front lines, literally, and can tell you about the cost of living and whether foreigners are plentiful or scarce. Many cabbies have offered keen political insight as well. In societies with high unemployment, a lot of smart people are driving taxicabs.

Even at five feet nine inches, I found the backseat of the tiny Ford taxi cramped. My knees were bent up under my chin and my briefcase was clutched under my arms as we took off for the short trip to the Central Bank.

If it wasn't the Bedford Falls Savings and Loan, the Central Bank of El Salvador wasn't exactly the Bank of England, either. Sitting at a small desk outside the office of the bank president I found "Manuel Garcia," a small, proper young man crisply dressed in white shirt and slacks. I introduced myself and asked, in Spanish, if I could sit down for a minute. It was hot out, I explained, and I needed a breather.

"I would like to make an appointment to see the president," I said, smiling an ingratiating smile.

"What is the nature of your business, Mr. Smith? Why do you need to see the president? He's quite busy, as I'm sure you understand. Perhaps I can help you."

Most Salvadoran men smoke, so I offered a cigarette, which Manuel readily accepted. Never underestimate the power of schmoozing. The real power in any office lies with the secretaries and assistants whose job it is to keep the boss organized and to insulate them from unwanted visitors like me. Generally, given the chance, most people like to talk about themselves and their families. From the photograph on his desk I could see that Manuel had a young family, as did I.

"Your younger son looks about the age of my son in Boston," I said. "What's his name?"

We spent a few minutes chatting about our children and I quickly learned that Manuel's older son was studying and living in Brooklyn.

"How wonderful," I replied, "What is he studying? Is he happy there? Is he a Yankee fan? Does he plan to return to Salvador? You must be so proud of him. Here, this is my home phone number in Boston. Have your son call me and perhaps we can arrange for him to visit. Boston's lovely."

Within five minutes I had made a friend of Garcia, and when I let it drop that I was at the bank hoping to secure a list of El Salvador bondholders, he said, "I can help you with that. You don't need to take up the time of the president with such a simple request." He went to the files and produced a three-page list, kept in pencil, with the names of the bondholders, the identification numbers of the bonds they held, and the amounts. He couldn't make a copy fast enough and I couldn't believe my luck.

"If my son needs some help, can he call you from Brooklyn?" Garcia asked. "Of course," I replied. "I'd be happy to help him."

The list wasn't exactly a state secret, that much was clear, but it also wasn't published anywhere, and it was invaluable to me because each of the bondholders on the list was a potential seller. In one quick visit to the Central Bank I had the list—the critical information—needed for the "sell" side of the market I had come to create.

As was my custom, I had cabs wait for me in San Salvador. I wanted to spend as little time on public streets looking like a foreign businessman as possible, and when the meeting was over I took my briefcase, with the gold mine—the list of bondholders—inside, and scurried for the cab. It had been a good day. I knew who the potential sellers were. Their names were all on the list Garcia had given me. Now I had to find out who might be interested in buying El Salvador bonds.

The tools of my trade were remarkably low-tech in the 1980s. I solicited buyers by placing modest ads in San Salvador newspapers popular with the business class, papers such as *El Caribe*. The ads were laughably simple and self-inflating: "Multinational company is interested in selling bonds of the government of El Salvador denominated in U.S. dollars. Interested parties should contact us by writing to Box Number X at this newspaper." I never mentioned the name of my company, Turan Corporation, or my own name, part of the plan to blend into the woodwork as much as possible. Primitive as they were, these small ads launched millions of dollars of transactions in El Salvador bonds. I have always said you only need one buyer, and in my case my best customer turned out to be Xerox.

I had limited operating capital at this point in my life and I could not afford to speculate in El Salvador bonds. By this I mean I wasn't going to buy them and pray I'd be able to flip them to another buyer at a better price. I had to have my buyer lined up and I had to know his price. Then I'd find my seller and I'd know, up front, the price I could pay and still make a nice profit. It was all about the spread.

Of the ten replies I received to my first ad, the only serious inquiry was from the offices of Xerox Corporation in San Salvador. The letter indicated that Xerox was interested in purchasing El Salvador bonds with a face value of $3 million. This was great news. But Xerox was only willing to buy those bonds if it could pay for them with colones. Not so great news, but not at all surprising. Xerox, like many foreign companies, was looking for a way to convert profits in the local currency into dollars.

My discussions with Xerox were held at first through their local Salvadoran representatives, but it quickly became clear that the shots were being called at the corporate headquarters in Greenwich, Connecticut. The Salvadorans in the local office were simply minions. In any event, before I could supply the bonds, I had to know what price Xerox would pay for them.

In the cat-and-mouse game that is a negotiation over price in any transaction, you have to be prepared to endure long silences to succeed. If you are the kind of person who feels compelled to fill in awkward silences, you will typically be on the losing end of a deal. I had no idea what price I'd be able to buy ("source," in industry parlance) the bonds for—bonds I intended to flip to Xerox—so I had to know Xerox's price.

In talking with buyers, it always paid to be optimistic about El Salvador's future—the war will end, the country will stabilize with American help, peace will prevail. In talking with sellers, it always paid to be a pessimist—the country's balance of payments deficit was growing worse, the elections are coming up and the right wing may prevail and the violence will get worse, the U.S. Congress is growing impatient with Salvador's military and its human rights abuses. But I never offered an opinion, to a buyer or seller, as to what the price should be. I never said more than, "I will execute this trade at the best price possible," leaving ambiguous the question of "best for who?"

Whatever corporate strategy Xerox had devised to repatriate profits, it was clear they were serious buyers. In this first transaction, they were willing to buy $3 million (face value) in bonds for 15,300,000 colones. In other words, they were willing to pay the equivalent of $2.55 million, at the unofficial or black market exchange rate of six colones to the dollar. They didn't put it that way and neither did I, of course, but in my own mind I always had to factor the black market rate into my pricing, because the black market was the only way I was going to be able to turn such a large sum back into dollars for myself.

If the bonds performed, in a couple years Xerox would have made a nice profit (high risk, high return) plus interest, but more important, that profit would be realized in dollars. (For clarity, I have simplified the terms of the transaction somewhat.)

Now that I had my buyer and knew his price, I had to find a seller who wanted to part with $3 million in Salvador bonds at a lower price; preferably a much lower price. My goal in a transaction of this size was to pocket a profit of about $150,000, more if I could swing it. I started working my list, the one I took away from the Central Bank.

But I had an obvious problem. Xerox was only willing to pay me for the bonds in colones and the seller was going to want payment in dollars. After all, that's why almost every holder of Salvador bonds bought them in the first place. (There were some exceptions, but not many.) To make the deal work, I was going to have to come up with a lot of dollars to buy the bonds, accept colones when I resold them, and then convert those colones back into dollars at a rate that would still allow me to walk away with a profit. In other words, I was going to be stuck with the very problem companies like Xerox were trying to solve by buying Salvador bonds in the first place.

Why all this pricing and reliance on the black market? Because the Central Bank had tiny foreign reserves, which it held tightly. It was hard enough to change $100 worth of colones for dollars at the official rate of five colones to the dollar. More than $2 million? As Tony Soprano would say, "Fuhgettaboutit." To convert the colones that Xerox was going to pay me into dollars, I'd have to find a *cambista*, a money changer, who had access to large amounts of dollars, and I'd have to pay more than the official rate for each dollar. *How much more* would determine the amount of my profit, if I could make a profit at all. Since currency exchange rates, official and unofficial, can fluctuate daily, I was going to be taking a huge currency risk. I would be at the mercy of an unpredictable currency black market. In two weeks, it might cost me twice as many colones for each dollar I wanted to buy. I had to be sure the spread I was making in the bond transaction would be enough to cover my currency risk.

My working assumption when I quoted the price to Xerox was that it would cost me about six colones for each dollar I was going to have to convert, 20 percent more than the official exchange rate. So I had to find a seller willing to part with $3 million in Salvador bonds for 80 cents on the dollar, or $2.4 million. Then, if all went according to plan, I'd buy the bond for $2.4 million with dollars borrowed from a U.S. bank, sell it to Xerox for 15,300,000 colones, use those colones to buy dollars on the black market at the rate of 6 colones to the dollar, and end up with $2.55 million. After repaying the bank loan, my profit would be a handsome $150,000. But if the unofficial exchange rate ticked up to 6.5 colones per dollar before I could complete the process of converting my colones back into dollars, that $150,000 profit would not only disappear completely, I'd be $46,000 in the hole.

Cold calling is a staple of our business. From my office in Boston (I had flown home to visit my neglected family), I started making calls on my rotary-dial phone, wearing out the tips of my fingers trying to reach the bondholders on the list from the Central Bank to see who might be interested in selling their Salvador bonds. In those days, it wasn't always easy to get a call through to Central America, so I did a lot of dialing, both to El Salvador and to the European headquarters of companies doing business there.

"Good morning. This is the United States calling, Robert Smith of the Turan Corporation in Boston. May I speak to your chief financial officer, please?" I wanted the person on the other end to hear a serious American voice calling internationally. I wanted to impart *gravitas*, not come across like a local hustler, and a call from the United States really was something special back then.

When I finally reached someone who seemed to have financial management oversight, I would state my interest in buying $3 million (face amount) of Salvador bonds. Most of the bondholders expected to hold these bonds to maturity, hopefully collecting principal and interest along the way. But the war raging across the country cast considerable doubt on the government's ability to pay. Latin American countries had defaulted on debts before, notably Mexico in 1982. Dollars were scarce, and inflation was eroding the ability of small countries like El Salvador to meet its obligations. I knew that, with patience, I'd find someone who wanted to unload their bonds, and probably at a deep discount.

British American Tobacco was ready to sell. But at what price? With illiquid assets for which there is not yet an established market, such as Salvador bonds, prices are entirely subjective. There are no comparisons to be made to help establish value. For me, that's perfect. In my business, an uneducated consumer was always my best customer.

In a $3 million deal—that is, a deal for $3 million of El Salvador bonds at face value—every penny in the spread is worth $30,000. After some haggling, BAT agreed to sell me the bonds for eighty cents on the dollar. If the colon didn't fall dramatically against the dollar by the time I was able to convert the bonds, I'd have my profit of $150,000, which I would never disclose to BAT or Xerox, of course. I have made a habit of always complaining to buyers and sellers that my margins are so low, I'm practically working pro bono. The buyer should always feel like he's stolen the merchandise and the seller should believe he's sold at the highest price possible. You don't let on when you've made a good deal and you never strut.

Today, bonds are traded electronically. In El Salvador in 1984, the mechanics were far less sophisticated. Once I paid for the bonds using a check drawn on a line of credit at Shawmut Bank in Boston, I had to physically take possession of them and then deliver them to my buyer.

When the terms were settled with both BAT and Xerox, I wired the money to BAT in London. BAT then telexed an acknowledgment. With the telex in hand, I caught the next flight to Miami, and then the next Taca Airlines flight to San Salvador. Crazy as it may sound, I brought my wife with me on this trip. I didn't like being an absentee husband, though a visit to a war zone didn't promise to be very romantic, especially with me feeling the pressure of executing this transaction and being able to leave Salvador with my dignity and my wallet intact.

The trip, which I would make frequently over the course of several years as I grew the market in El Salvador, took about six or seven hours if the connections worked well. The next morning, first thing, I presented myself at the offices of BAT, showed my identification and the telex that proved I had paid for the bonds, and took possession of the bonds I would now own for a matter of hours. (Sometimes the physical bonds would be in London or elsewhere abroad. In that case, they would be sent by courier to Shawmut Bank, where I would pick them up and carry them with me to El Salvador.)

With the bonds in my briefcase I headed for Xerox. Walking around with $3 million in bearer bonds is like walking around with cash, and I was desperate to blend into the woodwork as I moved around San Salvador. I wanted to unload the hot potato in my briefcase as quickly as possible. (My wife, Salua, had been more concerned about the safety of her Louis Vuitton bags on the airport luggage carousel than about the $3 million in cash equivalent I had on me.) So I dashed around in cabs from hotel to office building to office building. I was *shvitzing* like crazy, my suit was a rumpled mess, and my glasses were fogged up in the humid air. It was a nerve-racking day trying to keep the dominos in place until I could close the transaction.

Now came the hard part. For all of my efforts, I had a bank check from Xerox in Salvadoran colones worth more than $2.5 million at the black market exchange rate, *if* I could find a way to convert it. The financial risk was enormous. It was a race against the clock. The longer it took me to find a way to get dollars for my colones, the greater the risk that my profit from the transaction would evaporate, or worse.

A falling colon was only one part of the problem. Where were all these dollars going to come from? Where would a *cambista* get those kinds of dollars? The answer was that the dollars were going to come from the pockets of Salvadoran maids working in Beverly Hills, Salvadoran gardeners in Coral Gables, and Salvadoran taxi drivers in Manhattan.

It's impossible to know how many Salvadorans, legal and illegal, were working in the United States in the mid-1980s, but it was a lot. Tiny countries like El Salvador, with few exports to sell abroad and little economic opportunity at home, end up exporting the one commodity they have a surplus of: human labor. And all of those thousands of Salvadorans working in the United States were sending home to loved ones, every month, small money orders purchased from Western Union or the U.S. Postal Service; $50 here and $100 there, sent to family in cities and small villages throughout El Salvador.

I wasn't going to rent a car and go about the country buying up dollars a few at a time with my huge stash of colones, of course. But there were clever Salvadorans who did.

It worked like this: Toward the end of the month, when the lion's share of money orders from the States arrived by mail, a small-time money changer in a village such as Acajutla would buy them from the local residents for a slightly better rate than could be obtained at a local bank—say, 5.25 colones on the dollar, whereas the official or bank rate was 5 colones. He'd aggregate them and travel to a larger town like Ilabasco, where another middleman might offer him 5.50 colones on the dollar for all of the money orders he'd collected in Acajutla. The middleman in Ilabasco, of course, was aggregating money orders from many smaller middlemen throughout his region. Then, the middleman from Ilabasco would travel to the capital, where he'd find the likes of Jose Manuel Gomez in a small office on Avenida Roosevelt in San Salvador.

A business associate in Guatemala, where I had similar exchange-rate problems with bonds I bought and sold there, had given me Gomez's name and number. "You can trust him," Ricardo told me. Though he had never personally met Gomez, Ricardo was in the same business himself in Guatemala, converting *quetzals*, the Guatemalan currency, to dollars and vice versa, a black market operation that operated quite openly, if illegally. Ricardo and his boss had done business with Gomez and found him to be trustworthy.

In every country where hard currencies like the dollar are difficult to come by, there is always the official exchange rate (even if there are precious few dollars to be exchanged) and the unofficial exchange rate, essentially a free-for-all market where the cost of a dollar is strictly a matter of supply and demand and open to the ingenuity of the buyers and sellers. Though such transactions are illegal, they are often tolerated because they grease the skids of the local economy, and those who ran the *cambio* operations in Salvador and elsewhere in Central America were typically professional businessmen who understood banking and economics.

Cambio could be a very lucrative business. With modest start-up capital, an enterprising *cambista* could change $50 million of currency a year, making a 5 percent to 10 percent spread per transaction, a pure profit of $2.5 million to $5 million a year. These weren't the black market "retail" street cambistas stepping up to tourists in the main square. They were sophisticated businessmen dealing with major corporations and financial institutions in what might be called a "parallel" market. Theirs was a high-risk/high-reward world, but the risks weren't just financial. Because they operated outside the law, the means of enforcing agreements, either between customer and cambista or partners in cambio businesses, could be ruthless. Bad checks, scams, competition—whatever the beef—justice was meted out directly and summarily. Rumors of beatings and worse swirled around this community of underground financiers.

Jose Gomez was about thirty years old when I met him in San Salvador in 1984, a neatly dressed, educated man in Salvador's ubiquitous white shirt and dark slacks, standard business dress in the capital. He spoke fluent English and had an air of casual efficiency and professionalism about him. His wasn't a cloak-and-dagger operation; he had a simple office in a converted house one floor up from the street. There was no sign on the door. Like Ricardo in Guatemala, he operated quietly but not anonymously. There was no need to. Most, if not all, of Gomez's customers—people with dollars to buy or sell—would have been the rich and powerful: judges, military officers, government officials, politicians. In other words, people in a position to need the services of a moneyman who could deliver the cash.

Though Gomez had been recommended by a trusted friend, I was still apprehensive, to say the least. I had a lot of money at stake and I was going to be handing Gomez a readily negotiable check for millions of colones that would be cashed well before I knew whether Gomez would make good on the exchange. And even if Gomez could be trusted, I was petrified that my profit could go down the drain on any bad news that sent the colon plunging. There were other cambistas in San Salvador, to be sure, but I knew even less about them than I did about Gomez. Over time, Gomez would come to be a trusted associate, a friend, and part of my bond-trading business in Salvador, but at the time he was both my best hope for securing my profit and a huge risk.

In our first meeting, I tried—as best as a paunchy, balding, five-foot-nine-inch Jewish boy from Brookline can—to strike a "don't fuck with me" pose. I may have even intimated that if he screwed me I could have him killed. Gomez was courteous enough not to laugh in my face. He was in a country where life was already cheap. You could hire a killer for $500 or a thousand bucks. I was on his turf, and if things turned sour, he'd find a way to dispatch me before I

could wipe the condensation from my eyeglasses. Besides, I was very nervous, it was hot and humid, and I had soaked my clothing with perspiration. I looked as if I had showered in my clothes. I didn't exactly cut a threatening figure.

Gomez's desk was clear with the exception of three telephones and a small notebook, which sat open. A few old copies of *Time* magazine sat on a small table nearby. I could see Gomez's notebook was kept in a neat hand: columns of names, buyers and sellers, and numbers in which he reconciled his transactions, colones for dollars and vice versa.

"So, Mr. Smith," he said after we had introduced ourselves and made small talk. "How can I help a friend of my friend, Ricardo?"

The size of the transaction I described, in the neighborhood of $2 million, didn't seem to faze him, but he explained that it would have to be done over many days.

"I can't exchange more than $100,000 to $200,000 a day for you, Mr. Smith," said Gomez. "Even if I had the cash on hand, if I did your transaction all at once, it would look like there was a run on dollars and the price will shoot up. Wait here in San Salvador a couple of weeks or so and I will have your money."

Where did Gomez get *his* dollars? He'd buy all those money orders sent by Salvadorans working in the States and aggregated by small-time money dealers from the hinterlands, giving them, say, 5.75 colones on the dollars they bought for 5.50 colones from another dealer who bought them from the peasants in small towns like Acajutla for 5.25 colones. He'd deposit all those dollar money orders in a bank account he maintained at the Whitney National Bank in New Orleans, charge me about 6 colones for a dollar, and write me a check drawn on the New Orleans bank. Just like me, Gomez and all the other cambistas along the way were making money on the spread.

All of these parallel market transactions were done without receipts or documentation of any kind. Needless to say, the first time around this block, after signing over a check for more than $2.5 million worth of colones to Jose Manuel Gomez, a man I had just met in

his small office in San Salvador, I was a nervous wreck. Even if I had a receipt, what was I going to do? What I was doing may have been tolerated by the powers that be in El Salvador (after all, trying to control the flow of cash is like trying to keep water out of New Orleans), but it was illegal. If Gomez took me to the cleaners, who was I going to complain to? The authorities? Gomez could easily pay them off with my own money. Despite my tough talk, I was completely at Gomez's mercy.

"Come back later this afternoon," said Gomez, "and I will have your first $150,000." Later that afternoon he made good on this promise—well, at least I had a check drawn on an American bank for $150,000. Whether the check was good I wouldn't know until I tried to deposit it back in Boston. Perhaps, I thought, this is just a confidence game and he's setting me up for something even bigger.

For the next two weeks or so I bided my time in San Salvador, hanging around the hotel pool, touring the volcanoes, and frequenting the cafes in the Zona Rosa. I cringed at the thought that a falling colon would steal my profit, so I watched the exchange rate every day. And it started, as I feared, to creep up, first to 6.1 and a few days later to 6.2 colones to the dollar. Each fluctuation caused severe palpitations. My fear of a falling colon only dissipated at the larger fear that I might not see any more money from Gomez at all—that I'd been had and that I wouldn't know it until I got back to Boston.

Every day for the next two weeks, late in the afternoon, I stopped by Gomez's office and he'd have another check for me, drawn on his New Orleans bank: $200,000 one day, $125,000 the next, until, finally, I had dollar checks drawn on the Whitney Bank worth more than $2.5 million. I was lucky that the small daily upticks in the exchange rate were matched with downticks, which meant the rate had held relatively steady.

In 1984, I had two small children, a hot-blooded Brazilian wife with expensive tastes, and very little operating capital. If Gomez's checks were bad, not only would my profit disappear, but a $2.4 million loan from Shawmut Bank, the line of credit I used to buy the bonds from British American Tobacco, would have to be repaid. The loan was secured in part by the Boston condo my family was living in. I was, as they say in poker, "all in."

I flew back to Boston, to a family I hadn't seen in several weeks, feeling like a mother bird returning to the nest with no worms for the chicks. It would take several business days to find out whether Gomez's checks were as good as his promises, days that passed so slowly I thought I would go mad.

As I said, Jose Gomez became a trusted associate and friend. He was as good as his word, and we went on to do many more transactions, just like this one, over the next several years. He often would pick up and deliver bonds for me, saving me the trip from Boston. He became my go-to guy in El Salvador, honorable, decent, and completely trustworthy. We grew quite fond of one another.

I don't know why Jose was murdered in 1988. The crime was never solved. There were only rumors of a money transaction gone bad.

As the market in Salvador bonds grew, I was sometimes buying from a seller on one floor of an office building and selling to a buyer on another floor of the same building, without the buyer or seller knowing about it. In one deal, I bought from Texaco and sold to Shell. As the crisis in El Salvador deepened throughout the 1980s, bondholders wanted an exit strategy and were happy to unload their bonds for seventy-five to eighty-five cents on the dollar. At first, when I had virtually no operating capital, I only bought Salvador bonds when I had a seller. I didn't want to risk getting stuck with the bonds myself.

After several Salvador transactions, now confident in Gomez and with some money in my pocket, I felt more comfortable if I had to hold the goods a while before reselling them. Indeed, I would cherry-pick the bonds with the earliest maturities for myself. Why? Because I noticed something very interesting, something other savvy buyers also noticed, no doubt. The principal and interest being paid to the bondholders was coming not from the Central Bank of El Salvador, but in the form of checks from the United States Treasury Department. To bolster the government of El Salvador, its client, and to protect its interests in the country, the United States was going to ensure that El Salvador did not default. The real risk in these bonds was practically nil. The United States was virtually guaranteeing they would be paid—and paid on time. On top of that, the bonds with the earliest maturities were often being called and paid in full before the due date. With the big boys at Citibank, Morgan Stanley, and the other major investment banks out of the game—too dangerous, stakes too small—I had the playing field to myself, and what a field of dreams it proved to be.

The word *globalization* wasn't part of the lexicon in the mid-1980s, though one could argue that the process of globalization has been going on at least since the days that Spanish ships carried spices back from the Orient. But globalization as we know it today—integrated, global markets linked electronically and operating twenty-four hours a day, seven days a week—was still around the bend in 1984, at the height of my El Salvador business.

One can look back today and see clearly that the development of the global economy has not simply paralleled the emergence, growth, and pervasive integration of digital technologies into our lives: Rather, the global economy as we know it *owes its very existence* to the digitization of information. When the tools of my trade were the rotary phone, the telex, and an airline ticket, it took a lot of sweat and chutzpah to prowl around in the dark corners of the global economy. And they were dark precisely *because* information was scarce and easily held close to the vest once you had it. When I bought an El Salvador bond from Texaco and sold it to Shell, only a handful of people ever knew the buy or sell price, and only I knew *both*. Today, anyone with a computer can know the buy and sell price within seconds, not only because the information can travel at the speed of light, but because clever people set up trading, reporting, and regulatory mechanisms that exploit the capabilities of digital technologies. The game today is played on a digital playing field, because that's where all the players have congregated. No one in their right mind today would buy or sell a bond to me in any other way than through one of these highly transparent markets, and that's why my spreads are now a tiny fraction of what they once were. Today, I need an optometrist to see the spreads.

In El Salvador in the 1980s, I also learned an important lesson about capital—financial capital and human capital. Money, and people, will find ways around any barriers erected to keep them at home when the financial incentives are sufficiently high. Developing or poor countries often impose strict limits on the amount of local currency its citizens can convert into dollars from the Central Bank in order to maintain a certain level of foreign exchange required to buy desperately needed imports. They also typically place strict limits on the amount of foreign currency their citizens can take out of the country to prevent the flight of such foreign reserves. And they try, as El Salvador did, to fix exchange rates and impose arbitrary price controls to keep inflation under control. Such measures may work temporarily, or partially, by criminalizing natural economic behavior. But eventually and inexorably, people will act to protect their assets and feed their families and will find ways around such artificial barriers. Whether it's financial capital or human capital, it will move across borders.

More and more countries have learned this lesson over the years, at least with respect to currency exchange controls. They simply don't work and, in fact, tend to exacerbate the very problem they are designed to control: currency flight. Show me a country with strict currency exchange controls or with an arbitrarily fixed exchange rate and I will show you a thriving currency black market.

In countries like El Salvador, and other developing countries, including some on our own borders, such as Mexico, human labor is a major export and a critical source of foreign exchange as workers send some of their hard-earned wages to family back home. When I was exchanging some $2.5 million worth of colones through Jose Manuel Gomez, I already knew that the dollars I would buy were coming from the small remittances of Salvadoran workers in the United States. I had encountered precisely the same situation in Guatemala a year earlier. I had gone into business with a former Guatemalan finance minister to start an ill-fated business called American Check, a retail operation designed to facilitate the transfer of remittances of immigrant workers in the United States. The keystone cops story of American Check is told in Chapter 4, but the enormous impact of foreign worker remittances on the global economy wasn't apparent to me thirty years ago.

Such remittances remain a powerful force in the global economy today, though one easily overlooked in the vast ocean of money that sloshes electronically across international borders every day. In 2003, *Global Development Finance*, a publication of the World Bank, put the total of foreign worker remittances globally at $72.3 *billion* in 2001, with $18 billion of that amount coming from foreign workers in the United States. In 2006, the amount of total remittances soared to just over $300 billion, according to a report by the International Fund for Agricultural Development and the Inter-American Development Bank. Some people argue that such remittances, which exceed the amount of assistance to developing-world countries through governments and multilateral institutions, are a far more efficient mechanism for strengthening the economies of developing countries than foreign aid, because the money passes outside of large bureaucracies and directly into local hands, where it is spent or invested in the local economy. Much of this money—though how much is impossible to measure—inevitably finds its way back to the United States, often in the form of the purchase of American-made goods or, in my case, as checks stuffed in a briefcase.

In smaller countries, such as Nicaragua and El Salvador, remittances practically sustain the national economy and are a more predictable flow of capital than, say, private investment. In 2001, for example, remittances represented 13.8 percent of El Salvador's gross domestic product and 16.2 percent of Nicaragua's. Indeed, remittances are El Salvador's biggest industry, worth more than $2.8 billion a year and engaging nearly a third of all Salvadorans. An astonishing 2 million of El Salvador's 6.5 million people are living and working in the United States.

This is not to say that remittances have solved El Salvador's chronic poverty or closed the gap between rich and poor. Far from it. But El Salvador's economic and social problems would be far worse without them. And with many people in the United States proposing a virtual Berlin Wall along the southern border, we would do well to remember that no wall, no law, no border patrol can reverse the overwhelming power of people in pursuit of a livelihood. You may as well try to legislate the ocean tides. Such measures may be successful at the margins in restricting the flow of people, but there may also be unintended consequences. Those railing for get-tough immigration policies may be underestimating the stabilizing effect of foreign worker remittances in countries that less than thirty years ago were a major source of instability in the Western Hemisphere. People stuck in their own economically impoverished countries with no work, and prevented from moving freely across borders to find work, will eventually create the very kind of social and political unrest that made El Salvador such a violent and war-torn country in the 1980s.

I also learned one final lesson in El Salvador that has propelled me, sometimes recklessly, sometimes with more deliberate consideration, into other parts of the world where economic chaos, war, or political instability made it counterintuitive to seek my fortune there: No economy is too small, no political crisis is so dire, and no country is too bankrupt for a solo operator like me to find riches among the ruins.

CHAPTER 2

VIETNAM

The Early Education of an Economic Warrior

"PINCHUS SILVERBERG" was a big-time Chicago scrap metal dealer with a fondness for sharkskin suits, oversize pinkie rings, fat cigars, and gold teeth. Short, with an ample belly that strained against the buttons of his tailored shirts, and an accent suggesting he was originally from Brooklyn, Pinchus cut quite a figure in South Vietnam, where I first met him in 1968.

Ill-mannered, bombastic, and loud, Pinchus sprayed spittle and squinted when he talked, and it was in his nature to prattle incessantly. About fifty years old, Pinchus had bid millions of dollars to win the contract with the U.S. Department of Defense (DOD) to remove military scrap metal from the war-torn country. Burned-out trucks and jeeps, spent artillery shells, old guns . . . you name it: If it was made of metal Pinchus wanted it, because he could resell it at a handsome profit in Taiwan, Japan, or any one of a number of other countries in Asia.

Ever since the days of the American Revolution, when Pennsylvania farmers sold food to British troops stationed in Philadelphia, even as the underfunded Continental Army starved at Valley Forge, enterprising Americans have been making money off of war. Pinchus was part of this proud American tradition, and in 1968, as an associate commercial officer with the Joint Embassy/USAID Economic Section in Saigon, I was assigned to help Pinchus fulfill his patriotic duty.

It was assignments like this one, and many others I undertook in Vietnam, that laid the foundation for my career as a debt trader. Though I didn't trade debts in Vietnam, I got quite an education there in both finance and psychology, both of which were essential to my later success.

Of course, 1968 was a year when many of my contemporaries were either burning draft cards, conscientiously objecting to the war, taking long vacations in beautiful Canada, or hastily enrolling in graduate school to avoid going to Vietnam. I, on the other hand, was desperately looking for a way to get there. I was completely apolitical at the time and also completely nearsighted. So nearsighted that when called for my preinduction physical at the Boston Naval Base in 1965, I was promptly declared unfit for duty, a "4F" stamp, which I could hardly see, imprinted on my record.

Incredible as it may seem, going to Vietnam in wartime seemed a better option than continuing to work as a collections lawyer in my father's law firm. I was a recent law school graduate, but I detested the work—the routinized, unchallenging, mind-numbing work—of collecting small debts. Combat in Vietnam may have offered the very real prospect of physical death, but working in my father's collections practice offered the similarly real prospect of a death of the spirit and the soul. When I was found to be physically unfit for duty, I wasn't exactly disappointed; I didn't have a death wish. But it did force me to try and find another way to get to Vietnam.

I had already tasted life abroad and longed to escape again overseas. After high school, in 1958, I lived in France for three months with a host family under the auspices of the Experiment in International Living, an exchange program for high school students. After college, in 1962 and 1963, I went to Turkey and Belgium with the Association for International Students of Economic and Commercial Sciences (AISEC), a global nonprofit run by students and recent university graduates interested in world issues, leadership, and management. When it became clear in the mid-1960s that Vietnam would be the defining event of my generation, I wanted to be a part of the action. Not because I thought American survival depended on our winning the war, or because I believed Vietnam was the essential bulwark against the spread of global communism, but simply because Vietnam was the biggest, most controversial, and perversely glorious cause of the times, whether you were for the war, against it, or, like me, agnostic on the matter.

Since I wasn't going to go to Vietnam in uniform, I saw the U.S. Agency for International Development (USAID), the foreign aid division of the State Department, as my ticket. I had worked as a summer intern at USAID in 1964, before my last year of law school. I secured the internship with the help of the venerable Senator Leverett Saltonstall of Massachusetts, whom my father knew because he was active in Republican politics in the state.

During my USAID summer, I had the lofty title of Administrative Assistant to the Deputy Assistant Administrator for Private Investment and Guarantees—in short, I was an assistant to a deputy assistant. Our unit's job was to draft legislation that would provide tax incentives to companies investing in countries the U.S. government was trying to assist economically.

The offices of USAID in the early to mid-1960s were filled with bright, engaged civil servants who believed in their work because Presidents Kennedy and Johnson believed in the agency's work, too. One of the division chiefs who supervised me in 1964, Park Massey, vouched for my skills and my integrity when, in early 1967, I applied for a job with the agency.

After months of waiting for my security clearance, I was at last offered a job as a foreign service reserve officer to be posted to the agency's commodity import program in South Vietnam. Under this $300 million program, the United States would buy goods needed by businesses in South Vietnam from U.S. suppliers and sell them to the Vietnamese for *piasters*, the local currency of the time. The piasters would be deposited into a special account jointly administered by the U.S. and South Vietnamese governments, and then used for local development or military needs. The goal was to facilitate and encourage trade in Vietnam, and to generate cash that could be reinvested into the South Vietnamese economy.

My parents were incredulous, to say the least. For my father, my decision to leave his law practice for the war, even as a civilian economic officer, was a rejection of the life he had carved out for himself and had worked so hard to carve out for me. He was also filled with anxiety that he might lose his only son, literally and figuratively. Ironically, my father was a staunch Republican and a patriot who believed in "my country right or wrong." He had no use for war protesters, beards, and draft dodgers, and he faithfully supported Richard Nixon. Still, he didn't want his only son in Saigon.

My mother, too, was practically speechless. In her mind, I had a perfectly respectable reason for not going to Vietnam, a medical disqualification, and yet here I was ready to run headlong into a war zone. Nearly everyone my age was looking for an "out" when it came to Vietnam and here I was, their only son, the great white Jewish hope, looking for an "in." She couldn't fathom it.

My mother and father saw me as a great catch for a nice Jewish girl from Newton or Brookline and, at twenty-eight years old, surely ready to settle down, buy a house, and start delivering grandchildren. But it was not to be and I had to disappoint them. Shortly before I left for Vietnam in March 1968, I bought my mother a potted plant that she tended with meticulous care throughout my absence, afraid that if she allowed that plant to die, I would surely perish in the jungles of Southeast Asia as well.

When I stepped off the Pan American airliner that brought me to Saigon via San Francisco and Hong Kong, Vietnam's humidity hit me square in the face. Almost immediately, I discovered that the Saigon that Graham Greene described in his 1955 novel *The Quiet American* was dead-on. The city was alive, sultry, fragrant, decadent, seductive, noisy, tumultuous, and intriguing.

Some two months earlier, the Vietcong (formally, the National Front for the Liberation of Vietnam) and the People's Army of Vietnam had launched an assault of unprecedented ferocity against U.S. troops and the South Vietnamese military that would, they hoped, lead to a broad popular uprising against the South Vietnamese government. Part of the strategy behind this Tet Offensive (so named because it was set to commence at the beginning of the Lunar New Year, known in Vietnamese as *tét*) was to bring the war to the major cities, which, until that point, had been relatively untouched by the mayhem raging in the countryside. Much as Defense Secretary Donald Rumsfeld would, nearly forty years later, dismiss the embryonic Iraqi insurgency as the last gasp of a few Saddam loyalists and "dead enders," at the beginning of Tet, General William Westmoreland, commander of U.S. troops in Vietnam, deemed Tet to be the last desperate breath of the enemy. Both men would be proven badly and tragically mistaken.

As the war raged, everyone quickly became accustomed to regular, though random and intermittent rocket fire into Saigon. Indeed, after I'd been in Saigon for a few weeks, those rockets, which landed throughout the city, usually at night, seemed more of a nuisance than a real threat. The chances of getting hit by a Vietcong rocket in Saigon were probably lower than the chances of getting seriously hurt darting about in Saigon's chaotic traffic, and considerably less than the chances of catching a venereal disease from one of Saigon's ubiquitous bargirls. The explosions simply became part of life and part of the soundtrack of Saigon in wartime. On nights when the occasional

VC rocket would land near my apartment, I'd climb under my bed, where I kept an M1 rifle I never fired, and wait for things to quiet down.

Just five days after my arrival in Saigon, I wrote to my childhood friend, Matt Zion, back in Boston. With Matt, I shared some of my first impressions:

> Initial impression is the unreality—it's like any other city except for the pillboxes, searches, military vehicles, guard posts, sandbags, and bunkers. . . . Don't be naïve in thinking withdrawal is possible or practical for our capital investment, our bases, equipment, and sheer military presence are so overwhelming, that even if peace were declared tomorrow, it would still take a year just to withdraw. Make no mistake, we are here to stay.
>
> . . . In Saigon we all have a ball—the military ride around in their jeeps looking for girls while the bureaucrats are stuck in their air-conditioned offices writing memos and cable to each other. Occasionally your windows rattle and you hear thunder and lightning [a reference to the occasional rocket or artillery shell hitting inside the city] and you know that somewhere women and children are being maimed, villages destroyed, and 500 Americans per week are dead. You're sorry about that, but you never see it.

The war continued to seem surreally distant to me until the day in October 1968 when a rocket zoomed through my office and destroyed the desk next to mine. Because it was a Sunday, none of us were there at the time, but suddenly the danger was much more real. It was clear from the damage that had I been at my desk, I likely would have been killed or seriously wounded.

Despite the apparent dangers I was undeterred, and like so many others who have come to Saigon over the years, I fell in love with the city and the people. As a graduate of an all-male preparatory school and an all-male college, I didn't mind that Saigon was a sexual paradise, a lover's free-fire zone. (My father always told me nice Jewish boys didn't "do that" until they got married; he couldn't imagine why these all-male environments felt so suffocating.)

If the social life was colorful and exciting, the work at the embassy was routine. (Actually, our offices were in downtown Saigon, not at the embassy proper.) My main function in my first job in Vietnam was reviewing paperwork that would allow a buyer in Saigon to import some concrete from Sheboygan, Wisconsin, or some rebar from Bayonne, New Jersey. Within three weeks I was bored to tears and arranged a transfer to the embassy's commercial office, a job that promised to get me out from behind my desk. That's because the job of the commercial office was to monitor the South Vietnamese economy from the field and, occasionally, to give an assist to U.S. businessmen doing business in-country. Businessmen such as Pinchus Silverberg.

Pinchus may have had the contract to remove all of the DOD's scrap metal from Vietnam, but what he didn't have was the cooperation of the local South Vietnamese civilian and military authorities in Nha Trang, where much of this waste was piling up. He had been unable, despite (or more likely, *because of*) his tirades, threats, and temper tantrums, to get a barge loaded with his scrap metal in Nha Trang, a lovely coastal city a couple of hours' flight north of Saigon.

So Pinchus called Senator Henry "Scoop" Jackson of Washington State, the influential Democratic hawk with whom he had some kind of connection, and asked for his help. How he knew Jackson I don't know, but Jackson was a staunch supporter of Israel and Pinchus, who was Jewish, may have been a staunch supporter of Jackson for that reason. Many affluent Jews from all over the United States supported Jackson's campaigns.

Jackson arranged for Pinchus to meet the U.S. ambassador to South Vietnam, Ellsworth Bunker. Bunker instructed my boss, Dick

Devine, a Yale graduate and as lovely and refined a human being as ever walked the earth, to see what could be done on Pinchus's behalf. And Dick, in turn, asked me to help Pinchus and his associate, "Steve Schwartz," get his scrap metal moving out of Nha Trang, which is how the three of us ended up on an Air America flight from Saigon to Nha Trang in the fall of 1968. (Air America was an ostensibly civilian airline, but it was operated by the CIA.)

By the time Pinchus entered my life, I had been in Vietnam for about six months and had settled in nicely. I tooled around Saigon in a Volkswagen Beetle I had shipped over from the States, or a USAID jeep I had managed to commandeer for my own use, or on a little Kawasaki 125cc motorbike I had purchased after my arrival. The Kawasaki was small, but it was agile and quick, important attributes in a city where traffic, motorized and otherwise, was merciless.

When I wasn't working, I would hang out at the exclusive Club Circle Sportif, with its beautiful swimming pool, tennis courts, and other luxuries; relax in restaurants and cafes with friends; or visit some of the countless bars where American men went to meet Vietnamese girls. At the Club Circle Sportif, I would occasionally glimpse General Westmoreland and other high-ranking American military and civilian personnel playing tennis, as if the war were a job they went to during working hours. At the bars, as mentioned, I initially became known as "Cheap Charlie No. 10," meaning I wasn't worth a bargirl's time because of my reluctance to buy the girls "Saigon tea," a nonalcoholic, flavored concoction that signaled your interest.

In the evenings, I would join many other Americans in Saigon on the roof of the Caravelle Hotel, where we could watch the war in the distance. B-52s, the huge workhorses of the war, were carpet bombing Vietcong positions outside the capital and the explosions could be seen from miles away, reddening the night sky just as the sounds of the bombardment, arriving slightly after the flashes of light, would punctuate our conversation. People were dying, but these evenings always had a Fourth of July air about them.

"[T]his is one of the few live wars you will ever see," I wrote to my friend Matt, "including flares . . . aircraft of every description, bombing, and plenty of sound and repercussion—all for the price of a beer. . . . The other night one flare on the other side of the Saigon River caused the destruction of 200 houses. Someone on the roof thought we had hit a gook village [gook, of course, was the then-prevalent but racist term for the Vietcong] and bought everyone drinks."

Once I had transferred to the commercial office from the commodity import program, I was able to get out from behind my desk. One of my jobs was to pay visits to Vietnamese businesses—bicycle makers, auto-parts suppliers, construction companies, and the like—and write reports about them. Many of them were in Saigon, but others were in distant cities that required trips on Air America, which ran regularly scheduled flights to all major cities in the country and to some that were more remote. I'd ask questions, mainly in French, which many Vietnamese spoke, or else through an interpreter, especially where the owners or managers were Chinese (many businesses in South Vietnam were owned by Chinese). The questions were pedestrian: How much business do you do a year, how many employees do you have, what challenges are you facing, and so on. Routine stuff.

But I loved being out and about, whether on the streets of Saigon or off in the boonies. Generally I was treated with suspicion, however. I'd present my business card with the U.S. embassy seal on it, but most people were reluctant to talk. I suspected that a lot of their business was "off the books," and they had nothing to gain by talking to me.

Trips to the remote provinces were always the most interesting, and the most dangerous. I'd be dispatched to a corner of the country near the Cambodian border, for example, to try and take an inventory of foreign aid shipments of food stuffs such as wheat or sugar, and invariably I'd have to deal with a South Vietnamese army colonel who accompanied me and whose only mission seemed to be to distract me, often by suggesting I go off with a young village girl while he and his men "counted" and probably then subtracted from the food shipments for their personal use.

These small villages of a few thousand people, mostly peasants and their barefooted kids, made me nervous because the local population was often sympathetic to the Vietcong and hostile to Americans. On one such foray, I was supposed to take a 4:30 p.m. flight back to Saigon on a six-seat Air America Beechcraft, but by 6:00 p.m. the plane still hadn't arrived. I noticed that my South Vietnamese army colonel was as nervous as I was about the prospect of being abandoned in potentially hostile territory. When the plane at last arrived, more than two hours late, we both breathed a heavy sigh of relief.

Perhaps the most intriguing journey I made while stationed in Vietnam was to Vientiane in Laos. A lot of gold was being smuggled from Laos into Vietnam, and I was dispatched there on a DC-3 to try to find out how much gold was coming across the border and how it was getting there. This was one of the things I loved about Vietnam: Even a very junior civil servant would often be given enormous responsibility and independence because there was so much to do and so few people to do it. I nosed around Vientiane for a few days, then flew up to Luang Prang and was struck by its absolute poverty—people bathed in the same river they used as a toilet—but enchanted by the sheer beauty of this exotic place. It was everything my father's law office in Boston was not. I was thrilled to be there. And while I never learned much about the gold smuggling on that trip to Laos, I did learn that smoking cocaine-laced marijuana before boarding a propeller-driven DC-3 is highly inadvisable.

All of these experiences, however, would prove invaluable throughout my career. I learned how to approach strangers on their own turf and use casual conversation to establish a bond, which was precisely the skill I would use in El Salvador to get that list of bond-holders from the secretary to the president of the Central Bank. I learned how to listen critically and discern when people were telling me the truth and when they were bullshitting me, a critical skill in any trading profession. I learned to weigh people's motives and sometimes hidden agendas. But mostly I learned how to be at ease and operate in unfamiliar territory. And from Pinchus Silverberg, I learned other important lessons, especially about how *not* to behave in a foreign country when you wanted to get things done.

On our flight from Saigon to Nha Trang, I tried to ingratiate myself with Pinchus by letting him know that I was Jewish. It was about all we had in common. I think he expected someone more senior—he was old enough to be my father—and someone with real clout to be assigned to accompany him to Nha Trang. But he was one of those people whose sole criterion for evaluating others was whether they could be useful to him, and on that score he was clearly dubious about me. I could have been a rabbi or a Martian for all he cared, as long as I could help get his scrap metal moving.

On the flight north, Pinchus gave me a list of the people he suspected were impeding his progress. Some were South Vietnamese military, some were local officials, and then there was the indolent crew of the company he had hired to load the barge. It is likely all of them were looking for a cut of the action, but I also suspected that the Vietnamese simply found him obnoxious. I'd only spent a few hours with Pinchus and it was already clear he was rude, culturally insensitive, and utterly lacking in the social graces.

On the flight I suggested to him that he needed a Vietnamese ally who could handle the local politics of the situation for him. I had already learned in Vietnam, as I would again and again throughout my career, that people are more responsive to taking direction from their own. Find someone you trust who speaks the language and lives in the culture. They will almost always solve problems for you faster and better than you could on your own. When operating on foreign soil I have always tried to adhere to this rule. I always handled the business, but I always found a local partner to handle the politics.

"You have a local partner in the head of the company you've hired to load the barge," I told him. "Make him feel important. Make him feel invested in the process. Tell him you want him to handle all the local relationships." I had the sense my advice was going right over Pinchus's head.

When we arrived in Nha Trang, Pinchus was, as usual, loaded for bear. He'd been paying small bribes to local political and military officials, but his scrap was still parked at the docks. One of the little favors he dispensed was a wristwatch. He wore as many as a dozen of them outside his shirtsleeves and under his suit jacket, which made him look like a Times Square hustler. This seemed to be the extent of his understanding of the local culture—that everyone could be bought with a cheap watch. On top of the condescension implicit in such small bribes (larger bribes would have shown more respect and probably would have solved his problem), Pinchus berated and bullied every Vietnamese who stood in the way of his scrap metal and the barge that would take it from Nha Trang. It was all so counterproductive.

I also suggested that Pinchus let me do the talking for him. We first needed to meet with someone from the U.S. Department of Defense in Nha Trang. After all, it was DOD with whom he had a contractual relationship. He was, in a sense, working for them. I would gently make it clear to the local DOD officer in charge that the embassy had a strong interest in Pinchus fulfilling his contract, that I had personally been asked by Ambassador Bunker to facilitate the loading of Pinchus's barge (a harmless stretch; it was Dick Devine who asked me, but the ambassador had asked him), and that there would be great official displeasure if the situation couldn't be resolved immediately. That would be enough, I thought, to get someone from

DOD to lean on his South Vietnamese counterpart who, in turn, would lean on whatever local officials needed to be leaned on.

Every evening in Nha Trang, after we'd made our rounds and exhausted the day's possibilities for meetings, we ate at the U.S. Officer's Club, one of the perks of my embassy position. For a dollar you could enjoy a prime rib that would have done a Chicago steak house proud, and beer was only twenty cents. Evenings like this, especially in as tranquil and beautiful a place as Nha Trang, were always especially surreal. This was a war zone, and yet, away from the battlefield, it all seemed like a tropical vacation.

After dinner, Pinchus always wanted to sample the local bar scene, and I warned him, too late I would soon learn, that indulging with the local women in Vietnam could be hazardous to your health.

After a few days of meetings, we finally ended up face-to-face with the local South Vietnamese military commander who, we surmised, really had the power to solve Pinchus's problem. The Vietnamese were, generally speaking, very patient people who listened carefully to everything you had to say, even if they had no intention of cooperating. I started to explain how important it was to the embassy to see Pinchus's barge loaded, but he could barely wait for me to finish my little speech before he started ranting and raving about how the Vietnamese were refusing to load the barge. If my suggestions that he let his local partner handle the politics, or that he allow me to do the talking, had penetrated his skull at all, it didn't show. But no matter how agitated he got, the Vietnamese commander remained as calm as could be.

"Look," I said, "what's past is past. Let's try and solve this problem together. Mr. Silverberg has powerful connections in the United States and Ambassador Bunker has sent me here to enlist your help and support." This statement had the advantage of sounding like both a respectful request and a vague threat at the same time.

When the risk of having one's local fiefdom upturned by official interference from the outside becomes too great, intransigence usually gives way to cooperation. After all, why invite more scrutiny?

After my little spiel, the local South Vietnamese military commander figured he'd get Pinchus moving and out of his hair so that he could get back to business as usual, and back to flying under the radar of the U.S. embassy as well.

Four days after we arrived in Nha Trang, the scrap metal started to make its way from the docks and onto the barge. But, poor Pinchus. He just couldn't resist the opportunity to be the Ugly American one more time. Down at the docks, the crew hired to load the barge was taking its sweet time. In typical Vietnamese fashion, they were squatting in little groups in their wide conical hats, smoking cigarettes and chatting away, when Pinchus decided to try to speed up the process.

"They're too fucking slow," he muttered, loud enough for his displeasure to be apparent. He would show them the proper way to load a barge.

He stripped off his jacket, removed the few remaining wristwatches from his arms, and rolled up his sleeves. Then he grabbed an armful of small scrap, stepped onto the barge, and promptly lost his footing. I already suspected Pinchus wasn't feeling well: He confided to me one evening in Nha Trang that he'd caught gonorrhea in Saigon, an occupational hazard when you're in the scrap metal business in Vietnam. In any event, he twisted and broke his ankle and let out a stream of profanity that even the Vietnamese seemed to understand just from the context.

I was embarrassed to be with him and embarrassed that he was an American. The Vietnamese barely suppressed their laughter, and I made a note to never, ever act like Pinchus Silverberg, either at home or especially in a foreign country. I realized at that moment that when Americans travel abroad, each one of us not only represents ourselves, but to some extent our country. Pinchus's efforts to bludgeon the Vietnamese into submission with his tantrums were futile. There were better ways to get things done that kept your own dignity, and the dignity of others, intact. Indirectly, it was the most important thing I learned from him, a lesson that has stood me in good stead throughout my career.

It wasn't just Pinchus who taught me that lesson in Vietnam. My boss, Dick Devine, also taught it to me, albeit in a different way and from an entirely different perspective.

One day, Dick and I were driving in a USAID jeep toward the huge U.S. naval base at Cam Ranh Bay. We were in a free-fire zone, so-called because the area was so dangerous the rules of engagement permitted shooting at anything that moved. Much about Vietnam was surreal, and the roadside billboards that announced you were entering a free-fire zone were no exception.

As luck would have it, the jeep broke down inside the free-fire zone. Despite his seniority, Dick was on the ground and under the jeep in a moment trying to identify the source of the trouble while I, the junior officer, leaned against the hood and smoked a cigarette. A few moments later, a huge U.S. military refrigerator truck rumbled by and came to a stop.

"So," said the sergeant who stepped out to see if he could help, "you're in charge here?" He was looking directly at me. He assumed that the guy lying in the dirt with grease dripping into his face from the bottom of a leaky crankcase had to be the lackey. "No," said Dick from under the jeep. "I'm in charge."

That was Dick. He *was* in charge, but he exerted a quiet authority and didn't ask you to do anything he wouldn't do himself. He was a gentleman through and through. He earned your respect and loyalty that way and, in so doing, taught me another lesson that has stood me in good stead throughout my career: Treat people well and they will follow you to the ends of the earth; treat them badly and you sow the seeds of your own undoing.

When Dick Devine left Vietnam around Christmas of 1968, midway through my own tour there, I was truly sorry to see him go. I revered Dick. He was thoughtful on a personal level, but also on a larger political and cultural level. He had come to Vietnam with a deeply held reverence for public service. In Dick's position there were always local business people trying to curry favor, but he was incorruptible. I also appreciated the fact that he let me draft my own performance evaluations, which he would review before signing, of course.

Those glowing evaluations landed me a new position in January 1969 as assistant financial attaché working under Edgar Gordon of the U.S. Treasury Department in the Joint Embassy/USAID Economic Section. Gordon never thought as highly of my work as Dick Devine had, and when I was no longer allowed to draft my own reviews, my job performance seemed to suffer.

"Unfortunately, although well-equipped, [Smith] has not always shown . . . responsiveness to my work suggestions, nor much initiative on his own," Gordon wrote in my last fitness report, which he prepared just as I was getting ready to depart Vietnam in late 1969. "[A] request for a study of foreign private investment in Vietnam had to be repeated several times over a period of six weeks. A study was produced in draft that was a combination of a good description on the investment climate with a mass of somewhat unrelated statistics unadorned by analytical comment."

Then the clincher: "The rest of his work is better but sometimes sparse in quantity."

"But Edgar," I protested, "I always had glowing evaluations from Dick Devine."

"This is the Treasury Department," Edgar replied, unmoved. "We do things differently here."

Part of the job of the financial attaché's office at any U.S. embassy is to monitor the banking and financial sector of the economy, keeping an eye on inflation, exchange rates, and foreign currency reserves. My job, not expertly performed apparently, was to serve as a liaison between the embassy and Vietnamese and foreign banks and financial institutions.

It was from this perch that I received my early lessons in how currencies operate with respect to one another and, more important, how human behavior, emotion, and perceptions affect currency markets. If you want to make money speculating in currencies, it would help to have a degree in economics. But it would be even more helpful to have a degree in psychology.

When I would go to the officer's club for a one-dollar prime rib or a twenty-cent beer, or if I went to the PX to buy cigarettes, a blender, or even a television set, I was not permitted to pay in U.S. dollars. This rule applied to all U.S. servicemen, contractors, and civil servants in the country. (Don't think of the PX as a convenience store for small items; it was more like a forerunner of Costco, a huge warehouse where you could buy almost anything you could find stateside, including big-ticket items like appliances.)

The coin of the realm for Americans in Vietnam was the MPC, or Military Payment Certificate (sometimes referred to as "scrip"). These were colorful paper notes, many with images of submarines and other military hardware on them, issued in denominations from five cents to twenty dollars. This parallel currency was intended to solve a problem that arose when hundreds of thousands of Americans flooded Vietnam with real dollars in the early years of the war: inflation.

The dollar represented stability and safety to the average South Vietnamese and to the elites as well, at a time when the fate of their country was uncertain. If the war ended badly for South Vietnam, they would likely find all their piaster savings worthless. But those with the foresight to hoard dollars would always have something of value. Thus, South Vietnam experienced what is called in economic terms "a flight to quality." The dollar became the preferred currency of commerce, which, inevitably, drove down the value of the piaster.

If I wanted to buy a suit that cost 10,000 piasters from a local tailor and the official exchange rate was 100 piasters to the dollar, that suit would cost me the equivalent of $100. But the tailor might be happy to sell me the suit for $50, provided I paid in U.S. dollars. In effect, in this hypothetical transaction, the real value of the piaster was half of what the official exchange rate said it was.*

Psychology is all-important here. As the perception grew that the dollar was the preferred currency, more and more people began chasing the same supply of dollars. After all, no one wanted to be left out in the cold. The law of supply and demand made dollars more expensive and the value of the piaster sank. And the more it sank, the greater the urge to flee to the quality and the safety and stability of the dollar. Thus, a falling piaster became a self-fulfilling prophecy. As with any perceived shortage, hoarding only hastens the arrival of the very conditions people fear, yet human nature almost always, in an economic context, drives people to do what is in their personal, short-term interest, even if it is clearly not in their collective, long-term interest.

To try to tame inflation in South Vietnam and keep the country economically stable, beginning in 1965 Americans were required to accept MPCs or piasters (at the official rate of exchange) when they cashed their dollar checks from home or their paychecks at a U.S. disbursement office located on military bases and other U.S. installations in the country.

The MPC program was fraught with problems, however. In theory, MPCs could only be spent by American citizens at a U.S.-run PX, commissary, or officer's club. The assumption, which turned out to be flawed, was that MPCs would therefore have no appeal to the Vietnamese. What the U.S. Treasury Department and the military

---

*Even official exchange rates were complex in Vietnam and fluctuated over time, as official rates do. But it is fair to say that in the late 1960s, the effective official exchange rate was, generally speaking, about 100 piasters to the dollar.

did not anticipate was that the South Vietnamese would start treating MPCs just as they did the dollar, and for the same reasons—even this parallel U.S. currency was perceived to be stable and safe or, at the very least, preferable to the piaster. Thus, Americans were able to multiply the spending power of their paychecks by converting them into MPCs at the official exchange rate (which we were required to do) and then sell them to a money changer for piasters at the black market rate. The black market rate was by far more favorable than the piaster exchange rate available at U.S. disbursement offices. Those "cheap" piasters would then be spent at bars, local shops, restaurants, and brothels.

But, as the Vietnamese became accustomed to the MPCs, it wasn't only black market money changers who were willing to accept them for devalued piasters. Soon merchants, prostitutes, barkeepers, cyclo drivers (of the bicycle-drawn carriages used all over Saigon), indeed, all Vietnamese, began to accept MPCs as payment for all manner of goods and services.

Once MPCs became widely accepted, it was easy for Americans to game the currency exchange system. Because greenbacks were still preferred to MPC, you could take, say, $1,000 U.S. dollars you brought from home and find a money changer to give you $1,400 in MPC on the street. If you were going out of the country on R & R, you were allowed to convert your MPCs to dollars. So you would take the $1,400MPC that cost you $1,000 cash to the disbursement office where the official exchange rate was $1MPC to $1 and leave, say, for Hawaii with $1,400 in greenbacks. It was a great racket. In theory, when you returned to Vietnam from Hawaii you were supposed to convert any dollars you had left back into MPCs, but no one did because you could take those dollars, go back to your money-changer friend, and once again convert them into MPCs at a bargain rate. You'd make out coming and going, literally.

Another popular way to profit from Vietnam's Byzantine currency exchange system involved the purchase of automobiles. American personnel going home to the States were permitted to purchase cars through a special U.S. auto sales department at a steep discount from list prices. A $3,000 Buick, for example, might cost $2,000, but it had to be paid for in MPCs. The car would be picked up when you arrived back home from a local dealer.

But there was a way to make this sweet deal even sweeter. Most Americans in Vietnam had some saved greenbacks that had been sent from home, gathered in small transactions as they went about daily life, won in poker games, or held on to when coming back from R & R overseas. So you'd take your $2,000 cash to the black market where you could get $2,800 in MPCs, then use $2,000MPC to pay for the car and exchange the remaining $800MPC back into dollars at the U.S. disbursement office before leaving for home. It was like getting an $800 rebate on a car already discounted by $1,000. The effective cost of a $3,000 automobile became $1,200.

Although the MPC became widely accepted currency in South Vietnam, there was a catch, and it proved disastrous for many Vietnamese. The value of the MPC lay in its ultimate convertibility into a real U.S. dollar at some point. To stop the burgeoning use of MPCs among the Vietnamese, periodically, and without warning, the U.S. military declared a "conversion day" when all outstanding MPCs had to be exchanged for a new issue of MPCs that looked noticeably different from the previous notes. Vietnamese, who were forbidden from holding MPCs, were not allowed to exchange them for the new ones. After a C-day, as conversion day was called, the old MPCs were worthless.

Because only U.S. personnel were allowed to trade their old MPCs for the new, C-day was a day of panic for many Vietnamese, some of whom had their life savings in MPCs. On C-day they would frantically seek out Americans to exchange their old MPCs for them, often willing to accept pennies on the MPC dollar in order to salvage anything from the disaster of C-day. This was, of course, tempting for many G.I.s, who could reap a huge windfall at the expense of a Vietnamese. But finding an American to help was difficult for two reasons. It was strictly forbidden for Americans to exchange MPCs for the Vietnamese, and to help enforce that rule G.I.s were typically restricted to their bases on C-day. Any G.I. or U.S. civilian trying to convert a large sum of old MPCs would immediately be suspected of trying to do so illicitly for a Vietnamese friend or associate, and reprimanded or fined, accordingly.

As you would expect, C-day virtually erased the black market for the *new* MPC as well, because if the notes could suddenly become worthless once, the U.S. military could call a C-day again at any time in the future. Memories are short, however, and gradually a black market started to develop in the new MPC as the pain of C-day began to dissipate. It was a cycle repeated several times.

By the time I moved to my new job as assistant financial attaché in early 1969, I already had plenty of personal experience, as every American in South Vietnam on official civilian or military business did, with the local currency scene. I didn't dare dabble, as many did, in the black market, because it would have been unseemly, not to mention ruinous, for my career as an embassy officer to do so. But when I made purchases from local merchants, drank at a Saigon bar, or engaged the company of one of the bargirls, the price was always negotiable in three currencies: piasters, MPCs, and greenbacks, which, as noted, were preferred. Though using dollars was forbidden in theory, it was commonplace in practice. Every local Vietnamese would run various calculations through his or her head when haggling over a price, whether for a suit, a drink, or a sexual favor, as did every American.

There may have been three currencies in play in Vietnam, but there were *six* conversion rates one had to work with, and to understand the country's economy, and where the Vietnamese themselves thought the economy was heading, you had to factor in all of them. First, there was the official exchange rate between the dollar and the piaster. This was the legally sanctioned rate at which exchanges between the two currencies could be made at a bank.* Second, there was the black market piaster/dollar exchange rate. If you really want to know what level of confidence the local people in any country have in their economy, this is the rate that tells you; it's a barometer. Third, there was the official MPC/dollar exchange rate of one-to-one: a one-dollar MPC equaled one U.S. dollar. Fourth, there was another black market rate in play here. Though MPCs were widely accepted by the Vietnamese, the dollar was still king and black marketers often gave you $1.40MPC for a real U.S. dollar. And, finally, there were the official and the black market MPC/piaster rates.

Part of my job at the embassy was to monitor all of these rates by going out every few weeks to banks and merchants, and even onto the streets where the black markets flourished, and reporting back on the various cross-rates of exchange. Those rates were used to help assess and predict the prospects for economic growth, the risk of recession and inflation, the standard of living for the Vietnamese, and the overall strength of the economy.

I tried not to be too obvious about what I was doing, but it was hard to conceal my true intent. For example, every few weeks I'd pay a visit to an Indian tailor I knew on Tu Do Street (most of the tailors in Vietnam were ethnic Indians or Chinese). I always wore one of those safari-style shirts favored by journalists, and, in essence, I saw myself as a journalist of sorts because I functioned like one, ambling the streets and gathering information. I'd pretend to be interested in buying a suit, but really I wanted to negotiate the price to see what the going rate was in the various currencies. After a couple of visits, my tailor friend became suspicious. "Mr. Smith," he would say, "why don't you buy a suit or just change money? Why are you always just asking questions?"

---

*There were, in fact, many "official" exchange rates in Vietnam that varied from commodity to commodity and by category of importer, but for our purposes we can speak of one effective, official exchange rate.

I spent a year and a half in Vietnam, during which time I was constantly working with these various rates of exchange. It proved to be invaluable experience when years later, in El Salvador, for instance, my profit on a bond deal depended completely on the official and black market exchange rates for the colon and the dollar. I may have had some tense moments letting those Salvador transactions play out over several weeks when a plunging colon could have cost me the shirt off my back, but, thanks to Vietnam, I wasn't a novice at the game.

There was even, in a manner of speaking, another means of exchange in Vietnam. G.I.s and other Americans would buy goods from the PX, such as television sets, tape recorders, and even refrigerators, and sell them at a profit to a Vietnamese, usually for MPCs that could be used, in turn, to buy even more goods at the PX that would also be resold at a profit. Some Americans simply started using the PX as a supply house for their illicit trade. Eventually, when this kind of trade got out of hand, ration cards were issued to limit how many items of a particular kind any one individual could buy. But here, too, I drew an early lesson that I would employ later in my career: the value of barter schemes involving real goods to navigate around currency exchange barriers. (I'll talk more about barter schemes in Chapter 3.)

The big-picture lesson I took from all of this—one that has invariably been proved true over and over throughout my career—is that any attempt at currency controls, whether it's officially set conversion rates or limitations on the amount of currency an individual can convert or take out of a country, is also an invitation to circumvent the system. Money simply flows around all artificial barriers erected to try and control it. This is why, despite the fact that MPCs were intended only as a currency to be used at U.S. facilities, a Saigon bargirl might, in a good week, be able to sell $1,400 in MPCs to a black market operator for $1,000 in real U.S. dollars. Or, take $500 in real dollars and turn it into 100,000 piasters at twice the official exchange rate.

Everyone in Vietnam, it seemed, was a speculator, and when people speculate, psychology, more than economics, will dictate price.

The Vietnamese *perceived* the MPC as a symbol of economic strength, nearly as good as a real dollar, despite all the restrictions on the use of the scrip and even though, theoretically, there was no place a Vietnamese could spend it. But if your neighbor or the merchant down the street is willing to accept it, that legal restriction is meaningless.

That was why C-days became necessary. It was the only way to send the message that MPCs really were a closed-loop, limited-purpose currency. There may have been a few lovesick G.I.s trying to help their desperate Vietnamese girlfriends and willing to risk being caught, but otherwise most Vietnamese who had saved large amounts of MPCs lost everything.

These kinds of financial shenanigans were also the reason why it was so hard to make a true Vietnamese friend. Far more often than not, friendships, especially romantic friendships, were rooted in economics. There was almost always something your Vietnamese friend wanted from you and, sad to say, it almost always involved money, travel, a job; something other than love, for sure.

On the night of July 23, 1969, I went up to the rooftop of my apartment building at 3:00 a.m. with my reel-to-reel tape recorder and talked for about a half-hour into the microphone about my impressions of the country and the war. Listening nearly forty years later to my twenty-nine-year-old voice—which on that evening was competing with the sound of an occasional helicopter passing overhead—transports me back to those heady days when I felt like I was, at last, fulfilling my destiny to be a citizen of the world.

I had come to Vietnam apolitical, in search of adventure, nothing more. And far from sating my thirst for adventure, Vietnam only fueled it. But the war, and the way we were waging it, had made a deep impression.

"Regardless of one's political feelings prior to coming out here," I said that evening, "I think if you're here long enough . . . you'll begin to see the complete, utter folly of this industrial accident, I guess would be the best way to explain it. It's the first war in history whereby the victims, mainly, I guess, the Vietnamese, have managed to, in many, many cases, do very well. You hear about corruption . . . black market manipulation . . . bribery, and you probably don't begin to scratch the surface . . . and you really can't condemn it, because if you were Vietnamese you'd be doing the same thing."

It had also become obvious to me that the official sanguine appraisals of the U.S. military's progress in the war flew in the face of reality. By the summer of 1969 (I would leave Vietnam in September of that year), it seemed that the number of Vietcong rockets being fired into Saigon had increased, and that they were coming closer and closer to my apartment near the presidential palace. Their psychological impact was considerable, and I found myself spending many sleepless nights, which is why I was on the roof with a tape recorder at three in the morning.

Listening again to that rooftop tape, I can hear the death of my innocence and the beginning of my transition from an apolitical adventure-seeker to apolitical cynic.

"Our government lies. . . . It has propaganda, spies. There are many things that happened here that we never disclose . . . they're all the time optimistic . . . [but] they know they are deluding themselves and the facts aren't the way they say they are. . . . I suspect that we'll be here at least . . . for two or three more years."

In fact, Saigon fell almost six years later, on April 30, 1975, by which time my USAID work had taken me to the Dominican Republic, El Salvador, and Brazil. Regrettably, however, by April 1975 I was back in my father's law office in Boston and knew I'd be stuck there until I could figure out once again how to make a Houdini-like escape to some exotic spot far from home.

---- CHAPTER 3 ----

TURKEY

Selling the Letter "M" for a Cool Half Million

MY CAREER as a debt trader began in Turkey, that mystical coun-try at the crossroads of Europe and Asia, that island of moderation in a veritable sea of Islamic militancy, a country that during the Cold War was a base for American nuclear missiles pointed north toward the Soviet Union. Today, Turkey is knocking on the door of the European Union, setting off fierce debate in Europe about what it means to be European and reminding everyone that even an eco-nomic basket case like Turkey can, given enough time, turn things around.

I first went to Turkey in 1962, a recently minted graduate of Bowdoin College, under the auspices of the Association for Interna-tional Students of Economic and Commercial Sciences (AISEC). There I did basic foreign exchange for tourists at the Turkish office of an Italian bank, the Banca Commerciale Italiano.

For my parents, my brief sojourn in Turkey in the early 1960s probably seemed a misguided but temporary departure from the straight and narrow path that had been planned for me (Vietnam was yet another shock that came later). But Turkey was a whiff of that wide, wide world I first encountered in my uncle's stamp collection, and it would, coincidentally, some fifteen years later, be the key that unlocked the door to my career as a debt trader.

The 1970s were years of great turmoil, both economic and political, in Turkey. Throughout the decade, Turkey's economic distress and its growing ties to the West sparked violence between the nationalists and the communists. In 1971, the military forced the resignation of Prime Minister Suleyman Demirel and imposed martial law, which was enforced until elections were held in 1973, when the new prime minister, Bulent Ecevit, formed a fragile coalition government with the religious National Salvation Party. Ecevit would remain in power until 1979, when the deteriorating economy helped topple his government and Demirel returned to power. On top of the political and economic turmoil, natural disasters, in the form of major earthquakes, combined to cripple the country.

During the 1970s, many plans would be laid to stabilize Turkey's pitiful economy, which had been battered by high oil prices, inefficient and corrupt state-run industries, inflation, high unemployment, currency devaluation, and a massive foreign debt with no foreign reserves to pay it off. That's why, in 1978, slogging through a career as the collections lawyer my father always dreamed I would be, I was retained by a large Buffalo-based collection agency called the American Bureau of Collections (ABC) to collect a small $25,000 debt on behalf of an American client who had sold goods to a Turkish importer. The claim was one of many thousands held by American and European companies that had exported goods to Turkey but had not been paid because of a lack of hard currency in the reserves of Turkey's Central Bank.

By 1978, I had not only been to Turkey as a young college graduate, I had, under the auspices of AISEC, worked for Esso (now ExxonMobil) in Belgium. I had lived and worked in Vietnam, the

Dominican Republic, and El Salvador working for USAID, and I had lived and worked in Brazil, where I met my wife. I had all these adventures and had earned some good salaries, but now I was back in Boston doing collections for $125 a week and I wasn't happy about it. A well-trained monkey could do what I was doing. In fact, the mentality of your typical collections lawyer was like that of a gorilla—they liked to puff out their chests and beat them with their fists in order to scare people into paying their debts, and that simply wasn't my emotional makeup. Instead, I usually empathized with the debtors from whom I was supposed to collect. I didn't have the sadistic impulses it took to scare them into submission. I lost my verve and my ambition. I was depressed, withdrawn, and started to suffer from headaches. My wife, who had just moved from Brazil to Boston, was feeling isolated, and I was feeling the pressure of the high financial ambitions she had for me.

There is an old maxim and it never fails. Don't get discouraged when things aren't working out. Why? Because circumstances are going to change. All you have to do is be open to new opportunity when it arrives. General George Patton once described luck as the time when opportunity and preparation meet. In my case, the opportunity was the telephone call asking me to collect this modest trade claim in Turkey. The preparation was my years of living and working abroad.

In those days, international communication was typically done by telex, and we had a telex machine in our small law office on Beacon Street. The telex was about the size of a small refrigerator and had a keyboard and a roller to handle huge rolls of paper that would print messages sent and received. The machine made an enormous racket when pounding out messages, like a hundred typewriters being banged on at once, but I always associated that sound with the machinery of international commerce. At least if the telex was running it meant we were still in business. A telex had a grandeur about it that modern-day e-mail, all silent and coolly efficient, cannot match. When you heard that telex racket you knew important news or business was being conducted over the wires because, unlike e-mail, it cost money to send and receive a telex, so messages were direct, minimal, and had an air of authority about them.

If you've seen one demand letter from a collections lawyer, you've seen them all. There was never anything new or original in the work. I dutifully sent, by telex, my standard demand letter to the Turkish debtor, threatening to hire local counsel in Istanbul if the claim wasn't promptly paid. Within days I had a return telex. "Dear Dr. Smith," it said. "We are pleased to inform you that your client has now been paid in full," or words to that effect. By sheer luck, the International Monetary Fund (IMF) had just released loan monies to Turkey to settle small trade claims, those under $50,000, and mine was among them.

I wrote to the American Bureau of Collections, thanked them for the business, and told them that thanks to my hard work and important contacts in Turkey, I was able to collect the claim. I enclosed my bill for professional services rendered. Harvey Herer, the owner of ABC, called me right away. "Smith, you're a genius to collect this money."

"It's just another day's work," I replied.

"Well, here's another day's work," said Harvey. "We have additional claims for five to eight million dollars overdue from Turkey to American companies. Can you collect on these?"

I thought for a minute and somewhat impulsively said, "In order to collect debts of this size I have to take a trip to Turkey. If your clients can pay $2,500 for my airfare and hotel, I will be glad to go over. I'm sure I can solve the problem."

I stood to make a lot of money—hundreds of thousands of dollars—if I could collect these additional claims. My wife had been mentioning a few too many times that she didn't not want to be married to a loser, that she didn't come to Boston to watch me fall into despondency. In short, she gave me another kick in the pants. I didn't want her to be married to a loser, either.

If I could just collect these claims in Turkey, I thought, I would no longer be a loser. But it wasn't just the collections business that made me itch to go to Turkey. I had a vague sense that I needed to shake things up, get away to some foreign place just to see what opportunities might present themselves. In truth, I had no idea what I was looking for, but I just needed to taste the adventure of my earlier career—foreign languages, foreign currency, foreign culture, maybe a little taste of war or civil strife—to keep my sanity.

I turned to my paralegal, "Lynn Kaye," who was standing in my tiny office, and said, "Lynn, I'm going away for a few weeks to hunt for business. Handle everything."

"But Mr. Smith, I don't know what to do—"

"Think of yourself as a basketball player. Just keep bouncing the ball," I said. My employees usually find they can run the office better than I can. All my employees always find out they're more talented than they think they are.

A fellow named "Wayne Jasper" worked with me then as a collections attorney, handling all aspects of the business I couldn't be bothered with, which was basically everything. Jasper, a tall, thin Brahmin who went to Williams College, would, in my absence, go to court, make motions, and manage the practice while I was away desperately trying to come up with an escape plan.

On the plane I couldn't wait to once again see the dome of the famed Blue Mosque, built in the early 1600s, and the spectacular Church of Haghia Sophia, now the Ayasofya Museum, a former Eastern Orthodox church converted to a mosque in 1453 by the Turks. I was eager to wander through the packed bazaars full of copper and brass, rug merchants, exotic spices, and gold jewelry, all the vestiges of the old and new Byzantium Empire that I had first glimpsed fifteen years earlier, just after graduation from Bowdoin.

But the vibrant country I remembered didn't exist. Instead, what I found in Istanbul was an armored ghost town. There were tanks, but few people in the street. Violent demonstrations from both the left and right kept other people off the streets and, according to the business people I met, kept the money out of the country. The Wells Fargo representative office had just been bombed. The Intercontinental Hotel in Taksim Square was nearly empty. So was the exquisite Istanbul Hilton Hotel where I stayed; in those days it was Turkey's finest, on a hill with a view of the Bosporus. So serious was Turkey's political and financial unrest that the country was known as "The Sick Man of Europe," a phrase commonly attributed to Tsar Nicholas I of Russia referring to the Ottoman Empire, but no less apt in the late 1970s.

The morning after I arrived I began making my rounds, trying to get a handle on how to collect the claims that would help me cast off the "loser" tag my wife had gently laid around my neck. I visited the commercial attaché at the American consulate. I went to Citibank's representative office (these representative offices did not handle banking business, but rather were the eyes and ears of the institution). I looked up two local collection lawyers. I went to a local Turkish financial institution, Akbank, and spoke with some of the officers there. I visited the Central Bank in Ankara. I was simply trying to understand what plans Turkey might have for paying back its huge trade supplier and other debt, in excess of $3 billion, a tiny portion of which was held by my clients, because the Central Bank didn't have any foreign exchange with which to make payment. The country was broke, out of business, and under threat of military rule (indeed, on September 12, 1980, the military did take power). How could these debts, my client's claims, be paid? That was the question I turned over and over in my mind. Under the current conditions, the IMF wasn't likely to go further than it already had in easing

Turkey's economic pain. The restructuring of the economy necessary to meet IMF conditions was simply not going to happen any time soon.

After a few days of meetings, during which I tried to get a sense of the scope of Turkey's financial mess, it dawned on me that I was thinking about the problem the wrong way. I didn't have a collection problem on my hands because, in fact, most of those exporters who had sent goods to Turkey, like my client, had been paid; it was just that they had been paid in Turkish *lira*. (How trade claims are processed and paid can be a complicated matter. Suffice it to say here that most trade claims, including those I was chasing, had been paid, in Turkish lira, into accounts at banks in Turkey.) The real problem was a foreign exchange issue. We weren't dealing with deadbeats who wouldn't pay their bills; we were dealing with a Central Bank that simply couldn't provide the banks with dollars for all the liras it was collecting on behalf of exporters like my clients.

Now there was no way a little collections lawyer like me was going to be able to solve Turkey's foreign reserve problem. That was a job for the IMF, the World Bank, powerful governments, and international bankers. But I was determined to stay in Turkey until I had a plan to turn this hopeless situation into cash for my clients and, not incidentally, for me.

I went back to the Hilton dispirited by the realization that no huffing and puffing or threatening demand letter was going to solve my problem any more than I could change the weather. Night had fallen and the moon shone over the mosque domes and the fishing boats bobbing on the Bosporus. It was early March and a brisk breeze riffled through the chilly air. I went out on the balcony, lit a cigarette, and then another and another, sipped quite a few glasses of *Raki*, a traditional Turkish liquor, and thought well into the early morning hours. There had to be a way to save this situation. There must be some way to make this work; some way to get money out of Turkey and make the commissions that would give me the freedom to leave collections law behind and find a new career.

Turkey needs hard currency, I thought, but its major exports—nuts, tobacco, and agricultural products—simply weren't enough to cover their negative balance of payments. But I had noticed something interesting in my wanderings around Istanbul. Because they couldn't afford to import them, Turkey had become quite self-reliant in the manufacture of washing machines and other durable household appliances, but all were sold domestically. After all, if you were American, European, or Japanese and could buy quality brands like Maytag and Whirlpool, why would you buy a Turkish washing machine that would be unserviceable when it broke down? But if you were in Africa and couldn't afford a Maytag or a Whirlpool, maybe you could afford a Turkish machine if the price was low enough.

There had to be an idea here. I kept struggling. And then, well drunk at this point, I did have an idea. And like most ideas born on hotel balconies in the middle of the night under the influence of alcohol, it was positively brilliant. The next morning I wrote a proposal and sent it by telex to Harvey at ABC, because to make the scheme work I was going to need Harvey on board to convince his exporter clients that this was the way we could collect on their claims. In other words, Harvey was going to have to sell the scheme and I would implement it.

I knew it was a cockamamy plan, but it looked great on paper. In very simple terms, it would work like this: I would form an American company called Turam Corporation (for Turkish American), which, in fact, I did almost immediately. (How Turam became Turan we will come to shortly.) The exporters whose claims we were trying to collect would subscribe to the scheme by paying a small participation fee, in dollars, based on a percentage of the face value of their claim. If we were successful in satisfying their claim, we were to get another fee based on a percentage of what we were able to collect. We would then take the liras our customers had in Turkey and use them to buy nontraditional exports such as appliances from Turkish manufacturers, which Turam would then sell for hard currency in underdeveloped markets such as Africa. The assumption (not necessarily a sound one) was that there would be buyers in Africa who could pay for the merchandise in a hard currency like dollars or barter some other goods we could sell for hard currency somewhere else. (Believe me, it was far more complicated than this—indeed, so complicated that I can't, all these years later, remember exactly how it was supposed to work.)

The big incentive for Turkey in this scheme was twofold: First, millions of dollars in trade claims could be extinguished with no outflow of dollars, and second, the Turkish manufacturers providing the nontraditional exports would get liras to reinvest in the local economy.

Harvey called me in my hotel room after reading my telex the next day. "Are you serious? Can you really pull this off?"

"Of course I can," I said, brimming with overconfidence. In fact, I didn't have any idea whether I could make the plan fly. "You sell it to the creditors and I'll make it work on this end. You'll get a high profile in international collections."

"But it's a bit over-the-top," Harvey said. "Can you really do this much negotiating in a country you don't even live in? Imagine the bureaucracy."

"I can handle it. I know Turkey. I'm a member of the Turkish American Society. I know all the businessmen here." This was a huge stretch, but it was true that I had joined the Turkish American Society. I always join societies. The key to making money is having information. I always make sure, in whatever country I am in, that I am talking to as many people as I possibly can, and business groups are often a great way to network. Ideas abound that way. But at this point the truth was I knew hardly anyone in Turkey.

Harvey went for my balcony idea and agreed to try to sell it to his clients.

I called Salua to share the good news. "Your father called," she said before I could get a word in edgewise.

"What did he say?"

"I told him you are in Turkey, working."

"Ah."

"He said you must have a screw loose going all the way to Turkey to work with Muslims. What does he mean, Bob?" asked my Lebanese-Brazilian wife.

"He means I should be doing collections law in Boston."

"I'm lonely," she said.

"I'll be back soon." I didn't tell her that I was planning a long-term business venture in Turkey. You never know how things will work out.

"Well, don't hurry back if you are making any money," was her quick response. Salua always kept her eye on the ball.

I did come back, but continued working on the barter scheme I had dreamed up sitting on the hotel balcony in Turkey. Harvey and I went on the road, meeting with his clients, doing a dog and pony show, and explaining our Rube Goldberg approach to settling their claims. Over the course of the next six months, American Bureau of Collections and Turam became well known in international trade circles for our barter scheme, even though we weren't yet producing. We were written up in *Business Europe* and other journals and magazines widely read in the business community. The gist of all the articles was that ABC, acting through Turam, was administering a barter/trade arrangement to get hard currency out of Turkey to satisfy the claims of exporters with trade claims in Turkey.

"There is something in this deal for everyone," said Harvey in one of his many interviews. "The Central Bank gets some foreign exchange and a payment backlog off its books, the local Turkish manufacturers get some lira to pay their workers and finance their businesses, and the foreign suppliers get most of their money back." *Most* was the operative word. The rest was to be commissions paid to Turam and ABC.

To get my barter scheme off the ground, I was going to need some help in high places, so I started by going back to Turkey and taking the wood-burning train to Ankara to meet with "Tarik Angit," the secretary of the treasury. I had met Angit once before, a meeting facilitated by the commercial attaché at the U.S. embassy, when I came to the country on my first collection assignment for ABC. It is the job of commercial attachés to help Americans doing business abroad in the hopes of fostering trade and good commercial relations.

I was all sooty from the ride on the wood-burning train, but there was no time to change before the meeting. Ankara is a drab, bleak place, and to add to this charming atmosphere it was cold and windy when I arrived. Angit's office was in the Ministry of Finance building, a large, impersonal edifice that only added to Ankara's bleak cityscape. Angit is a bear of a man, six foot three inches tall, with a mustache and a businesslike but friendly manner. Unlike Ankara itself, he had an elegant sense of style and was wearing a perfectly tailored Savile Row suit. With his perfect English and air of authority, he exuded power. I showed him a rudimentary brochure describing my barter scheme. It all sounded quite brilliant. Angit was noncommittal.

"I see what you are trying to do," he said, "but what you really need is a partner who knows and understands Turkey extremely well. The guy for you to meet is 'Bob Dudley.' He is an expert in Turkey and worked for two American banks that did a lot of business here. He has lots of contacts here," he said, filling my pockets with Turkish cigarettes. "Go to 'Cendex Bank' where he is a director. Tell him I sent you."

I always follow a lead, because you never know if there might be a pot of gold at the end. I was familiar with Cendex Bank. "Cendex Holdings Ltd." used to be a trading company in London and in Turkey and competed with Deltec Bank in Brazil when I worked there. When I returned to the States a few days later, I went to New York to meet this Bob Dudley at his well-appointed office in midtown Manhattan. Dudley was in his early thirties, one of those young, intelligent, and focused men whose face should have been imprinted on a coin. Figuratively speaking, it would have been appropriate.

"Bob," I said to Dudley, "it's a pleasure to meet you. Tarik Angit and all the bankers in Turkey speak so highly of you. I've been given a mandate [which was a stretch, but then again everything I was doing was a stretch] to put together this barter deal using nontraditional exports from Turkey to help American creditors realize something on the value of their claims. The business will be extraordinarily lucrative [another stretch], but I need someone who knows Turkey and knows the banks there. Why don't you come to Boston, become 49 percent partner in Turam, and we'll work together?"

Timing can be everything in business and in life, and as it happened, Dudley was growing weary of Cendex and was itching to go out on his own. To my surprise, Dudley agreed to come up to Boston and see the world headquarters of the mighty Turam Corporation, which just happened to be located, as were so many other global enterprises, in the offices of my collections law practice.

Bob Dudley was a very educated, very sophisticated banker. He lived well, and he wanted only the best. We agreed he would visit Boston sometime in the near future. Several weeks later, Dudley called and told me he was on his way up to Boston and wanted to meet with me and discuss my proposal further. I had to move quickly to make my bland, underwhelming law office look like something an ambitious banker would feel compelled to join.

Wayne Jasper had access to some very expensive Turkish rugs. He had lived next door to the Gregorian family, well-known rug merchants in Boston, who sold the finest Persian carpets in the world. So Jasper borrowed some carpets of great distinction. We borrowed some artwork from well-to-do friends. We organized everything, which meant that we threw a forest worth of loose papers in boxes and stored them in the basement. By the time of Dudley's visit, the small law offices of Smith, Levenson & Smith looked like a smart boutique financial firm.

"Tom Morgen," whom I had hired to make collections calls, dressed up as a chauffeur and went to pick Dudley up at the airport in an elegant rented Lincoln Continental.

It worked. My office made a favorable impression on Dudley, and I managed to make a good impression on him, too. Dudley came on board for an agreed 49 percent of Turam, but as we will see, things started to fall apart before I even started the paperwork to make Dudley part owner of the Turam soon-to-be global empire. Here we were, Dudley, an up-and-coming forty-year-old banker, and me, an opportunistic forty-year-old collections lawyer. We were going to make money together. Dudley would become president of Turam and I was to be chairman of the board. Dudley moved to Boston and we were ready to make our first $20 million.

I moved everyone around the office and gave Dudley the fanciest desk and the office with the best view. I tried to keep up the appearance that he had joined a budding conglomerate. In truth, every day I feared Dudley would soon discover that the emperor had no clothes. It was practically inevitable. After all, between the time he came to visit and agreed to join Turam and the time he moved to Boston a couple of weeks later, the Lincoln Continental had disappeared. It was all very stressful. I just hoped we could get the money ball rolling before he cared much about the sleight of hand that got him to Boston. If we started making big money, it wouldn't matter.

The day after he arrived at Turam, Dudley walked into my office. "It's time we went to Turkey," he said. "I want you to meet my friend, 'Mehmet Sudak.' He's the head of 'MS Group,' one of the largest Turkish conglomerates. Our friend Tarik Angit has left the Ministry of Finance to become president of 'MSBank.'"

"Great. Let's go to Turkey," I agreed.

Mehmet Sudak was the Donald Trump of Istanbul at that time. He was a short, squat man in his mid-forties with a prominent mustache and a soft voice. His manner was very refined and very Westernized. Indeed, he had attended college in Massachusetts. There was something about his face vaguely reminiscent of a bird of prey. Sudak's name was attached to practically every new construction site in the Middle East where the various arms of the MS Group were busy financing and building apartments, shopping centers, and roads. He knew his best opportunities were in the Muslim world, where he would be seen as a Muslim brother first and an opportunist second. His office had a huge conference room with expansive, stunning views of Istanbul. Dudley, Tarik Angit, and I sat around the conference room table. I was impressed with myself for keeping such esteemed company.

It didn't take Sudak but five minutes to pour ice-cold water on my barter scheme. "Forget the barter bullshit you're doing," said Sudak. Now there was a good idea. It was, in truth, a *meshuga* idea, so complex and so dependent on so many ministries in Turkey and elsewhere that the red tape alone made it completely unworkable. In retrospect, it had as much chance of working as hitting the lottery. But Sudak didn't agree to meet with us just to give us a dose of reality about my barter plan. When people like Sudak meet with you, they almost always have an agenda; there's always something they *want* from you. Such was the case with Sudak. I was all ears.

"My company is going to purchase $20 million face amount of Turkish nonguaranteed trade arrears [NGTAs]," Sudak said, referring to precisely the type of trade claim I had been trying to collect on for Harvey Herer's exporter clients. "I will get you a list from the Central Bank of all the creditors owed money. I'll offer to buy the debt in dollars at a discount and then collect the money, in Turkish lira, from the Central Bank."

The idea here was that while Turkish liras were of little use to exporters who sold goods *to* Turkey, they were of great use to Sudak, who did a vast amount of business *in* Turkey, business conducted in liras. If DuPont, for example, was owed $1 million in American dollars by Turkey, dollars the Central Bank didn't have, DuPont might be perfectly happy to take $300,000 from Sudak and assign its claim to him. Better $300,000 in hand than a claim for $1 million that might never be paid, or might only be paid many years down the road. Since Sudak had use for liras, he could, in effect, get the equivalent of $1 million in Turkish liras for the bargain price of $300,000 at the official exchange rate. And the Central Bank would be delighted, too, because Turkey now had a $1 million debt off its books. Given the nature of his Middle East business, getting dollars was not a problem for Sudak. His construction contracts called for payment in dollars. There were plenty of petrodollars in the Middle East, so he had the dollars to buy these trade claims at a discount.

Sudak's scheme, and indeed my own barter scheme, the one Sudak shot down, were early iterations of a form of finance that has since become commonplace as a way to settle or retire debts, one that now appears in countless variations—the debt/equity swap. The basic idea is to convert a debt into an equity position in some enterprise, and it is a device used in both international and domestic finance. Indeed, the debt/equity swap has burgeoned into a ubiquitous device for retiring all kinds of debts. United Airlines and other major air carriers, for example, have climbed out of bankruptcy using debt/equity swaps in which creditors agree to exchange the debt they are owed into an equity position in the "new" company that emerges from bankruptcy debt-free.

But debt/equity swaps had their roots in the blocked currency problem encountered by corporations doing business in countries where it was difficult to convert local profits into a hard currency such as dollars. And Turkey was one of the first countries to use the debt/equity swap technique as a way to address its foreign debt problem and attract new foreign investment. Many banks also started using debt/equity swaps as a way of realizing value on defaulted or nonperforming loans to developing-world countries. In his book *The Global Bankers*, Roy C. Smith (no relation) describes the notion behind the debt/equity swap as it related to bank loans, an explanation that also applies, for the most part, to trade creditors as well:

> The idea was to retire dollar debt by exchanging it with the
> central bank of the country for local currency that would then be
> invested in a company, factory, or real estate in the country. [In-

deed, some countries, to bolster certain segments of its economy, might, by the terms of the deal, restrict the equity investment to specific types of investments.]

The result was that the seller of the debt could realize a much higher price than in the secondary market [that is, if the debt holder simply sold the claim to another buyer willing to assume the risk] if he was willing to convert the proceeds into a local currency investment that might be more profitable in the long run than the debt, though he would be left with the sticky problem of repatriating his profits into his own currency later on. . . .

The country involved could retire the debt being swapped at a discount and would receive new capital investment in income-producing and foreign-exchange-creating assets that would add to employment and help service the remaining debt. Countries were concerned, however, that limits be placed on the number of swaps that took place as the creation of the new local currency to be swapped for the debt could add to inflation.

Companies exporting goods abroad, say, Ford Motor Company exporting automobile parts to Turkey, expect to be paid in dollars. Simply put, Ford sells parts to a buyer in Turkey under an import license granted by the government of Turkey. This license, in a sense, implies that when the buyer pays for the auto parts in liras, the government of Turkey will convert those liras to dollars to pay Ford. In simple terms, the transaction works like this: The buyer deposits payment for the auto parts, in liras, into a Turkish bank or a foreign bank located in Turkey with instructions for the bank to pay Ford in dollars. But when a country like Turkey develops economic problems—a huge trade imbalance, rampant inflation, or loss of confidence—the Central Bank may not have enough dollars to satisfy all the demand from trade suppliers such as Ford. If the Central Bank can't make that exchange for Ford, then that's a trade supplier debt, and that's when companies like Ford start looking for other ways to collect dollars for the liras that have been paid for the goods they shipped and sold to the Turkish buyer.

For example, Ford could use all that local currency to build a local manufacturing plant in Ankara and export the cars to the United States or Europe for sale, where, of course, customers would be paying in dollars or euros. That's one way to turn a local, inconvertible currency back into dollars.

If creditors couldn't make use of the currency by building a foreign plant like Ford, or didn't want to take such a risk, they might participate in a debt/equity swap that gave them a stake in a local enterprise. Although this kind of arrangement merely offers the prospect of increasing their pile of local currency, trade suppliers might take the risk anyway in the hope that the currency crisis would ease at some future date, allowing them to cash out and realize even more dollars. As an inducement, governments sometimes throw in guarantees that give such creditors priority.

But many debt/equity swaps do offer the prospect of a dollar return. For instance, some creditors have swapped the debts they are owed for equity positions in luxury resorts that collect large sums in dollars and other hard currencies from vacationing tourists. Even Hollywood got in on the act in the 1980s when debt/equity swaps started to catch on.

Hollywood producers knew that they could significantly reduce the costs of shooting a film by moving production to countries such as Mexico or Turkey where labor, food, and materials were cheap. If you were shooting a western, for example, there were plenty of places in Mexico that looked just like Arizona or Texas. So producers would create budgets for their films with what were called "above" and "below" the line financing. Above-the-line expenditures were dollar costs—the money needed to pay the marquee stars and the U.S.-based production crew. Below-the-line financing was the money needed, say, in pesos, to pay local extras and cover food, lodging, equipment rental, and the countless incidental expenses that come with setting up shop with a hundred or more people in a small town in Mexico for a couple of months while shooting a film.

To raise the below-the-line financing, some Hollywood producers turned to me in the early 1980s to find companies and individuals that were looking for a way to convert local currency, such as pesos, into dollars. In other words, people willing to swap the debt they were owed (or the local currency they held but could not convert into dollars) for an equity position in the film—a film that would, hopefully, make millions, in dollars, when it was shown on movie screens across the United States.

Savage Harvest, a 1981 film shot in Kenya starring Michelle Phillips, was one of two films for which my job was to find (for a fee, of course) the below-the-line financing. The other, shot in Mexico, was *The Evil That Men Do*, a 1984 film starring Charles Bronson.

These debt/equity swaps, however configured, solved a problem in a way that usually had something in the deal for everyone. The foreign creditor had a way to satisfy a claim that might otherwise become worthless. The debtor country had a way to retire some of its foreign debt (which has all kinds of economic benefits). And the schemes encouraged local investment, created local jobs, and made the country a more attractive place to do business. The schemes were not without their critics. Some people argued that valuable investments were being given away at bargain-basement prices to accomplish only slight reductions in a nation's indebtedness. Others, rightly, raised concerns that since governments could simply print more local currency to pay off their debts through such schemes, currency then used for the local equity investment made these deals inflationary. Brokerage fees in such deals were usually very high and how much *new* foreign investment they really encouraged was questionable.

Nevertheless, just as El Salvador taught me that money and people flow across borders without regard for laws designed to contain them, I was learning from Sudak's NGTA scheme that in finance, every financial problem has a solution—or, more likely, a thousand of them. Financial creativity, too, is an organic process, and if there is a way to make money at something, someone will inevitably find it. Debt/equity swaps, in all their infinite variety, are proof of that.

"I need someone to approach the creditors and act as the middle-man," Sudak continued as he described his NGTA scheme to us. That was me: the consummate middleman. And people like Sudak needed middlemen. It's always best not to be transparent when you're doing this kind of business. Once people understand what you're doing, the price goes up. Why? DuPont might be happy with $300,000 for a million-dollar claim, but if they realize it would still be a great deal for Sudak at twice the price, they might not part with their claim so readily. Having a middleman is essential. With a middleman, DuPont and Sudak would never meet. Furthermore, under Turkish law, only foreign entities could buy the trade claims, so Turkish buyers either had to form a foreign entity, which could take months of bureaucratic red tape, or find a foreign partner. Turam was already up and running. "What would you fellows, Turam, charge by way of commission?" he asked.

Dudley, the banker, said, "Two percent." He was Mr. 2 Percent.

"Alright," Sudak said. "You'll get 2 percent of the face amount of all the exporter trade claims [nonguaranteed trade arrears] you purchase on my behalf." My head was spinning. I was deliriously happy. Two percent of $20 million was $400,000, which was a lot of money to a struggling collections lawyer. And this wasn't exactly heavy lifting. We already had the buyer: Sudak. It all seemed too good to be true.

"Mr. Angit, as president of my bank, MSBank, will do all the financial arrangements," said Sudak. "The NGTAs will be registered in the name of Turam and I will pay you 2 percent in dollars as commission. Turam will collect on these claims in liras and invest those liras in some of our companies in Turkey." This was how Turkish law was set up to encourage both liquidation of foreign trade claims and increase investment in Turkey. It all meant that in addition to the commissions we were going to make, we'd have a piece of the action in some of Sudak's many companies, specifically his spare-parts business. The deal was getting even sweeter. If I were a cartoon character, there would have been dollar signs where my pupils should be. I loved Sudak. He was going to make me a rich man.

"You'll need to apply to the Central Bank to get a license to invest as our foreign partner," Sudak said. "We'll help you with all the paperwork and get your application through the bureaucracy. Once the Central Bank receives the agreements assigning the trade claims to Turam, we will get the Turkish liras at the official rate." In other words, that $1 million claim Sudak was buying for $300,000 would be converted into $1 million worth of liras at the official exchange rate.

"Moreover," he continued, "I'm establishing an offshore bank because my contracting firm is doing big business in the Middle East. We're building housing in Libya. We have one of the first Turkish contracts to build there. The Saudis can look to us for hospitals, roads, and military barracks. With all that building going on, the other Turkish contractors will need spare parts for all their machinery. So we will supply those to the Middle East, too. After all," he boomed, "we're Muslim brothers and we are close by. You'll even have a participation in the bank and the spare-parts company."

I could see my father holding his head in desperation. Now he's working with the Muslims. *Oy vey!*

The purpose of the offshore bank was, coincidentally, an effort to squeeze Dudley's former employer, Cendex Bank, out of the picture. And to accomplish that feat, Sudak had just hired Dudley's best friend, "Simon Lowenstein," a director of Cendex in London, to become chairman of his new offshore bank. The new bank would finance the purchase of the trade arrears, the spare parts, and everything else Sudak needed to run his empire using huge lines of credit obtained from Western banks. Indeed, in short order, Lowenstein established the bank using tens of millions of dollars of credit lines obtained from English and European banks.

Documents and contracts were signed, and given that we were about to become millionaires—or so I thought—I felt Dudley and I should take Tarik Angit out to lunch. After all, it was Angit who had started this whole ball rolling by introducing me to Dudley. And now he had given up his government position to become president of Sudak's Turkish bank, MSBank. Angit had opened the door to all these riches and we were all now part of Sudak's happy family.

Dudley, Tarik Angit, and I got in the elevator. It stopped one floor below Sudak's offices. When the doors opened four tall, beautiful, dark-eyed models stepped in.

"Good afternoon, ladies," said Angit in Turkish, always charming.

They smiled and Angit turned to Dudley and me. "Sudak and his partner own a very successful modeling school on this floor. He usually takes his lunch break at the school."

"I see," my eyes now wide open, even more impressed with the reach of Sudak's empire. I hoped Dudley didn't expect us to buy a modeling school in Boston.

We walked into the Turkish sun and I looked at Dudley and thought, this is some partnership. After five days of being in business, we're going to be very rich, even if I had only the faintest idea of how Sudak's scheme was going to work. It seemed even more complicated than the one I concocted on the hotel balcony a few months before. But I had faith. We ate lunch at a fish restaurant looking across the Bosporus. I felt like I owned a whole string of modeling schools. We discussed future prospects. I was high on the future.

"I know, my friends, you boys won't forget me," Tarik Angit said to us somewhat obtusely during lunch.

"Of course not," I replied. It seemed an innocuous-enough statement. We were all friends. We wouldn't forget Tarik Angit.

We returned home to Boston the next day and got to work completing all the filings we needed to become Sudak's officially approved foreign partner, and within a month that task was done.

Our first assignment from Sudak was to find a good international law firm in New York to help him form the offshore bank. He would be coming to New York soon to interview them.

I called my old Roxbury Latin pal, John Goldman, a brilliant lawyer at the estimable firm of Milbank, Tweed. Goldman, unlike me, had been accepted at Harvard, as had many of my classmates. It was Goldman who had first introduced me to AISEC and, thus, indirectly, my first oversees work experience in 1962 in Turkey. John set us up with three prestigious law firms, including Alexander and Green, the oldest law firm in the country, founded in 1794.

Then Sudak and Tarik Angit informed us they were coming to New York on the Concorde. We would all meet at the Plaza Hotel and visit the law firms together. I could practically smell the money that was going to start flowing our way. I was at my desk, content as a Cheshire cat, doing a little bit of my collections work. In short order I would soon be rid of such work and counting the days until my newfound partners, Sudak and Angit, would arrive in New York to begin revving up the moneymaking machine. They were due to arrive in five days. My days as a loser were almost over. I couldn't believe how well this little collection matter in Turkey had turned out.

Now, I hadn't forgotten all those exporters who had signed up for my original but ill-conceived barter scheme hatched on a hotel balcony months before. Harvey at American Bureau of Collections had proved quite successful at signing them up for the deal. They were going to be the first holders of the NGTAs I would buy on Sudak's behalf. But things started to fall apart almost immediately when Dudley walked into my office and put an ultimatum on my desk. Dudley is as patrician and as cool as a banker can be. He was about to become as problematic as a partner in a partnership with no actual money can be when money is about to be made. (Partners quarrel when there's no money or too much money.)

"What's this?" I asked.

He pointed to the paper and I started reading. Dudley's chutzpah was astonishing. In essence, he was demanding 51 percent of Turam immediately; he wanted control of the board of directors and he wanted to appoint his former Cendex colleague, Simon Lowenstein, to the board. I couldn't believe it.

"Turam is my company," I said. "I started it and brought you in, and we agreed that I would have 51 percent of the company. By what right . . ."

Dudley interrupted before I could work up a full head of steam. "I'm going to tell Sudak about the bribe you agreed to pay to Tarik Angit."

The conversation had taken on a distinctly Kafkaesque tone. I didn't know what in the world Dudley was talking about. Then he reminded me of our lunch overlooking the Bosporus when Tarik Angit said something about "not forgetting him." I had simply replied, "Of course not," but the conversation was vague and I was only being polite. What was I going to say, that I wouldn't take care of him? The whole conversation had lasted all of two seconds and I ascribed no particular meaning to it. Now Dudley was using it to blackmail me into surrendering control of Turam.

"There was no bribe, Bob, that's ridiculous," I said. "All I said was that we wouldn't forget our friends. I never promised him anything!"

"Well," replied Dudley, "Sudak won't see it that way." Then, acting holier than thou, he added, "It's not the way I do business." What he meant was that not being the majority owner of Turam was the way he didn't do business.

But now I was really in a bind. It was Dudley who had brought me, and Turam, to Sudak. Dudley had the relationship with him, not me, and now he was threatening to expose me as corrupt and immoral. He wanted all of the anticipated riches for himself. I had no doubt that if he were to have 51 percent of the company, I would soon be a delivery boy for *The Boston Globe*, whose debts I collected.

"Sudak and Angit are flying into New York on the Concorde in a few days," he said. (This impressed us both a great deal, so we kept repeating it. At that time, flying on the Concorde was a rarity.) "I will tell him how dishonorably you're handling business. If you don't make me the majority shareholder in Turam, I'll resign."

There go my millions, I thought. Easy come, easy go. Maybe.

Dudley concluded his little speech by telling me that he would meet with Sudak separately in New York and tell him about my alleged "bribe."

I sat back and caught my breath as Dudley left my office. Where's my leverage, I asked? There must be a way to redeem this situation. I'm too close now to see it all go up in flames.

There were a few things I had going for myself. Turam, which I still controlled, had filed the necessary papers with the Central Bank of Turkey and was the officially approved, legally required foreign investment partner of the MS Group. It took many weeks to go through the registration process and there was a lot of complex paperwork, so there was a lot of incentive for Sudak not to lose Turam's participation. If I stuck to my guns with Dudley, I doubted Sudak would be eager to throw me, and with me, Turam, overboard. I also doubted he'd find my conversation with Angit terribly shocking, though who knew what story he'd hear from Dudley.

I left a letter for Sudak that he would receive as soon as he checked into the Plaza in New York. In it, I made sure he knew how much effort I had already expended on his behalf.

"Dear Mr. Sudak, Welcome to New York! I hope your visit is productive. I look forward to any way that Turam Corporation and I may collaborate with your efforts here. I would like to meet privately with you, as I am sure that Bob Dudley likewise has requested the same. I am enclosing the following documents for your perusal: a progress report on the contract for purchase of NGTAs by Turam on behalf of the MS Group and a preliminary outline from Haight, Poor & Havens, one of the three law firms we'll be meeting with during your visit. My associate, Wayne W. Jasper Esq., has had extensive contact with Grand Cayman Island counsel with respect to creation of the offshore bank. Also, please find an equipment-machinery and spare-parts joint venture proposal and a sample joint venture contract." The goal was to make sure that Sudak knew I was on the case before he saw Dudley and heard about my alleged bribery scheme with Tarik Angit.

I reached Tarik Angit by phone just before he and Sudak were to depart for New York and warned him about Dudley.

So the race to New York was on. Sudak, Angit, and their entourage were on the Concorde eating foie gras and drinking champagne. Dudley and I, separately, were using cabs and coupons on the Eastern Airlines shuttle.

The Plaza Hotel, before Donald Trump got his hands on it, was a splendid and exquisitely tasteful place; a fitting backdrop to the small international intrigue about to play out, one that I was sure would either render me a loser in my wife's eyes or catapult me to prominence as an international financier. In retrospect, it all seems a bit grandiose, but I was practically a kid then, in my late thirties, with big dreams.

When the shuttle landed, I sprinted for a cab and raced to the Plaza, adrenalin coursing through my system and mixing with copious amounts of cigarette smoke. It seemed like the most important day of my life.

The taxi pulled up in front of the Plaza and I rushed into the lobby and picked up a house phone. One of Sudak's minions gave me the bad news. Sudak was already meeting with Dudley, that lousy, double-crossing Dudley who came into my life through Tarik Angit, the very man I had allegedly agreed to bribe. I was devastated. I would now be on the defensive, and I had no idea how lavish Dudley's story of my corruption and deception would be.

I had no choice but to bide my time in the lobby and hope that Sudak would still allow me to plead my case. I called Salua.

"Don't be a loser," she advised helpfully. I vowed not to call her ever again. The pressure was getting to be too much.

Finally, Dudley emerged from the elevator. He barely looked at me and said he had to go uptown to see his divorce lawyer. Trying to separate from various types of partners was a common theme in his life at the time. In fact, it was his second divorce and he was still in his early thirties.

The moment of truth had arrived and I headed up to Sudak's suite. Like a trial lawyer, I had rehearsed my argument dozens of times. I knew exactly what I wanted to say. I hadn't said two words when Sudak held up his hand and said, "I'm staying with you. Let's go meet with these three law firms you've found."

I was dumbstruck and flattered. Maybe Dudley came off as unhinged. Maybe Tarik Angit had already taken the wind out of Dudley's sails. Maybe I am more impressive than I look. But the real reason, in retrospect, was that Turam was already registered with the Central Bank as the MS Group's official foreign investor to purchase the trade claims, and Sudak was eager to get moving.

Dudley promptly resigned from Turam (I had actually never gotten around to the paperwork that would have given him 49 percent) and formed his own company in New York, "Excell Management Ltd.," where he planned to broker his own Turkish nonguaranteed trade agreements. He knew the methodology and the documentation. And, indeed, in the years to come he did very well at it. For now, however, Turam remained in my hands, Dudley was out of my life, and my little ship was sailing on calm seas. Indeed, I would no longer have to split the millions that were about to roll in with Dudley. Things couldn't have worked out better.

Sudak and I visited the three American law firms I had identified for him, and he chose Alexander and Green to be his lawyers before heading back across the Atlantic. Like most magnates, Sudak was a globetrotter with offices in many foreign capitals, and our next meeting, about two weeks later, was in London at his wood-paneled office on Upper Brook Street. Sudak promised he would give me a list of 1,500 creditors holding trade clams against Turkey, creditors who might be interested in selling their claims at a deep discount to Sudak with Turam in the middle getting its 2 percent.

Salua came with me to London and enjoyed the theater and a hundred shops. She was beginning to sense that I had rounded the corner, and I began to realize that her expectations of me were what gave me the fight and the drive to turn this unexpected opportunity in Turkey into a real turning point in my life. But I was about to suffer one more shock.

I called on Sudak, who greeted me like a valuable member of his inner circle. He was very affable and polite and, as promised, he handed me the golden list of creditors and we shook hands amiably. "I am this man's man," I thought to myself. Until I came down the stairs and saw none other than Bob Dudley and Simon Lowenstein, just hired to run Sudak's offshore bank, in the lobby, laughing among themselves. The three of us nodded to each other civilly, but I said to myself, "I have big problems." I would later find out just how big.

On the plane back to Boston I paced the aisles smoking cigarettes (you could do that back then). Salua ordered glass after glass of white wine, and I racked my brains. "I have problems," I said. "But what are they?"

"Sit down, Bob," said Salua. "You'll find out soon enough."

Three days after returning to Boston from London, I got a call from Sudak. He told me, firmly, that he was going to buy Turam. I was speechless. I didn't understand. I'd just survived Dudley's coup attempt and now Sudak is telling me that he's going to buy Turam. This little company with no assets other than some furniture and some telephones was suddenly a hot commodity.

Why did Sudak want to buy Turam? It probably dawned on him after he'd helped Turam get registered as his official foreign partner that he didn't need to trust some unknown in Boston with his millions to buy the trade claims. He wanted to be in control and probably figured he could keep his ownership of Turam quiet and not lose its coveted foreign partner status.

"I see," I said to Sudak. "I'll do everything I can to help you. Let me get back to you." I was buying time so that I could figure out a way to salvage something from this fiasco, not the least of which was my dignity. A few days earlier I thought I was about to become a millionaire, and now I was about to be a collections lawyer again. If I refused to sell, Turam would be virtually worthless, since its major asset at the time was being Sudak's foreign partner and he could easily cut me out.

I didn't have a balcony at my offices in Boston, but I did have a fire escape with a view of the Charles River. This whole scheme was launched on a balcony overlooking one river; perhaps I could figure out how to end it, profitably, with a view of another. I went out on the fire escape, lit a Marlboro Red (did I *ever* smoke a lot in those days) and watched the M.I.T. crew gliding along the river. There I came up with a plan to salvage both my dignity and my dreams of riches. A few days later I called Sudak.

"You can have the company. How would you like to do this?"

"Well, the lawyers at Alexander and Green can come up next week to examine your books and records and we can make the transfer then," said Sudak.

"That's marvelous," I replied.

Wayne Jasper was doing all of my law firm's legal work by this point, busy as I was chasing a pot of gold in Turkey. After hearing that Sudak wanted to buy Turam, I walked into Wayne's office.

"We're about to do some real law," I said. "Start preparing documents authorizing me, on Turam's behalf, to borrow some money." If Sudak was going to buy Turam, I was going to make sure I had something to show for it—something to show Salua I wasn't a loser; something to show myself the same.

I rushed down to the "Fourth National Bank" in Brookline to see my old friend "Bradford Whitney," the senior vice president (ever notice how many people hold the title of senior VP at banks?) for whom I had done some collections work and where I had some personal and business accounts.

"I need a very quick loan," I told Brad. "I don't have time to go through a complicated process and there will be no risk to the bank. I want the bank to lend Turam Corporation $500,000, but it will never leave the bank. I just want it on the books of Turam. You can secure the loan with all of the assets of Turam." That meant some filing cabinets, an old telex machine, some office furniture, and one very real asset—the foreign registration in Turkey to be the MS Group's official foreign partner in the NGTA business. "Turam," I told Brad, "will deposit the money right back into a new account at the bank in the name of *Turan* Corporation," which I had just created.

The following week the lawyers from Alexander and Green came up to Boston and went through Turam's books. They went to the secretary of state's office to check our records and returned. Then they called Sudak. I listened through the wall.

"These books look very clean, Mr. Sudak. There's only one outstanding loan of $500,000 from the Fourth National Bank. Turam has no other liabilities."

I went back to my desk and entertained myself by opening up the mail at my collection law office. I never let the collection business die down while I was chasing the big bucks in Turkey. Who knew what would really happen? I could, as my father had said, depend on these self-addressed envelopes from debtors. "Bob, if you put postage on, they're more likely to pay," was one of my father's pearls of wisdom. "There's not a day that a check does not come in the mail and 30 percent belongs to you." So I kept opening envelopes.

Meanwhile, I knew Sudak's clock was ticking. When we'd started a couple of months before, you could have bought Turkish nonguaranteed trade arrears for twenty cents on the dollar, but now the market had moved up to twenty-six cents on the dollar, though the market was still thin.

He had two choices. He could create or find a new foreign partner, as required by Turkish law, a process that would take many weeks *with my full cooperation,* by which time he might have to pay thirty-five cents on the dollar for the trade claims. As others got wise to the money that could be made, the demand for the trade claims would go up and with it the price. If he delayed, even a few weeks, it was going to get more expensive to do what he wanted to do. His other choice was to buy Turam and swallow the half-million-dollar loan. It was a straightforward calculation.

When Sudak called the next day I was prepared. I had learned to always let the other party go first. You learn a lot about their thinking that way without selling yourself short.

"What will it really take to buy Turam?" he asked. I knew right then and there that he wanted to buy; he wasn't going to wait to find or create a new foreign partner and go through all the hassle that would entail. Surely there would be a lot of questions from the Central Bank, which would want to know why Turam had withdrawn and would probably require a letter of withdrawal, which only I could provide. The Central Bank was alert to sham entities created by Turks to get around the foreign partner law. Sudak didn't want to have to answer questions at this point or raise concerns that might interfere with moving ahead with his plans.

"If you pay off the bank loan, the company is yours," I replied. Sudak was a smart guy and a savvy financier. He knew the loan was recent and that it was all a way to get him to pay a half million dollars for Turam.

I didn't mention the figure to Sudak, though his lawyers had told him the amount. I didn't want to add salt to the wound and I thought the figure straddled that fine line between reasonable and extortionate. Why did I go through all the trouble to get the loan when I could simply have quoted him a price? It all has to do with making something that would be otherwise unpalatable acceptable to your adversary. It would be easier for Sudak to swallow a loan to the Fourth National Bank than to write a half-million-dollar check to Robert Smith.

"I will get back to you," Sudak said. He didn't sound happy.

I paced the floor and smoked cigarettes. Four hours later, I got a call from Simon Lowenstein. Sudak was sending the lawyers to do the final paperwork. "Oh, by the way," Simon said, "what are the wiring details for the Fourth National Bank?"

I sat back and congratulated myself. This putz that my father had long given up on was about to make a half million dollars against unprecedented odds at the expense of the richest, smartest businessman in Turkey. After all, I would no longer have to repay the Fourth National Bank. Sudak would do it for me. Meanwhile, I had the half million in an account I had opened for Turan Corporation, with an "n."

Unbeknownst to Sudak, I had Wayne Jasper create Turan Corporation to pursue opportunities in Turkey. After all, from American Bureau of Collections I knew the names of some of the NGTA holders who wanted to sell their claims, Sudak had given me the list of 1,500 creditors who might be willing to sell their claims, and Sudak wasn't the only fish in the sea—there were others interested in buying these claims, too, and for basically the same reason. In essence, I sold the letter "m" for half a million bucks. I'm sure Sudak was kicking himself for giving me the list of creditors.

Maybe I'm not going to be stuck in collections law for the rest of my life, I told myself. Maybe my wife didn't marry a loser. If I can do this, I can live the life I want. I will make money using my wits, not opening self-addressed stamped envelopes. The whole affair gave me the much-needed jolt of self-confidence I needed to try my hand at many different ventures. Even when I lost money in the future, as I sometimes did, I never again lost my self-confidence.

What I hadn't counted on was that gossip about the little Jewish collections lawyer who sold the great and brilliant Sudak an "m" for $500,000 soon made its way around Istanbul, and word came back that if Robert Smith ever returned to Turkey he would be lying at the bottom of the Bosporus in cement boots.

I laughed. Then I realized, "I can't go back to Turkey. How can I do my business? I have this list of creditors willing to sell the Turkey claims, which is invaluable, but how am I going to scour Turkey for buyers if I can't go back there?"

The answer was to find middlemen. Using the many contacts I had made there I was able to do many transactions in NGTAs with Turkish enterprises such as rug exporters and multinationals with operations in Turkey who were happy to have a cheap source of liras. I made a bundle buying claims against Turkey at thirty to forty-five cents on the dollar and selling them for fifty or fifty-five cents on the dollar. Instead of exchanging their dollars at the official exchange rate, they were able to buy dollar claims at about half their value. And the sellers, such as ABC's clients, got some of the highest amounts ever paid for such claims. The Central Bank, which could print liras with impunity, was happy, too, because it could now pay those dollar claims off with liras. Everyone was happy, except, perhaps, Sudak.

I bought and sold Turkish trade claims until 1982, during which time I made well over $2 million doing so. Then, as so often happens, the law that permitted NGTAs to be sold and converted lapsed and wasn't renewed. I was a company, Turan, without a country. What would I do now?

I dragged myself into the office each day, dreading it. Tom Morgen, my erstwhile chauffer who had escorted Bob Dudley to my office when I was trying so hard to impress him, said ruefully, "Well, we can keep collecting small debts." I looked at him in dismay. No more calls from Turkey. No more spreads. No more glamorous foreign travel.

I dropped in at my father's office seeking . . . what? Solace? Support? Some fatherly advice? I was morose sitting across from him. I had made half a million dollars selling the letter "m" to Sudak and another million or more on top of that. But it wasn't the money. I missed the adventure of it all and the thrill of living by my wits.

"What's the matter?" he asked. "What did you think, you were a Muslim doing business over there? What's wrong with our business?"

"I don't think I can spend my life collecting money from deadbeats," I said. My father winced.

What was I going to do? My staff was leaving and collections law was all I had left. Then, in December 1982, my father died, my honorable, decent, penny-pinching father. As I cleaned out his office and went through his files I fell into a depression and agonized over the fact that I had disappointed him. I had rejected the life he had worked so hard for. This son who always wanted something different missed his father. Maybe I would try to take collections work seriously. I will force myself to do it, I thought. All these schemes I get into, what good are they? A lot of worrying and skating on thin ice. My father would want me to settle down and have a serious career. No more cavorting among the Muslims.

But a few weeks after I buried my father, I got a call from a client, Baxter Healthcare, the medical device and pharmaceutical giant, with whom I had done business in the Turkish NGTAs. "We've just received these Guatemalan stabilization bonds," said my contact at Baxter. "Do you deal with them? Do you have a quote?"

"Of course I do," I said, though I hadn't a clue what they were. "Can you send me a copy of the bonds? I want to make sure they're not a forgery. I'll call you in twenty-four hours."

I went out on my fire escape again, lit another cigarette, and saw the future. Things change. There's always another train coming into the station. Even in Turkey they changed. Years later, I learned, Mehmet Sudak lost all his money and became a field manager for a construction company. His bank declared bankruptcy after three years. Dudley became a multimillionaire from his own excellent contacts in Turkey, and our paths would cross again a few years later, to our mutual gain, in Nigeria. (See Chapter 5.)

Some things did not change. Tarik Angit resurfaced on the boards of a few commercial banks. My wife went shopping. And I took a flight to Guatemala.

CHAPTER 4

GUATEMALA/PANAMA
Risky Business

IN 1954, the U.S. Central Intelligence Agency engineered the overthrow of the democratically elected president of Guatemala, Jacobo Arbenz Guzmán. Arbenz had radical ideas. He wanted a more equitable distribution of Guatemala's wealth, the vast majority of which was in the hands of a very few. He favored land reform, which would give Guatemala's poor a chance at a better life. And he wanted wealthy multinational companies, particularly the immensely powerful United Fruit Company—the American multinational that owned vast tracts of land in Central America and the Caribbean and exported huge amounts of tropical fruit to the United States and Europe—to have less influence on the country's economic and political systems.* That's why Guatemalans voted for him. And that's why

---

*United Fruit's primary exports were pineapples and bananas. Its dominance in countries such as Guatemala gave rise to the term "banana republic."

the CIA, suspicious of Arbenz's "socialist" ideas, engineered the coup that would lead Guatemala into more than three decades of bloody, "low intensity" civil war that cost more than 200,000 lives.

"Low intensity" is a relative term. Guatemala never erupted into full-scale civil war as El Salvador and Nicaragua did. It was more of a grinding, terror-filled period of political killings and disappearances carried out by a succession of U.S.-supported right-wing dictators against the peasantry, and for those on the wrong end of the bullets and machetes, there was nothing "low intensity" about it.

By the time I arrived in Guatemala in 1983, there was little outward sign of thirty years of bloodshed. Unlike El Salvador, hotels weren't being bombed and gunfire didn't wake you up in the middle of the night. But Guatemala was still an economic no-man's-land, a "third world" country (the now politically incorrect term for a "developing world" or "emerging market" country) where the poor were still very poor and without a voice, the rich still very rich and in power, and foreign companies struggled to find a way to expatriate local profits, just as they did in El Salvador.

When I received the call from Baxter asking if I dealt in Guatemalan stabilization bonds (GSBs), I did what I usually do when confronted with an unexpected new opportunity: I faked it. I had never even heard of GSBs, but that was no deterrent. A few years earlier I had finessed half a million dollars from the most successful business mogul in Turkey and then made a small fortune trading Turkish trade debt. I wasn't such a *schlemiel*, after all. I had wandered into unfamiliar territory and come out ahead, way ahead. I had a bright future in the world of high international finance.

"Of course," I said to my Baxter contact. "Send me copies of the front and back of your bonds." I had no idea what kind of instrument they were talking about and I had to figure it out, and to do that I had to see the bonds themselves and read the terms.

As in El Salvador (where I would further develop my bond business after Guatemala got rolling), foreign companies in Guatemala were holding dollar-denominated bonds with all the same risks—

mainly the issuer's ability to pay.* After all, Guatemala, like Salvador, was a tiny country with little foreign exchange. Its ability to make good on its dollar promises was far from a sure thing. But the call from Baxter made a lightbulb go off in my head: Maybe there's something happening in Guatemala that no one knows about, I thought. Maybe there's money to be made finding buyers and sellers for these Guatemalan stabilization bonds. I decided to go to Guatemala to investigate.

Even with the foray into Turkish nonguaranteed trade arrears, and my short-lived adventure as a future multimillionaire operative in the Mehmet Sudak empire, I was still, despite my aspirations, essentially a collections lawyer. And around the time Baxter was asking me about Guatemalan bonds, I got a call from "Frank Biers," a Chicago lawyer representing Bally Export Corporation, a subsidiary of the Bally Corporation, the giant resort casino and gaming enterprise. Bally had sold a million dollars worth of slot machines to a company called Juliano Internacional, a Panamanian casino operator, the purchases made through a third company called Balicar, a company registered in the Cayman Islands. Juliano and Balicar never paid, and Biers hired me to try and collect.

I knew right away that I might be overmatched. It's a safe bet that gambling businesses registered in the Cayman Islands and Panama generally aren't run by retired schoolteachers and church ladies. But

---

*While the risks were similar, the reasons that companies had these dollar bonds were somewhat different. In El Salvador, companies were looking for a way to convert profits in the local currency into dollars, and El Salvador bonds were a vehicle for doing so. But foreign companies that had sold goods to Guatemala were virtually forced to accept dollar-denominated bonds as payment because the country had so little foreign exchange. In short, in Guatemala, the bonds represented what we call *trade supplier debt*.

never-say-no-Bob-Smith-because-you-never-know-where-your-next-paycheck-might-be-coming-from said to Biers, "I'll be on the next flight to Panama." As long as I was going to Guatemala, I figured, I might as well make a stop in Panama.

Little did I know, however, that I was about to become a bit player in an underworld drama whose contours are still unclear to me to this day.

It wasn't that I had no experience collecting debts abroad. Indeed, in the early 1980s I had the idea that there was relatively easy money to be made in international collections as a middleman. (That's the story of my business life, the man in the middle. Whether in a bond deal or a collection, I was always making money as a middleman.) Many U.S. lawyers had clients who did business abroad and they advised them on all kinds of matters: contracts, customs, labor, and taxes, for example. But few wanted to be in the debt collection business. It wasn't intellectually challenging and was generally considered bottom-of-the-barrel business. Consequently, when their clients got screwed overseas, they looked for a collections specialist.

I didn't generally get on planes to do the heavy lifting myself. What did I know about the local courts, the local players, the business mores, or the cultural norms in these places? Besides, I was hardly an imposing figure. Knocking on a debtor's door in Panama or Costa Rica, or sending a telex from Boston and threatening to sue, wasn't going to scare anyone.

So, rather than try and collect debts myself, I'd take my nonrefundable processing fee and hire local counsel in whatever country the deadbeat was in. I was careful never to introduce my client, usually a law firm or collection agency, to the local counsel and vice versa. As far as my clients knew, I was the guy collecting the money. And as far as my local lawyers knew, I was the guy collecting directly for the creditor. As in my bond deals, if the parties on either end knew one another, they wouldn't need me.

This kind of business could be easy money. In addition to the processing fee, I'd get 35 percent of any monies collected and pay local counsel a percentage of that. If they didn't collect, I owed them nothing and still had my nonrefundable processing fee. Doing little more than finding a competent local lawyer in a place like Panama or El Salvador, I could make a good dollar. At least until foreign law firms in those countries got wise and started listing themselves in the various directories American lawyers and U.S. collection firms used to find people like me who claimed expertise in foreign collections.

That's one reason why, when Biers called, there wasn't much business being a middleman anymore. Besides, he was very explicit that I personally call on Juliano. Clearly, I'd have to go down to Panama and try and collect this one myself.

Guatemala was my first Central American stop in 1983, though, and it was there that I first learned how to buy and sell bonds in a previously nonexistent market. I had to become the market maker.

There was an enormous amount of reconnaissance involved because I was starting from scratch. What was a Guatemalan stabilization bond? Who would buy one? Why? At what price? What plans did the government have to pay the interest and principal on the bonds as they came due? What were the payment terms? Were there any special conditions attached to the bonds? A bond is, in essence, a contract, and all kinds of conditions can be attached to the promise to pay that can affect their value. And few of these details could be learned at a distance, or even from looking at the bond itself. You had to dig deeper to really understand the whole picture. You had to be on the ground.

My rounds on my first visit to Guatemala included the Central Bank, the Ministry of the Economy, the U.S. embassy, banks, law firms, and perhaps most important, the Guatemalan chapter of Rotary International. In Latin America, Rotary, an international network of community service organizations, has long been the crossroads of politics and business. In Guatemala it was also the social hub for all the movers and shakers in the business community. In such a tiny country there is only a relative handful of people, as few as three dozen, perhaps, who really exercise power in business. For that reason, the smaller the country, the easier it is to learn the ropes.

GSBs, I learned, were dollar-denominated bonds issued by Guatemala to help retire its foreign trade debts and thus stabilize the country's currency. The *quetzal* had long been on par with the dollar, but it was slipping of late. I also learned that few people were buying or selling GSBs because there was no mechanism for doing so. Potential buyers had no way of knowing who might want to sell, or even who owned them, and a potential seller like Baxter, who had accepted the bonds from the government as payment for goods, had no way of finding a buyer short of just asking around. There was no stock or bond exchange listing them and no central meeting place for buyers and sellers, which is what an exchange is in its simplest form. I was going to have to be what they call "a beater" on a jungle safari—the guy who goes into the brush to flush the animals out for the tourists to see.

When a market is virtually nonexistent or in its infancy, there is no transparency, no liquidity, and no barriers to entry. Any Tom, Dick, or Harry with a little moxie can try and create some action. I wasn't the only one. There was "Bongo" Bill Thompson (I gave him the nickname), who I called a "bathroom broker" because whenever I talked to him on the phone he always seemed, from the background sounds, to be doing business from the throne in his New York apartment. Once I got some business going in Guatemala he used to try and sell me GSBs on behalf of Procter & Gamble. How he became P&G's broker is anybody's guess, but he was in the game just like me.

At first, I simply started going through the Yellow Pages to see which international companies had offices in Guatemala City. Since Guatemala was paying its trade supplier debt to foreign companies with these bonds, it stood to reason many of those companies were holding GSBs. But the process was tedious, and to find out if any of them—Pfizer, General Motors, Sherwin-Williams, and many others—were selling, I'd have to call them, cold, one by one. That's why the list of bondholders was the holy grail in those days, if you could get your hands on it. Not only did it save you countless days and weeks of work, it would provide you with amounts, maturity dates, and other information that a cold call would almost never yield.

That's when I had the brilliant, if mundane, idea to advertise in the *Wall Street Journal* and the *Financial Times* of London announcing that I was interested in buying GSBs, and in local newspapers in Guatemala, such as *La Prensa Libre*, announcing that I was selling them. The strategy would prove successful both in Guatemala and later in El Salvador. Surprising as it may seem, small ads with a P.O. box number saying "International corporation interested in selling [or buying] Guatemala stabilization bonds" are what launched me into many millions of dollars of bond deals.

Again, to be a successful middleman, you can't introduce your buyer and seller. After making my rounds and learning what I could about Guatemalan bonds, I decided to take the plunge. I surmised from all my reconnaissance that there was, somewhere out there, a buyer for Baxter's bonds at about fifty cents on the dollar, or $1.5 million for the $3 million (face amount) they wanted to sell. But I was going to have to buy the bonds from Baxter and find the buyer, since I didn't yet have one lined up. If I had, it would have been a far less risky and anxiety-provoking proposition.

When I returned to Boston I again went to see my banker, Brad Whitney, who'd played such a key role in selling Turam to Mehmet Sudak. "Brad," I said, "I need a short-term loan to buy these bonds, and you can hold them in escrow as collateral until I can find a buyer."

Brad was wary—he'd never seen a Guatemalan bond before—but he knew and trusted me. I hadn't let him down on the Turkey business, and the risk seemed manageable. And indeed, within a few weeks I had my buyer, an intermediary named Galvaes who was working for an unidentified client. He'd seen my ad in *La Prensa Libre*.

Later, in both Guatemala and El Salvador, I would take the huge currency risk of accepting payments in local currency and finding a *cambista* to convert my local currencies into dollars. But I didn't have to take that risk on this occasion because Galvaes personally delivered to me in Boston a certified dollar check drawn on a U.S. bank for Baxter's bonds, which he then retrieved from the Fourth National Bank, where I had put them in escrow with Whitney. That first trade—my very first trade in so-called "jungle bonds"—netted me $150,000.

"I could make a nice living at this," I thought, perhaps a little overconfident from that first, relatively easy success.

Then I got *very* clever. In response to my second ad in *La Prensa Libre*, I received a call from Xerox in Guatemala City, suggesting that I get in touch with the corporate headquarters in Greenwich, Connecticut, because Xerox was interested in buying Guatemalan bonds. I called the corporate finance department and was directed to a gentleman named "Roger Pratt" who managed the company's finances in Latin America.

"Did you recently buy $3 million in Guatemalan stabilization bonds?" I asked.

"How did you know that?" asked Pratt.

I had caught a big one. I didn't know. I was fishing.

"Because I supplied the bonds to your broker [Galvaes]. I should come to Greenwich and help you develop a plan for repatriating your local profits using these bonds," I said.*

Now I could deal directly with Xerox. There was no need to pay a commission to Galvaes if the company could deal directly with me. Galvaes had been playing exactly the same game I was, trying to keep his buyer (Xerox) and seller (me) from meeting. But with one well-

---

*As noted, generally Guatemalan stabilization bonds were accepted as payment for trade supplier debt. But they also became a strategy for dollarizing profits earned in the local currency, the quetzal, by companies such as Xerox.

placed question I knew who Galvaes's client was. Now I had to make sure Xerox didn't find out who *my* seller was. But first, I had business to attend to in Panama.

In 1976, the voters of the state of New Jersey passed a referendum making it only the second state in the nation, after Nevada, to legalize gambling, though gambling in the state would be limited to Atlantic City. They did so, in part, based on the promises of politicians that an independent casino commission would ensure the mob would never infiltrate gaming in the state. This was like politicians promising to keep the waves from breaking on Atlantic City's beaches, of course, but voters were persuaded that gambling was the answer to Atlantic City's chronic poverty and urban decay. Today, more than thirty years later, Atlantic City comprises an island of extravagant casinos amid the same sea of poverty and decay.

In 1977, a year after the referendum, Bally created a New Jersey subsidiary, Bally Park Place, to build and operate a casino in Atlantic City. By 1980, Bally's investment in Park Place (no doubt named for the same Park Place made famous in the Monopoly board game, which is based on street names in Atlantic City) was close to $300 million.

All that stood between Bally and a lucrative casino license was the New Jersey Casino Control Commission, which took a dim view of any connections between casino operators and organized crime. This is why Bally, whose manufacturing subsidiary had been supplying Juliano and Balicar with slot machines for gambling operations in Panama, suddenly needed to put some distance between itself and the two companies.

I didn't know it in 1983, when I was hired to collect Bally's million-dollar claim against Juliano and Balicar, but both were front companies for the Chicago mob, and specifically for Hy Larner, the most powerful mob figure in Chicago, and perhaps in the country. Indeed, Larner, who kept a very low profile, was an associate of the infamous mobster Meyer Lansky. Both were Jewish, but their businesses were anything but kosher. Wherever they set up gambling operations, local politicians and top military men such as General Manuel Noriega and his predecessor in Panama, Omar Torillos, had a piece of the action.

In late 1979, desperate to try to cleanse itself sufficiently to pass muster with the New Jersey Casino Control Commission and salvage its $300 million Atlantic City investment, Bally began distancing itself from Juliano and Balicar, and other Larner front companies, by refusing to honor orders for gaming machines, primarily slots, and spare parts.*

But supplying these front companies wasn't Bally's only problem. Its chairman, William O'Donnell, was a longtime friend of Hy Larner's. As a condition of Bally's casino license, O'Donnell was required to step down as chairman and put his company stock in a trust, at least until the commission's complete investigation into Bally was completed.

As I said, when I arrived in Panama four years later to try to collect Bally's $1 million from Juliano and Balicar, I didn't know any of this. All I knew was that there was a 100 percent chance that any gambling operation in a country like Panama was run by organized crime in partnership with corrupt local officials, and probably even the country's top political and military leaders.

Manuel Noriega had become the country's military dictator in the summer of 1983, shortly before I arrived there. A CIA-paid operative for some thirty years and the country's top general, Noriega was,

---

*The story of Bally and Larner is told in more detail in *Double Deal: The Inside Story of Murder, Unbridled Corruption, and the Cop Who Was a Mobster*, by Michael Corbitt and Sam Giancana (New York: Avon Books, 2003). Indeed, some of what I learned about what was happening behind the scenes during my 1983 trip to Panama, when I tried to collect Bally's claim, I learned from this book.

in fact, deeply engaged in the drug trade, the arms trade, the country's gambling operations, and virtually every other illicit moneymaking scheme that ran through Panama. Seven years later, the United States would finally have its fill of Noriega and oust him from power in a military invasion, but in 1983, Noriega was the most powerful man in the country.

To this day, I don't fully understand why Juliano and Balicar were refusing to pay Bally in 1983. But the claim dated back to at least 1980 and may well have been payback for Bally's refusal, in late 1979, to continue to supply Hy Larner's various operations with slot machines and spare parts, a refusal that no doubt cost Larner millions of dollars in lost gambling revenues.

Even though I didn't have any specific knowledge of the connections between and among Juliano, Balicar, Noriega, the mob, Larner (whom I had never even heard of), O'Donnell, and Bally, I knew I wasn't walking into a garden-variety collections matter, either. Surely the fingerprints of the mob were somewhere in this transaction. I just didn't know where, and that made me plenty nervous—but not nervous enough to turn down the opportunity to earn a commission that could run into hundreds of thousands of dollars. That fat commission was dangling out there. I just hoped the price for grabbing it wouldn't be too high.

On the flight to Panama, I thought to myself, "This is a fool's errand. The debt is four years old and it's been in litigation for three. Why are they going to pay now? Because I ask them nicely? Because I'm a nice Jewish boy from Brookline? Because I'll threaten to sue them? They were already being sued! Why have I really been hired for this task?"

I was aware that Bally had cut off Juliano and Balicar; Biers had given me the background regarding Bally's need to sever ties with any company even suspected of ties to organized crime. But I wondered whether the litigation itself, and sending me to Panama, was part of an elaborate charade to continue to show the New Jersey casino commission that Bally really was at arm's length from Juliano and Balicar. Perhaps all these efforts to collect the debt, including my trip to Panama, were all show. I really didn't know. But by the time I arrived in Panama City, I started to think I might be spending eternity at the bottom of the ocean off the Panama coast. It wasn't a far-fetched fear. Juliano's president had disappeared on a boat trip several months earlier. Foul play was suspected.

In any event, the people at Juliano were expecting me when I arrived, because I had sent a telex telling them I was coming to Panama and hoped to have an amicable negotiation about how the debt to Bally might be resolved.

Shortly after I checked into my hotel in Panama City the evening I arrived, the phone rang. I picked it up but there was just silence. I didn't think much of it, but it happened a second time about an hour later and then a third. In my already-anxious state, I started to read all kinds of sinister meaning into these calls. By the third one, what seemed like a nuisance now seemed like a veiled threat of some kind, or at least a deliberate attempt to unnerve me. The bond business in Guatemala is going well, I thought. Why do I need this assignment?

I had an appointment the next day with "Linda White," secretary of Juliano Internacional. I was tired—I hadn't slept well—and I had worked myself into a state of high anxiety imagining all kinds of worst-case scenarios involving water, concrete, and large men in dark suits. When I arrived at Juliano's offices in a modern building in downtown Panama City, I was trying hard not to betray my inner state.

White, an attractive blonde American in her mid-forties, suggested we go to the Hilton, where one of Panama's largest casinos was located, for a drink and lunch. We chatted amiably on the way over. Over lunch I told her Bally wanted an amicable solution. In retrospect, White probably knew a hell of a lot more than I did about what was really driving relations between the two companies, and she almost certainly knew what I only suspected from what Biers had told me—that Juliano didn't simply have ties to the mob, it *was* the mob.

"Give me some ideas," White said.

"I think I can persuade Bally to ship you $200,000 in spare parts for your slot machines," I said. "In return, though, Juliano has to prepay Bally $400,000; $200,000 for the spare parts and $200,000 toward the one million owed. If that works, we can continue in a similar vein until the debt is repaid."

White was noncommittal. "That's interesting," she said, knowing full well that Juliano desperately needed spare parts to keep the money rolling in from its slots. As it was, they were bastardizing parts from one broken-down machine to fix another.

This was a meeting of two people with no real power, however. I had no authority to make an offer and White had no authority to accept one. I was just thinking on my feet. I was going to have to sell the proposal to Biers and Bally, and White would have to sell it to whomever it was she reported to. I went back to Boston and put the proposal to Biers by phone.

After getting Bally's agreement, Biers asked me to return to Panama to meet with White again and, hopefully, her superiors. But she was steadfast that I wasn't going to meet with anyone else at Juliano.

"In principle, this is acceptable, but I will have to take it up the chain of command," she said. "But it's hot in Panama, so we move very deliberately."

Again, paranoia came over me, and I wondered whether there was a hidden, threatening message in this statement. I still had the sense that I was playing a small part in someone else's play, a play whose script didn't call for it to end well for the messenger. When I got back to Boston, I hoped to see my commission and never see Panama again, at least not as Bally's collection's agent. In the end, however, I saw neither the commission nor Panama. The deal I proposed went nowhere, Bally and Juliano continued their litigation for several more years, and I was happy to be rid of the entire business. I had a young family and a promising bond business in Guatemala. Life would be good.

With nothing to show for my efforts in Panama, I refocused my attention on Guatemala.

To appreciate just how underdeveloped—or nonexistent, really—the market in instruments such as Guatemalan stabilization bonds was at the time, consider the story of Lloyds Bank of London (not to be confused with Lloyd's of London, the insurance giant).

Shortly after I started advertising for buyers and sellers of GSBs, I received a call from "Paul Prince" who worked in the bond department at Lloyds Bank.

"I saw your ad in the *Financial Times*," he said. "We have some Guatemalan stabilization bonds we want to sell. Do you have a buyer?"

As luck would have it, I did. A potential buyer had responded to my ad in *La Prensa Libre*: It was the Guatemala branch of a major international bank headquartered in London—the Guatemala branch of Lloyds Bank of London, as a matter of fact. Lloyds Bank of Guatemala was a subsidiary of Lloyds Bank of London that functioned autonomously.

These are big boys, I thought to myself, marveling at the coincidence. But if it is a cardinal rule to never introduce the buyer and seller, it was doubly true in this case.

"The bonds we want to sell are in the vault at the offices of Lloyds of Guatemala," said Prince. "See what price you can get from your buyer." Unbeknownst to Prince, I already had a letter of commitment from Lloyds of Guatemala to buy several million dollars face amount of GSBs at a certain price. I factored in a $100,000 commission for myself and sent a buy quote to Prince in the name of Turan, which he accepted. I wired the money to Prince in London and received back a letter of instruction directing Lloyds Bank of Guatemala to deliver $2 million face amount GSBs to Robert Smith of Turan.

Armed with the necessary paperwork and the letter of instruction, I flew down to Guatemala to pick up the bonds that Turan would briefly own. I took possession of my bonds in the basement vault at Lloyds Bank of Guatemala, endorsed them, got into the elevator, and went to the seventh floor to deliver the bonds to "Rodney Sinclair," the English president of Lloyds Bank of Guatemala. This was a major transaction for them, so I was delivering the bonds directly to the bank's president.

Sinclair was nonplussed, to say the least, when he realized that the bonds he had just purchased from me had been sitting in his vault, the property of Lloyds Bank of London, the entire time. Imagine the phone conversation that must have taken place between Prince and Sinclair, for neither one ever did business in GSBs with me again. (When Prince left Lloyds some years later we did do business again, but it was a full ten years before the Lloyds to Lloyds deal came up in any conversation, and then we enjoyed a good laugh about it.)*

But the fact is, both parties got what they wanted from the deal. London was trying to reduce its exposure to high-risk creditors such as Guatemala, and Lloyds of Guatemala was looking for a way to convert some of its quetzal profits into dollars that could be remitted to the home office in London. The right hand may not have known what the left was doing, but each had made a sound business judgment, given their different objectives, albeit not one they would have made if they were fully informed.

---

*In large financial institutions, it's not entirely uncommon for the left hand to be unaware of what the right hand is doing, and vice versa.

The larger point, however, is that I was able to thrive precisely because there was not yet any real market in these instruments back then. Everyone was stumbling around in the dark with no information. Everyone, that is, but me. I had just enough to make a go of this bond business.

With Galvaes out of the picture at Xerox, I thought, "Wow, this is great! I have a steady customer and the spread doesn't have to be shared." But once I introduced Xerox to the idea of using Guatemalan bonds to repatriate local profits, I created, albeit knowingly, another problem for myself. Once Xerox started buying GSBs not just as an investment vehicle but as a means of converting local profits into dollars, they would only pay for the bonds in quetzals, the local currency. After all, that was the whole point: Xerox wanted a way to convert quetzals to dollars, and they weren't going to do it on the black market. I would be paid for GSBs in quetzals. Converting them to dollars would be my problem, and that's how I first entered the world of the *cambista*. And in Guatemala, Felix "the Cat" Guitierrez was my guy.*

Like many in the *cambio* business, Felix was originally from Nicaragua and had fled the 1980s war between the U.S.-backed Contras and the leftist "Sandinista" government of Daniel Ortega, a war that would lead to one of the most sordid scandals of the Reagan administration: the secret sale of arms to Iran in exchange for the release of hostages held by Hezbollah, the radical Islamist group, with the proceeds of the arms sales going to support the Contras. When they fled the war, many educated Nicaraguans—Felix had an MBA—left

---

*The currency transactions I did with Felix, with all of the attendant risks, were very much like those I later did with Jose Manuel Gomez in El Salvador, as described in Chapter 1.

valuable businesses and property behind and took only their life savings. *Cambio* didn't require huge amounts of cash to start, and the returns could be as high as 10 percent, so it was enticing. Though technically illegal, the business was fairly open and operated out of respectable offices: in Felix's case, out of an office on the Avenida Reforma, just across from the U.S. embassy. The façades for Felix's *cambio* business were a finance company and an export/import operation. *Cambio* was so integrated into the fabric of Guatemala's business and financial worlds that Felix was one of several *cambistas* that founded the Guatemala Stock Exchange in 1987–88.*

My early success in Guatemala was making me a bit cocky, and I started to fancy myself a real prince of international finance. So when I learned about Caribbean-Central American Action (CCAA), I decided to get involved.

CCAA was a nonprofit organization created to support legislation known as the Caribbean Basin Initiative (formally known as the Caribbean Basin Economic Recovery Act), which was passed by Congress in 1983. It was part of the U.S. effort to resist Soviet influence in the region by improving local economies. Anastasio Somoza, Nicaragua's pro-American, right-wing dictator, had fallen to the Sandinistas in 1979 (he fled to Florida); civil war was raging in El Salvador; Guatemala continued to simmer at a low boil; and the Cubans were confronted by the United States in the Grenada invasion. The Caribbean Basin Initiative was a nonmilitary front in the Cold War. By allowing manufacturers in Central America and the Caribbean to export goods to the United States duty-free, the act was intended to support private enterprise in the region, which, it was believed, would make it less susceptible to Soviet influence.

CCAA, of which I later became a trustee, attracted a lot of big names. David Rockefeller was very involved; prominent politicians addressed our annual meetings in Miami, including then Vice Presi-

---

*Tragically Felix, under great financial pressure, committed suicide in 2006.

dent George H. W. Bush. Many government officials from throughout the region also participated. That's how, in 1983, I met "Guillermo Santos," one of Guatemala's wealthiest businessmen and a former Guatemalan minister of the economy.

Suave, fluent in English, and charming, Santos had vast holdings in Guatemala, including a pharmaceutical business, a flour mill, and a private hospital, among others. Five feet nine inches tall, with smooth, white skin that betrayed his French and Swiss heritage, Santos was a handsome man in his mid-fifties with a ready smile and a slight limp, and when he spoke to you he looked you directly in the eye. He was well respected and well connected, the kind of person you would feel comfortable having as a business partner. He exuded success and power without arrogance. He had been educated at a major state university in the Midwest and had married an American woman with whom he had nine or ten children.

Naturally, when we met, Santos was curious to know what had brought me to CCAA. I told him that I had just started trading GSBs and explained how I was hunting through the Yellow Pages just to try and figure out who might own them. It sure would help, I said, to have a list of the bondholders, and I suggested to Santos that if he could supply the list, I would give him a percentage of every deal. A short time later he called me in Boston.

"I spoke to the Central Bank," he said. "I can get you the list. I am sending my son to get it."

I was beyond excited. Santos was going to deliver the bond trader's holy grail. I could see my business in Guatemala taking off at warp speed. But days became weeks, weeks became months, and no list materialized. When I finally worked up the gumption to ask, all he told me was that he'd sent his son to the Central Bank and they kicked him out.

"But don't worry about that," he said dismissively. "I have some other ideas for us; ideas more lucrative than this bond business. The wave of the future is in remittances. There's huge money to be made helping foreign workers in the States send their wages back home."

This was the first time I had ever even considered the huge economic impact of all those Latin American workers making beds and tending lawns up north. But Santos knew the scale of the phenomenon was extraordinary, and he had a plan to profit from it.

Santos envisioned a nationwide chain of kiosks across the United States strategically placed where immigrants tended to gather—bus and rail stations, inexpensive hotels in cities such as Miami, and discount retail chains. At the kiosks, staffed by a single person, people could bring the dollars they wanted sent home. A key part of the plan was that the intended recipient could pick up the money in Guatemala, El Salvador, or wherever he lived within twenty-four hours. This was faster than Western Union, and faster and more reliable than sending postal money orders through the mail, especially since money orders were often lost or stolen. Our company, which we eventually called American Check, would charge a flat fee for the service based on the amount of the transaction, collecting dollars and paying out in local currencies. Our competitive advantage, one we would use to sell our service, was supposed to be speed and safety.

To manage the payouts at the other end, each branch of American Check in Latin America would have a U.S. bank account it could use to draw dollars for exchange into local currencies. By aggregating what we expected would be large amounts of dollars for exchange every day, we could buy local currencies from *cambistas* at favorable rates. So we'd make money not only by charging fees for the service, but in the currency transactions as well.

I was very impressed. Not only did this very successful, former Guatemalan minister of the economy want me as his 50/50 partner, but the business sounded simple and had limitless potential. I had some cash from my GSB deals and I couldn't give Santos my $200,000 initial investment fast enough.

Before we could start, we needed to register as a foreign exchange house with the Florida Banking Commission (our first kiosk was to be in Miami) and post a $500,000 cash bond to protect customers against any malfeasance or default. No bond company would write us a bond, however, so I forked over another half million to be held in escrow by the banking commission. After we'd established a good track record, that money would be refunded to me. And being able to say we were registered with the commission, and that deposits with us were secured with the bond, would give customers a sense of security that would, we thought, help the business. For his part, Santos raised a million dollars for the business by creating a bank, the Caribbean Basin Investment Bank, that he incorporated in, of all places, the remote Pacific island nation of Vanuatu.

Shortly after we incorporated American Check in Florida, Santos and I hired a public relations firm to conduct focus groups that would allow us to gauge the potential interest in our service among the people it was designed to serve. We traveled to New York, Texas, and Florida to survey the potential market. We met with community activists and talked with people outside small check-cashing operations in areas where there were large concentrations of immigrants. Encouraged by what we were learning, we hired a consultant to develop a computer system to process and monitor transactions. Then, with great optimism, we opened our first kiosk at the Everglades Hotel in Miami, ran television and print ads in the Spanish-language media, and waited for the money to roll in.

Except it didn't. The flaws in our plan became readily apparent, as did the incompetence and lack of initiative of twentysomething "Ernesto Santos," Guillermo's son, whom he had insisted on installing as the manager of our Florida operation. (This was the same son Guillermo had dispatched on the botched mission to get the list of GSB holders from the Guatemala Central Bank.) Ernesto's assistant was the girlfriend (and later wife) of an associate of Guillermo's who simply needed a job. She and Ernesto were not the most dynamic team to run a start-up. Not that I could have been of much help. I was never expected, nor was I inclined, to play any day-to-day role in the business. So while I was up in Boston trying to trade bonds and collect a few debts, Ernesto and his assistant were screwing up in Miami.

In fairness, it wasn't just the two office personnel in Miami that were the source of our problems. Because the computer system never worked, every request for funds had to be faxed to Santos's office in Guatemala, or to the office of some friend or associate of his in Salvador or Nicaragua, wherever the money was supposed to be delivered. This jerry-rigged system was cumbersome and unreliable, and to meet our twenty-four-hour delivery promise, someone had to be found to go out and source the local currency overnight for delivery to the intended recipient. This situation, in turn, exposed another huge flaw in our business model, one so obvious that in retrospect it's hard to believe we didn't anticipate it. Many of the intended recipients for money being sent home from America didn't live in the capital cities of Guatemala City or San Salvador or Managua. They lived hours away in the countryside, without cars, so they were dependent on buses that might take ten or twelve hours or more, each way, to reach the capital. Unless the intended recipient lived in the capital, we often couldn't deliver at all. Our delivery system, like our computer system, was a disaster.

It also became clear that for American Check to succeed, beginning with a single kiosk was a hairbrained idea. You couldn't generate enough daily business to do currency transactions of the size needed to make a decent profit on the currency exchange. We'd have needed at least a dozen or more locations right from the start to have a prayer.

As American Check floundered—it was costing us $10,000 a month to run the business while revenues were about $6,000 a month—I received a call from Ernesto. He had great news. He'd found a client who wanted us to remit $15,000 every day to Guatemala. It never occurred to him, apparently, that this was almost certainly an effort to launder drug money. Who else would want to convert this kind of money every day? Certainly not a landscaper or a taxi driver. Accepting that kind of business could land us in prison. "Tell him no," I instructed Ernesto.

Not ready to abandon the business, Santos asked me to increase my investment, but less than a year in, I wanted out and pleaded poverty. For $1, plus reimbursement of the $500,000 I'd placed in escrow with the Florida Banking Commission, I sold my half interest back to Santos and pondered what lessons I could take from the experience.

First and foremost, I realized that I simply wasn't comfortable trying to profit from the poor—from the blind, like Lloyds Bank and other large institutions, yes, but not from the poor. Second, I learned not to be overly impressed by people of power and wealth. I adored Santos; he was a lovable, charming guy, and even though I lost $200,000 with him I couldn't be angry. After all, he didn't force me into this business. But for all of his achievements in business and government, he wasn't a genius, and partnering with him was no guarantee of success.

I also took note of the one thing I did right with American Check: I didn't try to salvage the sinking ship by getting in even deeper. There is a time to take your losses and look for a better day: "Know when to hold 'em, know when to fold 'em," Kenny Rogers used to sing. And since American Check went nowhere after I bowed out, I had obviously made the right decision.

Losing $200,000 at the time wasn't a major hit, but it did cause me to reflect on where my talents lay. I had, in retrospect, expected Santos to bring to the table a practical, operational business sense that I never had, but you can't expect others to fill in your own gaps. It's too easy to ascribe such talents to others when you lack them yourself, especially when those people are as successful as Santos. Of course, in any good partnership you hope people's strengths complement each other. But I was overawed by Santos simply because he was rich and successful. I never made that mistake again.

After the American Check debacle and my anxiety-ridden ad-venture in Panama, I also decided I would do better by my family and myself, not to mention financially, if I simplified my business life. There was no need to go off on excursions of the ego—which was what American Check was—where I thought success in my fledgling bond business meant I was a financial genius who could make money in all kinds of schemes. And there was certainly no need for me to go running around places like Panama, where the head of the country and the mob were engaged in a joint venture and my life wasn't worth a five-dollar poker chip. At least when I was buying bonds from Lloyds Bank of London and selling them to Lloyds Bank of Guatemala, I wasn't risking my life.

Debt. That's what I knew and understood, and that, I decided, was where my future lay. And, indeed, when a big opportunity to make money in Nigerian promissory notes presented itself, that's where I went next: to the heart of Africa.

CHAPTER 5

NIGERIA

Promises, Promises

IF YOU HAVE an e-mail address, you have probably received a so-called "Nigerian 419 letter" in your mailbox sometime in the recent past. In fact, you have almost certainly received more than one, and perhaps as many as a dozen or more. These e-mails, named for a section of the Nigerian criminal code, come from someone identifying himself (or herself) as a Nigerian government official or heir to a fortune in Nigeria who needs help getting a large sum of money out of the country. In return for information about you, typically a bank account number, they promise you a share of the fortune. But first you need to wire the sender money for some bogus reason. People naïve enough to get sucked into the scheme are soon sending more and more money, because the expected fortune is always just one more elusive step away. At the end of the day, victims of a 419 letter are not only out thousands of dollars, they've set themselves up to be victims of identity fraud. It's one of the most prevalent scams on the Internet today.*

When I started doing business in Nigeria in the 1980s, the country had a well-deserved reputation for being fraught with corruption and fraud, and you had to operate with caution. The whole country seemed to be a giant "419" scam.

Indeed, in the 1980s, Nigeria was one of the world's most corrupt and undemocratic countries. In 1985, General Ibrahim Babangida took power in a palace coup, promising to return the country to civilian rule. But, according to Martin Meredith, author of *The Fate of Africa: A History of Fifty Years of Independence* (New York: Public Affairs, 2005), he "soon acquired a taste for wielding power himself and set up an avaricious personal dictatorship more ruthless than anything Nigeria had previously experienced." Babangida and his henchmen appropriated billions of dollars in oil revenue for themselves, were heavily involved in the drug trade, and, according to Meredith, "engaged in systematic commercial fraud on an unprecedented scale." Political opponents were tortured, persecuted, and murdered. By 1991, according to the World Bank, Nigeria was the thirteenth poorest country in the world.†

In the early to mid-1980s, I did a small amount of business trad-

---

*Ironically, the day after these words were written I received just such an e-mail from a woman claiming to be the widow of a former Nigerian ambassador to Canada. In the e-mail, she professed to be a born-again Christian battling oesophageal [sic] cancer and with only a few months to live. Her husband, she wrote, had, before his death, deposited $40 million with a Nigerian financial firm for her benefit, which she now wanted to use, in her dying days, to help hurricane victims. Her family, she said, would steal the money, so she was looking for a third party to take the money and use it for her designated charitable purpose. In this initial e-mail she is asking only for a favorable reply so that she can designate me the beneficiary of the $40 million fund. This is the bait.

†Babangida handed over power to an interim government in 1993, after losing an election the year before, but not without a struggle. Nigeria has since endured a succession of governments and has moved, albeit haltingly, toward democratic rule.

ing Nigerian promissory notes (NPNs). The government had issued these instruments, which were quite similar to bonds, to settle its trade supplier debt—money owed for goods imported into the country—from the 1970s. In 1983, the Nigerians had precious little in foreign currency reserves and were having difficulty repaying this debt. They rescheduled the notes, made one or two payments, and then defaulted. Note holders, eager to salvage something from this wreck, were unloading their notes for pennies on the dollar.

By this time, thanks largely to the business I had developed in Guatemala, I was gaining my reputation as "king of the jungle bonds," as the *Boston Business Journal* once described me. However, there was virtually no market for NPNs. My one major customer was Citibank, which had a debt/equity swap arrangement with the Nigerian government that allowed Citi to buy NPNs cheaply from Turan and convert them, at face value, into equity positions in Nigerian domestic enterprises. As I pointed out in relating my adventures in Turkey, such arrangements are a way for debtor countries to retire some of their indebtedness without having to come up with cash. To supply Citibank with NPNs for its debt/equity scheme, our challenge at Turan was to find out who held NPNs. Once we did, we almost always found them to be an eager seller. Nigeria was a poor credit risk and the NPNs represented the broken promises of the Nigerian government to pay its creditors.

But I knew, as did everyone else in the world of finance, that Nigeria had enormous untapped resources in the form of oil, if only it could get its act together and get that oil out of the ground and onto tankers bound for Europe, Asia, and the United States. Some people thought the government was too chronically corrupt and incompetent to realize this wealth, but I have always been an optimist on these matters: If there is money to be squeezed from a stone, especially if there's oil underneath it, someone, especially me, will squeeze for as long as it takes. I felt the same way about the Nigerian government. Someday it would figure out how to make a fortune from its oil. After all, there was an awful lot of incentive to do so. Thus, although we sold most of the NPNs we bought to Citibank, I wasn't afraid to hold on to some of them myself. I had faith.

I always traveled to every country whose debts I traded, but Nigeria especially intrigued me. One of Africa's most populous countries, it was also, potentially, one of its richest. And its rampant corruption and chaos gave it a sense of danger that gave me an adrenalin rush.

Before I made my first trip there in 1985, I sent one of my associates, a Hasidic Jew named "Moshe Goldberg," to the capital, Lagos, on a scouting mission. It was a crazy idea, really. The poor guy had to bring all the groceries he could carry because the chances of finding kosher food in Lagos were zero. He had ten kids (Hasids almost always have very large families) and a wife who must have thought he was insane to go to a place where it would appear as if he was from Mars, and he prayed three times a day. Just the thought of a white man in a yarmulke, with his *payot* (uncut side locks of hair) hanging in front of his ears, walking around the Nigerian capital was quite an arresting image. But Moshe was a financial genius with a lot of experience and he often made me, and himself, a lot of money.

When I finally went to Lagos and experienced the feeling of sticking out like a sore thumb as a white man among throngs of black Africans, I could appreciate just how alien Moshe must have felt walking the teeming streets of Lagos. In a place like Guatemala or El Salvador, blending into the scenery wasn't too difficult; for a white man in Nigeria, it was impossible. Anyone who wanted to target an affluent foreigner—and, by definition, a foreigner in Nigeria was affluent—would have no trouble picking me out of the crowd. Nigeria was the kind of place where you might pray *more* than three times a day that you would survive to see another dawn.

Though I am generally an unflappable traveler, I had qualms about going to Lagos. I had heard all kinds of horrific traveler's tales about European businessmen who'd been beaten and robbed on the highway from the airport shortly after their arrival; about the practice of disposing of one's enemies by forcing an automobile tire over their head and around their torso and setting it ablaze; about the unbridled corruption that was business as usual in Nigeria; and about people falling seriously ill from eating contaminated food.*

The quality of the food supply is an issue in most developing world countries, but I was especially concerned about Nigeria, in part because if I fell sick it was a long way back to the States for good medical care. By contrast, Central America was just a two-hour flight from Miami and I always knew I could get home quickly in an emergency. In Lagos I stuck strictly to hotel food, which tends to be more reliable, and ate cautiously. If I had something for dinner my first night there and didn't get ill, I'd order the same thing every night. I didn't tempt fate in local restaurants or by eating exotic foods. And I never bought from a street vendor.

To a financier or an economist, the terms *third world, developing world,* or *emerging market* when applied to a country are understood primarily in financial terms: What is the country's balance of payments; how much do they export; what is the per capita income; how well educated is the labor force; how big is the economy; what is the gross domestic product? To a tourist, those same phrases are understood in more prosaic terms: Does the water run; is there reliable electricity; is the food and water safe to consume; does a dilapidated public bus meant for forty passengers instead carry eighty people and a few farm animals as it spews out unfiltered exhaust? Nigeria's "third world" personality was immediately evident along the pothole-filled, trash-strewn roadway from the airport where countless sellers hawked pots and pans, vacuum cleaners—you name it—along the roadside.

I always thought of myself as a financial tourist and tried to ob-

---

*I used to have a saying: If you can get from the airport into the city, you can do business in a country. Lagos really tested that hypothesis. Writing about his first visit to Lagos, George Packer described it this way in a 2006 article for *The New Yorker*: "When I first went to Lagos, in 1983, it had a fearsome reputation among Westerners and foreigners alike. Many potential visitors were kept away simply by prospect of getting through the airport, with its official shakedowns and swarming touts. Once you made it into the city, a gauntlet of armed robbers, con men, corrupt policemen, and homicidal bus drivers awaited you."

serve the countries I visited from both perspectives, which is why the view from my hotel window at the Holiday Inn in Lagos was so telling. Between repeated knocks on my door by aggressive Nigerian prostitutes, I would gaze out my window to the hotel's swimming pool below, virtually empty except for a shallow layer of filthy rust-colored water. On closer inspection I noticed a few dead cats floating on the surface. Nigeria, I thought, makes Guatemala and El Salvador look like Monaco. It also made me think, "This is what happens to good people with bad leaders. Their country falls apart. No one cares anymore."

On my first trip to Lagos, I made my familiar rounds in an effort to get the lay of the financial land. I visited the major foreign banks doing business in the city—Barclays, the Bank of Boston, and Chase Manhattan, among others. I called on the commercial attaché at the U.S. Embassy where my status as a former commercial officer at the U.S. Embassy in Saigon opened a few doors. I stopped by the Nigerian Central Bank and the Lagos offices of some of the multinationals there. I tried to get a handle on oil production, the balance of payments, and plans to restructure, yet again, the NPNs. I'd ask the multinationals if they held NPNs, if they'd bought or sold them recently, and if so, from or to whom. As in Guatemala and El Salvador, there was no real market for NPNs and a little bit of information could go a long way. I was a sponge for every tidbit I could uncover about who was holding, who was buying, and who was selling: in other words, who was doing what to whom and for how much.

Nigeria had to find a way to make good on these notes eventually or no one would continue to export goods there anymore, and a country like Nigeria, which manufactures very little itself, desperately depends on imports. What oil Nigeria *was* pumping out of the ground was selling for about $15 a barrel, not enough to lift the country out of its crushing debt, including about $6 billion in trade supplier debt alone. There were billions more in commercial bank debt and money owed to the IMF and World Bank as well. But, despite the dead cats in the swimming pool and the bad debt on its books, I saw better days ahead for Nigeria—maybe even a pool filled with clean, chlorinated, cat-free water suitable for swimming.

Over the next two to three years I continued to do a small amount of business in NPNs, but it was in 1988 that the great NPN bonanza finally arrived, and by virtue of my "jungle bond" reputation, I was perfectly positioned to take advantage of it.

Early in 1988, I made a second trip to Lagos just to keep myself up to speed on developments that might affect the value of NPNs. I knew that a couple of years earlier, Chase Manhattan Bank, under contract to the Nigerian government, undertook a process known as debt reconciliation. It was Chase's job to compile a complete list of the current holders of NPNs, to document the specific imports for which each note was issued as payment, and to monitor payments from Nigeria's importers to the Central Bank. It was such payments for goods received, made in the local currency, the *naira*, against which NPNs were issued. From that point on, Chase was to be the payment agent on the notes; that is, the disburser of interest and principal payments. The Law Debenture Corporation of London would become the official registrar whose job it was to track ownership of the notes as they changed hands over time.

All this activity suggested that Nigeria was preparing to climb out of default and make good on its NPNs. Maybe it was instinct, or maybe just luck, but I had a feeling Nigeria's time had come and that there was going to be big money in trading its debt. When I went to Lagos in 1988, I made sure to meet with the Chase people tasked with the debt reconciliation and got the sense that Nigeria was serious about putting its financial house in order.

Lagos hadn't changed much. It was still the filthy, overcrowded, fetid city I had visited a few years before. Hoping for a slightly better view, I stayed this time at the new Sheraton Hotel, where I promptly met two ebullient Englishmen, nattily attired, in the lobby. When I saw them the next evening they looked distressed and shaken: Their hired car had been stopped on a roadway in Lagos by a crowd that surged toward them and started rocking the car back and forth, apparently intending to overturn it. Luckily, two policemen arrived on the scene, dispersed the crowd, and sent the Brits on their way, but not before robbing them of everything they had. There but for the grace of God, I thought. Such was life in Lagos.

Yet something was afoot in Lagos that would make me tens of millions of dollars with virtually no risk, assuming I could get home safely, and the opening act in the drama unfolded at a conference facility attached to England's famed football pitch, Wembley Stadium.

In March 1988, the Nigerian Central Bank hosted a meeting of the country's trade creditors at Wembley. The purpose, ostensibly, was to announce new terms of payment on the promissory notes. As a note holder, I was invited to attend.

Rather than travel to England for the meeting, I made the mistake of asking my London attorney, "John Smythe," to go on my behalf. I was less interested in the *terms* of the rescheduling than I was in knowing exactly *who* attended. As always, I needed to know the players—the potential buyers and sellers—and having failed during my two trips to Nigeria to obtain a list of the note holders, there was still much to be learned by finding out who was at the meeting and who they represented. Despite my explicit instructions, or perhaps because he simply didn't appreciate that knowing the players was more than idle curiosity, Smythe reported back only the terms of the proposed rescheduling. Lawyers, in my experience, aren't very business savvy, which is why they are lawyers billing by the hour and not entrepreneurs. Sending Smythe to the meeting was a huge wasted opportunity.

Then my luck changed. In April 1988, just a month after the creditors meeting at Wembley Stadium, I got a call out of the blue from none other than Bob Dudley, with whom I had had such a bitter falling out almost a decade earlier over our business in Turkey. I was surprised, to say the least.

In the years following our Turkey misadventure, Dudley and two partners, Simon Lowenstein (who had joined Dudley in trying to take control of Turam) and "Raymond Scheer," had formed an investment company called "Global InVest."

My conversation with Dudley, our first in more than eight years, was awkward. We circled each other like two wary fighters. After some small talk about families and business, Bob got to the point of his call, and it made me realize that the Wembley Stadium meeting was just window dressing for another scheme the Nigerians had developed to settle their trade supplier debt.* Through Global InVest, the Nigerians wanted to start quietly buying back their own debt on the cheap. (Dudley's partner, Scheer, it turned out, had excellent contacts at the Nigerian Central Bank from his earlier days at a large brokerage house that had advised Nigeria on debt rescheduling. That is why Global InVest was chosen for the job.)

If Nigeria were able to buy back, say, $4 billion of its NPNs at twenty-five cents on the dollar, it would cost them just $1 billion to retire $4 billion in debt. And in 1988, NPNs were selling for anywhere from eighteen to twenty-five cents on the dollar.

To advance the buyback plan, the Nigerians made sure that the new repayment terms announced at Wembley—twenty-two years at 5 percent interest—would encourage a lot of note holders to sell their notes as soon as a buyer came along. These notes had been in default for several years, and the only thing the note holders got at Wembley

---

*As a result of the debt reconciliation process undertaken by Chase Manhattan, only about $4.7 billion of the outstanding $6 billion of trade supplier debt was recognized, probably because some note holders were unable to prove that their notes represented legitimate or approved imports.

was another long-term promise to pay from a country that had repeatedly proved to be a bad credit risk.

The key to such a buyback scheme, however, is discretion. If word of a government-sponsored buyback got out, the price of the notes would rise, perhaps significantly, as holders realized there was a ready buyer for their otherwise illiquid asset. The entire purpose, from the Nigerians' point of view, would be defeated, or at least become significantly more costly. And, to work, the buyback had to be executed over a period of years. Any sudden increase in demand would also drive prices up and fuel speculation about a government-sponsored buyback.*

"I've heard that you've been doing some business in NPNs," Dudley said to me in that first conversation since our falling out over Turkey. "I'm interested in buying as much Nigerian debt as you can provide."

To try to keep the plan secret, Global InVest needed to spread the business of "sourcing the debt" around, and it needed players such as Turan involved. Since we were already buying NPNs, and Global InVest was only peripherally involved in trading developing-world debt, using us wouldn't raise suspicions that a buyback was afoot, especially if we spread our purchases out over time. Were Global InVest to go out and start suddenly buying large quantities of NPNs directly, the game would be up. Furthermore, Global InVest wasn't equipped to go out and beat the bushes and chase down sellers. Few who fancy themselves international mavens of finance want to

---

*There is no doubt in my mind that the World Bank and the IMF gave at least tacit approval to the Nigerian buyback plan. As major lenders to Nigeria, they would have been very concerned had they seen unexplained outflows from the Central Bank. And the buyback, if successful, would make it more likely that Nigeria would be able to repay its debts to the World Bank and the IMF.

do the grunt work. But this nitty-gritty, door-to-door work of sourcing the debt was right up our alley.

Now, Dudley didn't say anything about a buyback during our first conversation. He didn't have to. I knew Bob Dudley wasn't suddenly interested in speculating in large quantities of Nigerian debt. It was clear that he was buying for someone else, and given what amounted to the open-ended buy order he gave me, it didn't take a genius to realize who his customer was. When he later sent me a list of holders who owned small quantities of NPNs so that I could easily scout for sellers (small, in this case, meaning holders of notes with a face amount of $500,000 or less), there was no room for doubt. He was buying for the Nigerians themselves, and the Nigerians had given him the list.

The copies of the list Dudley provided literally had holes in them, however. Dudley wanted to control events, and me, as much as possible. He viewed me as a loose cannon. Because he was still suspicious of me, he would cut out the names of the major note holders before sending me the list, limiting me to chasing the small fry. This was fine with me: The smaller the note, the better the price, generally speaking, because the small guys have less leverage and are typically more eager to sell their distressed merchandise. It would cost me less to buy four $500,000 notes than one $2 million note, though I'd have to work harder to get it. But when it came time to resell, if I aggregated those small notes into a larger package, the better the sell price.

Another reason Dudley kept control of the list is that he didn't want me to go to the Nigerians and say, "I can do this for you directly: Cut out Global InVest as the middleman and I can save you tens of millions in commissions."

There was a rich irony here. Dudley was turning to the very company he once tried to steal out from under my nose because he needed me to help him execute one of the biggest deals in his life. And I, in turn, was chaffing at the bit to do business with the one person in my business life who tried to destroy me. Why? Because with a built-in buyer, doing business in NPNs was like having a personal mint. There were many millions of dollars to be made practically risk-free.

I say "practically" because there was always the chance Dudley would try and hang me out to dry again. I could go out and buy up NPNs and have him turn around and refuse to buy them from me. I'd be left holding the bag.

Because of our mutual wariness, we initially agreed to do all of our NPN transactions through an intermediary bank. Dudley would deposit money into an escrow account to pay for the notes and I would deliver the notes to the bank in order to get paid. We documented every trade with several pages of legal paperwork. Later, after we had done our first $50 million in NPN business, some modicum of trust was restored and we were able to speed our transactions and save on escrow fees by dealing directly with one another. We even did away with the legal documentation, relying on simple written confirmations of our transactions. Indeed, we even reached the point where Dudley sometimes paid Turan in advance on notes we hadn't yet delivered and we, in turn, sometimes turned over notes he hadn't yet paid us for, all to keep the deal flow moving as freely as possible.

The terms of my deal with Dudley were quite simple and, with regard to price, flexible. Dudley would tell me how much he was looking to buy over, say, the next month's time, and assure me he would buy from Turan whatever we were able to buy from others. Since markets fluctuate every day, there were no fixed prices; we were in an ongoing negotiation over every NPN, or group of NPNs, we were able to supply. I knew Dudley had a spread to make, and he knew I did as well.

As I said, in our business, the smaller the deal the better the price, *if you are the buyer*. So, when I set out to fulfill Dudley's initial order for $100 million in NPNs, my goal was to bundle as many of the smaller notes as possible into larger packages. On the *sell* side, the law of the spread is inverted. The seller of a large block of merchandise can command a better price because the seller now has leverage. How much Dudley would then sell that package to the Nigerians for I didn't know, just as he didn't know how much I was paying my suppliers. The cardinal rule in my business is to never give away your spread or it will shrink. I learned early on that as soon as your client knows your commission, he thinks it's too much. As it turns out, Dudley was charged with buying back in excess of $3 billion in debt. Whatever his spread, he and his partners stood to make upwards of $80 million to $100 million. We were all going to make plenty of money.

I started buying NPNs for Dudley in the summer of 1988 doing business as I always did: out of a little pocket-size spiral notebook in which I kept crude records of my purchases and my sales. This really was no way to keep track of $100 million in transactions, so in September my partner, Saleh Daher, came to Turan. Not only did Saleh have a keen, Stanford- and MIT-educated mind, he'd worked in major banks and, consequently, brought a level of management acumen and sophistication that went well beyond recording multimillion-dollar deals in little pocket notebooks with a pencil. Saleh knew computers and the software that was now driving the world of international finance. He systemized our operations and procedures and turned Turan from a little back-of-the-envelope operation into a truly professional firm. I could now concentrate exclusively on what I liked to do best—make the deals.

And make them I did. By late 1988 and early 1989, we were committed to buying $100 million in NPNs from various sellers around the world, transactions that would require anywhere between $20 million and $25 million in capital. I suddenly got very anxious. I believed from previous experience that Dudley was unstable and Machiavellian (the trust we eventually achieved was still a few months in the future at this point). "What if he backs out?" I said to Saleh. "I'll be ruined. I'll never work in the business again." All it takes is one default to people you've promised to buy from and no one will sell to you again. I had put my entire financial and professional future in the hands of the one person who once tried to ruin me.

On the other hand, if everything went as planned, with Turan providing the lion's share of billions of dollars of Nigerian debt to Dudley, we were looking at tens of millions in profits for Turan. A bonanza, in fact. It was a risk I was willing, indeed eager, to take.

One of the quirks about the Nigerian buyback scheme was that Indian businessmen, banks, and financial institutions based in places such as Hong Kong, Singapore, London, and Geneva held substantial quantities of NPNs, by some estimates as much as 40 percent of the total. India, like China and Lebanon, did extensive trade in Africa.* With Bob Dudley's list of NPN holders in my pocket, I made a special trip to Hong Kong to try and buy as many NPNs as possible from Indian firms based there. It was quite remarkable: Many of the Indian businessmen in Hong Kong had offices on Wyndham Street and I started, literally, calling on businesses at the top of the street and worked my way down the steep hill. (Hong Kong is hot and humid, so it was easier to work going downhill.) News of my arrival and the nature of my business traveled downhill faster than I did: By the time I knocked on most doors, people already knew who I was and why I was there. It became impossible to negotiate a better price for NPNs after I struck my first deal at the top of the hill because everyone further down the hill already knew the price I had agreed to at the top!

---

*India hadn't yet reached its full-tilt economic stride, though today it boasts one of the fastest-growing economies in the world. However, dating back to my days in Vietnam, I noticed that while India was an impoverished country, I never met a poor Indian abroad. Indeed, at one point the approximately one million Indian expats living and working abroad had a gross domestic product equal to the more than one billion Indians living in India.

Over time, however, Turan developed a good reputation in the Indian expat community and we ultimately bought between $300 million and $400 million in NPNs from Indian note holders around the world—notes we resold to Dudley. We made millions of dollars on these transactions.

As our procurement of NPNs proceeded, Dudley and I continued to regain one another's trust. I not only put a steady stream of NPNs on his table, but I honored his relationship with the Nigerians. I never did anything that would even appear to be an effort to try to work directly with the Nigerians myself, even though I could easily have saved the Nigerians money and made more myself by going around Dudley. And for his part, Dudley honored all of his commitments to me.

But no matter how many NPNs we were able to source, Dudley's appetite for more was insatiable. The Nigerians would advance him more money, but he wasn't having much success building another supply stream, other than Turan. Knowing that we could almost certainly increase the supply, not to mention our profits, if we could identify the larger note holders, the ones whose names Dudley had excised from the list he gave us, we decided to try to get the entire list on our own. I was concerned that asking Dudley for it directly would rouse suspicions that we were trying to outmaneuver him with respect to the Nigerians, but that was not my intent.

To our pleasant surprise, getting the entire list turned out to be a relatively easy task, easier than it had been during my two trips to Lagos. Saleh called a friend, "Steve Dale" at Chase Manhattan, the paying agent on the notes, and asked how we might get the list. Dale told us that only the Law Debenture Corporation, now the official registrar, could do that. One call to London and we learned that any holder of an NPN was entitled to the entire list. We got our hands on it as fast as we could.

Now I could package notes of many different sizes. Thus, a $10 million package of notes might contain some smaller notes purchased at eighteen cents on the dollar, some notes in the $1 million to $2 million range purchased at twenty cents on the dollar, and a $5 million note purchased for twenty-two cents on the dollar. (Remember that the smaller the note, the better the price.) For his part, Dudley wasn't going to bargain with me on each piece of the package. The larger the package the higher the price per unit and the larger the spread, *if you are the seller*. Therefore, I might sell the $10 million package of NPNs for twenty-four cents on the dollar, making a larger profit on the smaller notes in the lot than the larger ones.

Obviously, once we started putting larger denomination notes on Dudley's desk he was going to know we'd gotten hold of the entire list. But I reasoned, correctly as it turned out, that as long as I kept providing the notes to him and didn't attempt to interfere with his relationship with the Nigerians, he wouldn't really care. The Nigerians were making more money available to him to buy NPNs than he could provide. By increasing our supply to him we all stood to make more money. As long as we were working through Dudley, he would be hard-pressed to complain.

The NPN business, once it got rolling, was quite a spectacle. Saleh and I started working very odd hours back in Boston, sometimes sleeping in the office, because we were calling note holders all over the world in dozens of different time zones to keep the NPNs flowing to Dudley, not to mention ensuring the flow of our own risk-free commissions. I felt like a Las Vegas tourist in one of those Plexiglas booths where twenty-dollar bills are blowing around and you get to keep as many as you can grab in one minute. There was so much potential business we didn't know where to start.

We fell in love with Nigeria. The country was making us rich. In our small trading room we played Nigerian music on our tape player and even took to wearing *filas*, traditional Nigerian caps, for good luck. In retrospect, we were a little punch-drunk with our success. Maybe too drunk, literally.

One day Dudley called with an urgent request for $12 million in NPNs, which we didn't have at that moment. Our inventory was only about $2 million. Nothing drives me crazy like missing out on a deal (Saleh will tell you that it's excruciating for me to feel like I'm missing any of the action). So, when Dudley said he'd call some of his other sources to try and find the notes, I was beside myself. It wasn't just that I was missing out on a deal, it was that I was missing out on an especially good deal because, as I said, the larger the package of notes, the larger the markup for the seller—in this case, me.

Saleh and I kept a bottle of scotch in the trading room (I don't recommend this practice, by the way) that we'd sip from when celebrating each success in our booming NPN trade. But this time I poured myself a double to try and drown my disappointment. The $10 million in notes we didn't have meant losing a commission of perhaps a quarter-million dollars or more. Fortified by the liquor, I picked up the phone and called Dudley back.

"Bob," I said, "as luck would have it, we've been able to source an additional $10 million for you. Don't make your calls. We can close in two weeks. We've got it covered." Except, of course, we didn't.

Now we were obligated to sell Dudley $10 million in NPNs that we didn't have, and for the next two weeks Saleh and I scrambled like madmen. We had, in effect, sold short and would have to produce by the agreed-upon date no matter what price we had to pay to get the goods. And since we didn't know how many NPNs Dudley might have been looking for in this round of buying—he could have wanted $20 million, asked us for $12 million, and been shopping elsewhere, too—it was possible this bump in demand would push prices up and we'd be forced to buy, and then sell to Dudley, at prices that would reduce or eliminate our commission. Theoretically, we might even have to take a loss.

Saleh, to put it mildly, wasn't happy. He's the sensible, measured half of our partnership. I'm the impulsive, go-for-broke half. Saleh understands that I'd rather be waterboarded than watch a potential deal slip away. For better or for worse, we were committed.

We immediately called one of our largest and most reliable suppliers of NPNs, the London-based investment bank "Morrison Cabot," only to learn that they had precisely no NPNs to unload. This was a major setback. I was hoping to get the lion's share, if not the entire $10 million from Morrison Cabot. Because they had been involved in helping Nigeria restructure its debt, they were very familiar with NPNs and were trading them regularly. (Ironically, Morrison Cabot never quite differentiated between Turan and Global InVest; they assumed that when they were dealing with us, they were dealing directly with Global InVest, otherwise they might have approached Dudley directly and made better deals.) When we struck out with Morrison Cabot it was high panic time: Now we were going to have to build our package of $10 million piece by little piece, and $10 million in two short weeks was a tall order. As panicked as we were, we had to struggle not to betray it or we'd have paid through the nose to fulfill our commitment to Dudley.

Over the next two weeks we must have made sixty or seventy calls to NPN holders large and small all over the world. Some wanted to sell, some didn't; some wanted to sell a little bit now and more later. Later didn't help. We needed notes now. Two weeks later, five pounds lighter, and blood pressure thirty points higher, we managed to cobble together $10 million in NPNs. With that and the $2 million we had in inventory, we met our obligation to Dudley, but it was a very close shave.

As I said, meeting commitments to buy or sell is essential to success in our business. Reputation is everything, and one default can ruin you. It can be a precarious position when you operate in the middle, as we do, because your ability to perform as promised depends heavily on others keeping *their* promises.

At one point during the course of our Nigeria business we had agreed to purchase $5 million in NPNs from "Thackery Stipple," a British investment company, and based on their written commitment to sell at an agreed price we had, in turn, made a commitment to sell to Dudley. After the deal was struck, but before the notes had been delivered, I got a call from Thackery Stipple.

"The price of NPNs is up," they said, "and we want to renegotiate."

I was livid. Renegotiating is unheard of in our business, and indeed in any market-based trading business. Everyone knows market conditions can fluctuate; it's the risk everyone takes.

One of my talents is finding the right lawyer for the right job, and I quickly phoned a lawyer I had met during my collection days, named "Erskine Marx." This was no job for easygoing John Smythe, who had botched the Wembley assignment. Marx proved to be the most arrestingly aggressive and abrasive attorney it has ever been my privilege to work with. He was also an imperious snob with a faux aristocratic accent. His titanic ego was inversely proportional to his height but directly proportional to the prodigious whiskers that ran from ear to ear and under his ample nose. Marx was perfectly suited to the task, and his reputation for bare-knuckled legal brawling preceded him. On the very day I hired him, Marx phoned Thackery Stipple and threatened to file a petition for involuntary liquidation of the firm *that afternoon* if the $5 million in NPNs weren't delivered at the agreed price. The $4,000 I paid Marx was the best money I ever spent.

As the buyback proceeded, it became harder and harder to keep it a secret. People eventually started to wonder, "Why all this interest in NPNs?" Nevertheless, though suspicions and rumors of a government buyback started to circulate among the larger institutions that held NPNs, the price people were willing to sell for still allowed us to make a handsome profit. Some sellers even suspected Turan was working directly for Nigeria, or, like Morrison Cabot, they thought that we were an in-house part of Dudley's operation, not an independent player, and we never disabused them of these notions. Had they known, why would they have sold to us when they could have sold directly to Dudley at a better price? After all, both Turan and Global InVest had to get their spreads, driving the price at which we could buy and still make our commissions lower.

In the end, over a period of three to four years, Nigeria bought back about $1.5 billion of the roughly $4.7 billion in debt represented by the NPNs, and Turan sourced more than $1.2 billion of those notes. (Nigeria also continued to retire some of its debt with debt/equity swaps, as they did with Citibank.)

Note holders who held on to their NPNs fared even better than those who sold. Thanks in large part to high demand for oil, Nigeria did, as I always expected, find a way to tap its enormous oil wealth, and the NPNs as restructured in 1988 have almost all been paid in full, both principal and interest. The ever-rising price of oil was a major factor.

Even the most optimistic holder of NPNs, and that would probably be me, never expected to see the day when Nigeria would fully pay off its 1970s-era trade supplier debt. But by 2010, that is exactly what will happen. How do I know? Because in 2007, Nigeria deposited $480 million with Merrill Lynch, and Merrill accepted the liability to pay the amounts that remain owed on the notes. (Merrill's assumption is that the $480 million can be invested and can then throw off more than enough cash to repay the outstanding notes in full. If they invested this money in subprime mortgages, however, that was not a wise assumption.)

And there is more good news about Nigeria. Not only has it now settled most or all of its trade supplier debt, oil money has also enabled it to pay off most of its bank debt, too. In short, Nigeria's foreign indebtedness is a small fraction, about 2 percent, of its gross domestic product (roughly $3.5 billion at the end of 2007), and its foreign reserves have grown dramatically to approximately $75 billion in 2008.*

One basic lesson to be learned from my Nigeria experience is that sometimes misperceptions can play a big role in the price of an asset. In the 1980s, Nigeria was widely perceived as an unsalvageable wreck, in part because the only direct experience many investors had with Nigeria were fraudulent scams such as those 419 letters. (The Nigerian 419 letter predated the Internet. E-mail has only made it easier and less expensive to perpetuate the fraud.) Those who dared to venture to Nigeria saw only a frighteningly dilapidated airport and an equally dismal capital in Lagos. Many investors were simply scared off by Nigeria, and the value of assets such as NPNs reflected that fear.

Nigeria also taught me the extraordinary value of circumspection. Even today, when there is so much more financial information readily available in real time on computer screens throughout the world, circumspection is essential in a business such as ours. The Nigerian buyback succeeded, in part, because everyone involved kept their own counsel about what was unfolding. There was nothing fraudulent or even unethical about it, at least not by the commonly accepted standards of institutional finance. In our business, everyone is secretive because information is truly power in the zero-sum game of making money. Therefore, those who know don't say, and those

---

*For purposes of comparison, in 2005 the net foreign debt of the United States was a staggering 24 percent of gross domestic product, as reported in "The Overstretch Myth," by David H. Levey and Stuart S. Brown, *Foreign Affairs*, March/April 2005.

who say probably don't know, or they've just had too many drinks. Thus, when I was scouring the planet for NPNs to sell to Bob Dudley, I never said, "Sell me all you've got," or "I need to buy $20 million in NPNs, how many are you selling?" Rather, I kept my stated desires modest. If I knew from the list that XYZ Corporation had $50 million in NPNs, I'd say, "Our client is interested in buying $5 million worth." Inside I was salivating at the prospect of buying them all, but you never betray that desire to a seller. Sometimes the seller would say, "Well, we'd really like to sell $10 million," and I would "grudgingly" agree to do so, which kept the price down. Whether you're buying a car or a Nigerian promissory note, play your cards close to the vest or you will lose your leverage. Always suggest your need is limited, not infinite, and put a firm time limit on your offer so that your counterparty doesn't have much time to shop around.

Such circumspection worked to our advantage in Nigeria in other ways, too. Because everyone in our business protects information, people and institutions don't tend to share what they know. (The exception was the Indian expats on Wyndham Street, and because they shared information I was never able to negotiate a better price for NPNs than the price I paid at the top of the hill.) As a result, the buyback was able to proceed for five years with prices for NPNs ranging from twenty-two to thirty-eight cents on the dollar. Though many sellers suspected a buyback, most of them were never sure.

Nigeria was my first exposure to the buyback as a technique for reducing indebtedness and improving a balance sheet. The debt buyback is now a widely used method by both corporations and governments that have seen the price of the long-term debt obligations reduced to bargain-basement prices. They need not be, and often aren't, secret. Most are widely publicized so that debt holders know of the opportunity. While news of a buyback is likely to push up the price of an asset and increase the cost to the buyer, it nevertheless offers an attractive way to retire debt cheaper than if the obligations remain outstanding until they mature.

A final lesson from the Nigeria experience echoed the philosophy of George Washington, who believed that countries don't have permanent alliances, only permanent interests. So it is in business, though I would add that in business, one doesn't necessarily have permanent enemies, either. When mutual self-interest is involved, even former enemies will bury the past to make millions of dollars in the future. I'm sure I was the last person Bob Dudley, my former enemy, wanted to depend on to help him execute the Nigerian buy-back, just as he was the last person I wanted to be dependent on to make tens of millions of dollars. Yet here we were, each perfectly positioned to help one another.

Finally, in Nigeria I learned that there can, in fact, be something close to a free lunch. Never have I made so much money with so little risk as I did in Nigeria. But life has a way of evening things out, a hard lesson I would learn just a few years later in the "new" Russia. If Nigeria was "easy come" when it came to money, Russia was "easy go."

CHAPTER 6

RUSSIA

Boom to Bust and Back

YOU CAN LEARN a lot about a country from its airport when you first arrive. Arriving at Guatemala's La Aurora Airport in the 1980s, for example, one was immediately struck by the presence of heavily armed soldiers, an unfamiliar site in American airports back then, but far from unusual for a country with a brutal right-wing government and a history of political violence. Switzerland's Zurich Airport, of course, was all fine watches in the shops and cool, brightly lit efficiency, just like its famous banks. Before the collapse of the Soviet Union in 1991, Moscow's Sheremetyevo Airport was no less than a crash course (no pun intended) in the country's economy.

Ill-lit, reeking of acrid tobacco, and staffed by humorless customs and immigration agents, Sheremetyevo was strictly utilitarian and unremittingly grim. The sense of foreboding began with the immigration officer who checked your passport while sitting up in a booth that allowed him to look down into your eyes, which he usually did three or four times, flashing back to the photo in your passport to ascertain that the person in the photo was actually you. Clearly, the officers had been trained to do their jobs without betraying the slightest trace of humanity or goodwill. When capitalism began to take hold after the collapse of the Soviet Union, many of these same immigration officers would attempt to wrangle a few dollars by soliciting a small bribe to put an official stamp in your passport, which, though not required, many visitors desired as a small souvenir.

In the Soviet era, it was possible to arrive in Moscow and wade into a vast sea of taxicabs at the airport only to find not a one that wasn't "off duty." Paid a fixed salary by the state and forbidden, at least by law, from accepting foreign currencies, the cabbies had no financial incentive to take you anywhere. They got paid the same whether they idled in a drunken stupor at the airport or hustled to get you to your hotel. Most of them simply napped. Being implored to work hard for the glory of the Soviet state by many huge billboards, which featured the grim visages of current members of the politburo, just wasn't enough incentive.

Things didn't get any better once you got out of the airport and into the city. Empty restaurants wouldn't seat you because all the tables were "reserved" for phantom guests who wouldn't place any demands on the restaurant's underworked staff. Off in the corner, idle, shabbily clad waiters watched cartoons on old television sets, oblivious to the few customers around them unless they were trying to sell you a tin of caviar on the side in exchange for some hard currency. You didn't want to know what went on in the kitchen.

On every hotel floor grim-faced "key ladies," usually grossly overweight *babushkas*, took your key every time you left your room and returned it to you when you came back. They, too, often had something to sell on the side, perhaps a bottle of Russia's horrendously musty bottled water. Who they might have "lent" your key to in your absence was anyone's guess. But such meaningless, mind-numbing jobs were one way the Soviet state created what it claimed was a full-employment society.

Churchill's famous description of Russia as a puzzle wrapped inside an enigma wrapped inside a mystery was apt. Almost nothing made sense in Russia. Carpets were often cleaned with wet mops. Old women removed snow from Moscow's sidewalks using dead tree branches tied together with rope. Usually spring would have its way with the snow before the sweepers did. And then there were the schedule and departure times for all domestic Aeroflot flights, which were given in Moscow time, even though the country spans ten time zones. If the "wings of communism" were taking you from Tashkent, several hours ahead of Moscow, to Vladivostok, ten hours ahead of Moscow, you had to determine when to get to the airport by calculating the time in Moscow. The Russians may have launched the first earth-orbiting satellite, sent the first man into space, and figured out how to plant a nuclear warhead in Times Square launched from 8,000 miles away, but they never quite solved the time zone challenge. Aeroflot, the country's only airline, symbolized Moscow's central control over the vast territory of the Soviet Union and the pervasive effect of centralized planning, an immutable fixture of Soviet life.

Nearly two decades on from the demise of the Soviet state in 1991, it's difficult to remember just how stunning and monumental the end of the Cold War was to anyone who grew up practicing "duck and cover" drills in grammar school. This massive empire that once posed an existential threat to "the American way of life" simply disappeared overnight, and into this vacuum capitalism rushed in. It was one of the most chaotic, confusing, corrupt, and often murderous economic transformations to ever unfold. In short, it constituted the perfect conditions for me to visit and do some business.

In June 1998, I traveled to Russia to attend an investor conference and get a sense of what was going on in the country's new economy. Though I had been there many times before, prior to and after the fall of the Soviet Union, economic events were moving so fast that the place was visibly different from year to year. In the early 1990s, Russia launched into free-for-all capitalism like a Sputnik shot into orbit. Massive state industries were privatized (a euphemism, in most cases, for looted), often by the Communist bosses that had been running them in the Soviet era—or they were virtually given away to a favored few. Organized crime, protection rackets, and political and economic assassinations were commonplace. Huge fortunes were made overnight and just as quickly disappeared into overseas banks. Russia had adapted the most aggressive of Western business practices but without any of the legal and financial frameworks needed to make an orderly transition from communism to capitalism. Still, you never know what you'll find in a country recently renamed an "emerging market." And in 1998, *everyone,* it seemed, was doing business in Russia. After all, it was a vast untapped market of about 125 million people.*

When I landed at Sheremetyevo Airport in June 1998, I was met by one of the infamously comely Russian girls holding a sign that read: "Mr. Robert Smith, MFK Renaissance." MFK Renaissance, the powerful Russian investment bank, was the conference sponsor. Follow her? Gladly. It was definitely preferable to getting into a gypsy cab with someone's brother-in-law in front and then driven down a side street and relieved (at the point of a gun) of my passport, watch, and dollars.

Paul Caseiras invited me to the conference. Paul knew that I had, for several years, been trading the debts of Russia's Foreign Trade Organization, debts known as FTOs, and as one of MFK Renaissance's top salesmen Paul was eager to cultivate our relationship. Paul

---

*The population of the Soviet Union at the time of its dissolution in 1991 was approximately 290 million, and the Soviet republic of Russia accounted for almost half of it.

himself had nearly been murdered during an attack that began with a ride in one such gypsy cab. The men who picked him up followed him to his Moscow apartment and attacked him in a robbery attempt. Such crime was virtually nonexistent in Soviet days, but Moscow was now one of the most dangerous cities in the world, swirling with drugs, thugs, gangs, prostitution, and organized crime.

The MFK Renaissance conference was to be a six-day affair, and in order to attend I had to skip my fortieth high school reunion where I could have shown the august members of my Roxbury Latin class what had become of this low-ranking graduate. I could have told them that I now spent my life meeting with world finance ministers, providing life support, albeit in self-interest, to hemorrhaging governments. We could have all had a laugh at the imminent rigors their sons were going to endure in Roxbury Latin's new Robert P. and Salua J. A. Smith Theater, a performing arts facility that I had donated to prove a point about my less-than-stellar academic career. But, no, I decided to forgo those vain pleasures to go where the action was, where there was money to be made. Even an economic mercenary has priorities.

I followed the Russian beauty sent to meet me at the airport to a luxury bus, where I saw receding rows of men and women in their thirties who'd never seen a market crash, but who, despite their youth, were big-time traders and bankers from London, Geneva, and New York. I was about to turn sixty years old, and my first thought was, "Maybe I'm getting too old for this business." Then, happily, I spied my friend "Francis McDowell" from the investment bank "Connors Foreman." Francis was the philosopher king of our business, the steady oarsman, the Oxford don type who now found himself as an expensive hired hand pouring money into emerging markets. I sat down next to him, and he gracefully acknowledged my presence.

"Well, Francis, what do you make of things?" I asked.

I was interrupting him. He was not your typical financier. He was reading Cicero.

"I think it should be a fascinating trip," he replied, looking up briefly. "Bob, give me just a minute. I want to finish this section." He turned back to his book.

"You know, Francis, that Churchill referred to Russia as a riddle wrapped in a mystery inside an enigma," I said, trying to match his intellectual intensity with a well-worn quote almost every visitor to Russia has heard a dozen times.

"I know," he said, returning to his book.

I decided to eavesdrop on the conversations around me and take the pulse of this group, which, in theory, should have been relatively in the know about what was happening in the Russian economy.

"Goldman just oversubscribed $1.2 billion of Russian Eurobonds and they must know what's going on," said one voice. This meant that Russian bonds denominated in dollars that Goldman Sachs was underwriting were in great demand, driving the price up and the yield down. A bullish sign. (Two weeks later, Deutsche Bank would help Russia borrow another $2.5 billion through a similar bond issue. Lots of people were bullish on Russia and eager to lend it money.)

"The IMF just lent the Russians $22 billion," said another in the group. "The U.S. won't let them go down. They're nuclear, for God's sake," said yet another voice. Another good sign.

But then I heard the familiar voice of "Abby Frost" of "Sterns Capital Management" saying to someone, "We've sold all our GKOs [Russian short-term bonds denominated in rubles and shorthand for *gosudarstvenniye kratkosrochniye obligatzii*, which translates as "short-term obligation"]. The place is rotting."*

---

*GKOs paid an exceptionally high interest rate, generally between 30 percent to 50 percent and even as high as 150 percent in the spring of 1998. Though initially restricted to Russian buyers, by the spring of 1998, foreigners held approximately 28 percent of the outstanding GKOs. But, in the absence of a reliable tax collection system, the GKOs were a giant pyramid scheme in which the Central Bank had to keep selling more and more of them to pay off those that were coming due. When investors lost confidence and the money coming in from the purchase of new GKOs couldn't cover the costs of paying those that had come due, the shortfall had to come from the government somehow. The month after my trip, Goldman helped Russia "retire" $6.4 billion of its GKO obligations with a swap in which GKO

Oy vey, I thought to myself. Maybe I should have gone to my high school reunion, after all. I sat back in my seat and young "Arthur Higginbottom," Francis's associate, smiled at me. Someone started passing Cuban cigars around. I smiled back at Arthur and looked out the window at the gray sky. Let the games begin, I thought.

On the ride into Moscow I was struck by the change in the landscape. Gone were the billboards with proclamations about the mighty accomplishment of the Soviet state and other propaganda. The highway was dotted with billboards advertising Western goods, nightclubs, and casinos. My mind drifted back to the Russia I once knew.

I had first come to Russia in 1983. In those dark days, Moscow was a city of decaying buildings, an apt metaphor for the decaying Soviet state. I stayed at the Cosmos Hotel, one of several hotels for foreigners only that Russians (except for the prostitutes and money changers who bribed the security guards) were prohibited from entering. The Soviets were paranoid that mixing foreigners and Russians could result in the dreaded spread of ideas. The hotel was across from the Exhibition of Economic Achievements, a complex intended as a showcase for Soviet economic success. One morning I noticed a huge line had formed outside the park. I walked over to see what all the fuss was about and came face-to-face with the grim reality of Soviet

---

holders would give up their GKOs for dollar-denominated bonds paying between 8.75 percent and 11 percent. This short-term fix would only drive Russia deeper into debt and delay the day of reckoning. It was one of many factors that would, unbeknownst to me in June 1998, lead up to a massive debt default by Russia in August of that year. There is an excellent discussion of the events leading up to Russia's default in David E. Hoffman's *The Oligarchs: Wealth and Power in the New Russia* (New York: Public Affairs, 2002), and another in Paul Blustein's *The Chastening: Inside the Crisis That Rocked the Global Financial System and Humbled the IMF* (New York: Public Affairs, 2001).

life. At the front of the line was a group of tired-looking Russian women selling mangy bananas that no American supermarket would dare sell. No park ever had a more ironic name. That was Russia: a third-world country with a first-world nuclear delivery system.

In 1985, Mikhail Gorbachev came to power, and with his policies of *perestroika* (reform) and *glasnost* (openness) he unwittingly set in motion events that would six years later lead to the demise of the Soviet Union, and his own political demise at the hands of Boris Yeltsin. It was Yeltsin and his band of reformers who would put Russia on its chaotic path to capitalism.

"It's not like the old days," I said to Francis, interrupting his reading once again. I was commenting not only on the billboards that announced Russia's new capitalism, but on the fact that our bus was filled with business people interested in investing in the new Russia.

Francis looked up. "There are three other buses. Thirty fixed-income investors and ninety equity guys—U.S., Europe, Asia. All of us."

I nodded, quickly calculating that we probably represented somewhere between $75 billion and $100 billion going in and out of Russia.

Arthur leaned over. "What are you interested in?"

"Everything," I said obtusely. "What are *you* interested in?"

Francis answered for him, "The nightclubs." Since the fall of the Soviet Union, Moscow had become famous as an "anything goes" playground with wild nightclubs that attracted both Westerners and Russia's young, emerging entrepreneurial class. "Arthur, I'm sure Bob will know which nightclubs to take you to," Francis added.

Nightclubs, indeed. The mention of nightclubs brought back memories of another trip to Russia, this one in 1993, where I'd begun my serious market research on the country.

I was in Moscow to attend a conference sponsored by a trade association of Russian banks that were hoping to find U.S. partner banks with whom they could do business. There were about fifty dele-

gates there, but very few major U.S. or European banks were represented, only banks with names like "Pine Tree Bank" from Shawnee,
Kansas. Even the small players were looking for some insight into
the Russian economy. We all stayed in the monstrous, state-owned
President Hotel, visited different banks, and were introduced to high-
ranking government officials.

At that conference I met an old banker from "Lindor/Hoffman
Banc." "Walter Klinghoff" was a tall, elegant Swiss gentleman who
was very busy taking money out of Russia for Russian entrepreneurs
and politicians and depositing it in private accounts in Switzerland.
The money was literally being taken out of the country in suitcases.
He was one of many people facilitating the notorious capital flight,
said to be about $20 billion a year, that was bleeding the Russian
economy.

"Bob," he said, "you've got to see how the Russian economy
really works."

"That's wonderful," I said. "What do we do?"

"I suggest we go out for a night of drinking at Nightflight," he
said. "As Nightflight goes, so goes the Russian economy."

Nighflight was a joint Swedish-Russian enterprise with a good
steak restaurant upstairs and a discotheque downstairs. No Russian
men, at that time, were allowed in: only Westerners and Russian girls.
Drinks could be paid for only in dollars. Every Soviet girl from Minsk
to Neftegorsk with capitalist aspirations went there to begin her journey toward marriage, babies, emigration, and a house in Ibiza or
Great Neck. You could learn a lot about the state of the economy by
talking to these friendly girls about their standard of living. One
young woman I spoke with told me that she was a nurse. "And my
whole family of six lives in two rooms," she said. "I work for Moscow
General Hospital and I earn $30 a month." "I'm a schoolteacher,"
said another, "but I also do secretarial work for the bureau of exports." In short, for the newly rich, Russia's nascent capitalist economy life was grand. For ordinary folks, it was a day-to-day struggle.

These young women, far more beautiful than the stereotype of

Russian women would lead you to believe, would tell me about their lives with astonishing candor. I was a stranger, but a stranger, they suspected, with money, and they were looking for a way out of Russia to a better life.

At this point in time Russians, even those who were struggling, still had some hope that their lives would improve. By 1998, they were souring on capitalism, which had so far failed to improve the lot of the average citizen. The regimented but secure life that Russians once knew (a guaranteed job, an education, basic health care) had become a life of tremendous economic dislocation for many and a windfall for a few. Russians grew jaded, and many of those sweet young women looking for a way out in 1993 were now raking in hard cash as expensive prostitutes in 1998. The underbelly of capitalism was really showing itself.

The bus rolled on and we crossed the Moskva River. The sun had come out, turning the normally brown river waters to gold. I hoped it would be a good omen for the rest of the trip.

"What's the Kempinsky Hotel like?" I heard Martin Quintin-Archard say.

Martin was a young, quick-thinking, Rhodesian-born bon vivant who always wore a red vest, satin shoes, a Savile Row suit, and a monocle. Known by the James Bondesque nickname QAQA, with his long, unkempt hair and fancy clothes, QAQA cut a striking figure in the conservative world of international finance and everyone knew him. Though not especially good-looking, he had a *savoir faire* and self-confidence that allowed him to be quite a ladies' man. He also had nicknames for everyone (I detested mine: Budweiser Bob) and was always the center of attention, a testament to his gregarious nature. He was the clown prince of our business, but a very clever and successful one. And to think at one point earlier in his life, he was parking cars at a London nightclub.

QAQA died in 2000 at the age of forty-five while climbing Mt. Kilimanjaro as part of a charity fund-raiser in his native Africa. But in 1998, he was president of Intercapital Brokers and, like the rest of us, was looking to cash in on Russia. It was QAQA who first started posting quotes for emerging-market sovereign bonds on electronic screens in the late 1980s, ending the lack of transparency in a market that had been my bread and butter since the early 1980s. He had, in a way, made my life very difficult, but it wasn't personal. Actually, technology made it inevitable. QAQA was just the first to think of it.

There was no doubt that when it came to investigating the Russian economy through its nightclub scene, QAQA would be the lead investigator. When on the road, he was indestructible. At least he was then.

"I hear the hotel's very German," Higginbottom yelled from the back.

"Let's hope the presentations aren't in German," someone responded.

"The hotel is across from Red Square," I said helpfully. The spirit of camaraderie was rapidly rising as we realized that for the next six days we were all going to be in close company.

From the bus window, it was clear that Moscow, too, was a different city than it had been just a few years before. Yuri Luzhkov, its powerful, autocratic mayor, had spared no expense or bluster as he prodded, bullied, and demanded that once-dowdy Moscow be transformed into a grand, elegant, modern city. Buildings had been repaired and painted, streets paved, and parks and boulevards spruced up. Moscow was gradually reclaiming its former glory as a major European capital. Signs of the capitalist revolution were everywhere. Brightly lit shops that could be in Paris, London, or Zurich lined some of the newly refurbished boulevards. Stretch limousines and Mercedes raced by at frightening speed.

"How's business?" I asked Francis.

"I've been mostly in South Africa and Bosnia. Some here, of course. You?"

"Nigeria. Angola. Some here." I didn't want to admit that 50 percent of my business was now in Russia. Traders never admit anything.

"Going well?" asked Francis.

I nodded. You never say how well, but it had, in fact, been going very well. From 1993 onward, my partner, Saleh, and I had been making a lot of money collecting and brokering FTOs. Just as in Turkey, there were many companies that sold goods to the Soviet Union and had never been paid—companies like Upjohn, which had sold pharmaceuticals, or Xerox, which had sold copiers, or Italian shoe leather manufacturers, which had sent in goods for vests, hats, and lining. Now those were debts of the Russian government, but getting paid was still a nightmare. The Russians were arduous to deal with, and many businesses simply wrote off their Russian claims as bad debts. They got tired of carrying the losses on their books.

But those debts could be collected. They were monies owed. Our business in Russia took three forms. First, in some cases we acted, in essence, as collection agents. To ensure that companies would continue to export essential goods such as pharmaceuticals and high technology to Russia, priority lists were established for repayment of trade claims. We had contacts in Russia who could help us get creditors onto that priority list, so we'd go to a company like Upjohn and say, "We believe we can collect fifty cents on the dollar for your claim if you give us six months to try to collect." Then we'd work with people who would do all the bureaucratic legwork needed to validate the claim (in a country like Russia this could mean repeated visits to a half dozen ministries, banks, and other institutions). In many cases, our goal was to collect sixty cents on the dollar, pay Upjohn the fifty cents we promised, and make our money on the spread. More often than not, we were successful.

We also brokered trade claims matching sellers who wanted to unload what amounted to a Russian promise to pay with buyers who believed the Russians would eventually issue bonds to the debt holders with interest dating back, in some cases, to 1985, when the debts were incurred.

And, finally, at one point we created a $30 million investment pool from a handful of sophisticated, institutional investors that traded in Russian debts. There was good money to be made. All told, there was approximately $6 billion worth of Soviet-era trade debt still outstanding and we only had to share the universe with one major competitor, Morgan Grenfell, the British investment bank. There was plenty of room for both of us. In 1992, we were buying these debts for fourteen to twenty cents on the dollar. Saleh and I, as managers of the fund, took 20 percent of the upside and a one percent fee. We liquidated our first portfolio in 1994 at seventy-three cents in less than a year and a half. We loved Russia. By June 1998, just before Russia's August default, those debts were selling for eighty-five cents on the dollar, a real vote of confidence in the Russian economy.

That's when the Russians came up with a new plan for settling their commercial and trade debts. Shortly before the MFK Renaissance trip, a term sheet was released outlining the deal. The Russians were offering the trade claimants thirty-year dollar-denominated bonds as payment for the principal, and ten-year bonds in payment of the accrued interest on their claims.

In mid-1998 that looked like a pretty good deal. Russia was rich. The country was swimming in natural gas and oil (there's more crude oil underneath it than anywhere else in the world, save for Saudi Arabia) and clinking in nickel. Its diamond and gold reserves alone made it rich, not to mention its wealth in aluminum, copper, magnesium, and uranium, as well as in steel, farmland, and fishing fleets. Then there's the commodity we all love: cash. Russia had $14.5 billion of foreign exchange reserves, not a lot for a country of its size, but not chicken feed, either. President Bill Clinton was making public statements of support for Russia and its economic reforms, promising to ride to the rescue should it falter. His administration had a lot riding on Yeltsin remaining in power as Yeltsin, for all his flaws and vices (alcohol being one of them), was seen as key to Russia staying the course on the road to capitalism and democracy.

A subtext to all this support was the fear that should Russia descend into economic or political chaos, its thousands of nuclear weapons could fall into the wrong hands. The so-called "loose nukes" issue was very much on everyone's mind as Russia staggered forward in the post-Soviet era, and it was a major reason why the West was so heavily invested in keeping the Russian ship afloat. If the country became strapped for cash, might it be desperate enough to sell some of those weapons? Might its unemployed or unpaid nuclear scientists be tempted to work for other bosses?

Clinton had plenty of resources at his disposal to back up his rhetorical support: The IMF and the World Bank, though nominally international institutions, are very much under American and European influence (the IMF by tradition always has a European managing director and the World Bank an American president). Russia had already been the beneficiary of a $9.2 billion IMF loan package with billions more from the World Bank, and with those loans came strict conditions for fiscal reform. President Clinton wasn't the only American expressing faith in the Russian economy, either. Former President George H. W. Bush, flown to Russia by Goldman Sachs to tout its new Russian bond offering, was also expressing confidence. In the past, the United States, the World Bank, and the IMF had bailed out other countries of far less strategic importance than Russia: Mexico, South Korea, and Brazil, to name a few, had all been saved by the international financial cavalry. I saw all this as a virtual guarantee that the international community would not let Russia default because the implications were simply too dire.

This is not to say that Russia didn't have big problems. The country had about $50–$60 billion in total private-sector debt, on top of tens of billions more in "official debt" owed to governments, the IMF, and the World Bank. Though rich beyond measure in natural resources, Russia hadn't figured out how to manage these golden assets, which were "sold" to a handful of shameless and powerful individuals, including our hosts, Boris Jordan and Vladimir Potanin, the founders of MFK Renaissance, at bargain-basement prices in questionable auctions.

Jordan was the president and CEO of MFK Renaissance. He was only thirty-two, the grandson of a Russian immigrant to the United States, had grown up in Long Island and attended New York University. He was already a very rich man, with a fortune made in the post-Soviet era gold rush called privatization. Potanin, another of Russia's fabulously wealthy new oligarchs, was Jordan's principal partner in MFK.

While huge equity stakes in the country's most important firms were given to a few chosen banks in exchange for loans (more on this practice shortly), the debts remained as debts of the state. No one was paying taxes either, because the tax system was virtually nonexistent. Profits were going to a handful of men and investors in Russia who were quickly spiriting their fortunes out of the country. The entire process of privatization was, to put it mildly, a mess.

A slowdown in the global economy, and a serious downturn in emerging markets triggered by devaluation of the Thai *baht* and the "Asian flu" that followed, also dragged on the Russian economy. Oil prices were dropping fast, some 25 percent between 1997 and 1998, from over $20 a barrel to below $14, the level at which the cost of extracting oil exceeded the price. The Russian economy was floating on oil, and right now that was one leaky boat.

It is human nature to want to see the possibility of success. Success lies, we believe, somewhere just over the horizon. We just have to find it. There are sure to be some bumps along the way, but we still believe in the destination. That's why I was missing my high school reunion and was instead pulling up to the stark, elegant Kempinsky Hotel with 130 other people interested in finding that land of possibility somewhere over the rainbow. In a country as big and as rich in human and natural resources as Russia, there had to be a pot of gold somewhere.

Anatoly Chubais, a young economist from St. Petersburg, was the brains behind Boris Yeltsin's privatization plan for Soviet industry. A major element of the plan was the issuance to every Russian of vouchers that could be exchanged for small equity stakes in the new companies being calved from the large state industries. It was Boris Jordan, and a few others, who had the rather cold-blooded insight that most Russians, who had no experience or understanding of capitalism, would not understand the value or the purpose of the vouchers. And each voucher represented such a tiny stake that their owners were effectively shut out of the auctions being held to privatize industries, anyway. So Jordan developed a nationwide system for offering the workers small amounts of cash, around seven dollars, for their vouchers, and most workers were happy to have something for what they saw as a worthless piece of paper. From the workers' point of view, whatever Jordan was offering was more than they already had. They felt lucky to get the extra few rubles they got to buy vodka or an extra piece of beef, if one could be found during the difficult days of 1992–94 when the voucher scheme was in place. The irony, of course, was that Marxist dogma had it that workers owned the means of production, but after all these years of toil, the workers were being paid a pittance for all their decades of labor.

Jordan, who was working for CS First Boston, a major international financial services company, before he founded MFK Renaissance, became the biggest buyer of Russian vouchers. When a Russian stock exchange finally opened, he made spectacular profits for CS First Boston and a multimillion-dollar bonus for himself. As a result, these vouchers, whose cumulative value was supposed to represent, according to Chubais's privatization plan, 29 percent of the value of all state industries, effectively put the value of all of Russia's vast industrial and mineral wealth at an absurdly low $5 billion. That's one reason why Jordon and others who bought vouchers by the truckload were able to reap huge windfalls: The true value of the assets they were buying was astronomically higher. Gazprom, Russia's largest natural gas company, sold for $250 *million* at voucher auction prices and was valued, by Russian stock market prices four years later, at $40.5 *billion*. Lukoil, Russia's largest oil company, went for $704 million at voucher prices and had a market value four years later of almost $16 billion.

After his voucher success, Jordan decided to open his own investment house, originally called Renaissance Capital Group. He then partnered with Potanin, who owned a bank known as the International Company for Finance and Investment, or MFK.

The merged companies, known as MFK Renaissance, had equity capital of $400 million, another billion in managed funds, and total assets in excess of $2 billion, not to mention a staff of 600, all of whom seemed to be in their mid twenties. Jordan wanted to create a Russian Citibank, with a coterie of different financial revenue streams, so he had his staff selling such offerings as life insurance door-to-door in Moscow. This was an idea that might have been useful, given the amount of crime in the city, but it was one that was not yet comprehensible to the average Russian.

However, to Westerners looking to invest money, Jordan had set up a truly impressive operation. He was a genius at hiring young foreigners from places like J. P. Morgan and Merrill Lynch, particularly in the brokerage and capital markets area, and then letting the hedge and mutual funds abroad have the illusion that Western banking practices and Russian ethics had something in common.

Boris Jordan introduced the program on the first day of our conference and said we would be witnessing all the new transparencies in corporate governance in Russia (meaning we would know what they do with our money) and how the country's rich manufacturing companies were thriving. He painted a bright picture of the country's economic future. He was brief and then turned the program over to his speakers. This was probably just one of many investor conferences for him.

Boris Fyodorov, Russia's top tax collector and a well-respected government official, gave a presentation in well-spoken English and said that Russia, after years with no real tax code or tax collection system in place, now had an equitable system we could have faith in. Most Westerners living in Moscow worried that they would be the only ones asked to ante up, since the Russians themselves knew nothing of taxes.

"If they mean to collect from the Russians," Arthur Higginbottom mumbled to me, "that must mean they're sending soldiers in with tanks." Arthur had arrived late, following a late-night inspection of the city's nightclubs.

The next day, the minister of economy and the president of the Central Bank gave presentations stating, "We're establishing shareholder regulation regimes."

"Right," said Arthur, opening his eyes briefly.

It was becoming clear that the message the Russians wanted to convey was that the country would no longer operate like the Wild West but like a rational, Western-style economy with safeguards that would protect investors. Until now, Russia was high risk/high reward, because it had been a kind of capitalist free-fire zone where anything goes. If it wanted to attract the smart money and long-term investment by foreign companies, and not just the money of gamblers and speculators, it had to get its economic house in order, and that meant a fair and enforceable tax code, regulated stock markets, and a regulated banking sector. The message, not completely convincing, was: "Everything is fine. Not to worry."

But, in fact, the Russian stock market had lost half its value in May and was down 75 percent from its peak in October 1997, though it had rebounded by about 20 percent on June 2 and June 3, just prior to the MFK Renaissance conference. It was, to be sure, one very volatile market, but it didn't alarm me. The price of FTOs, the principal form of my multimillion-dollar Russia investment at the time, bore no direct relationship to the equities market. I was definitely a glass-half-full guy when it came to Russia.

I knew we were witnessing a sophisticated dog and pony show, but I was still bowled over by the intelligence of these Russians and how quickly they seemed to be adapting to and shaping a new economy. This was, after all, one of the greatest and fastest economic transitions in the history of the world and the learning curve was steep. While perhaps whitewashing the severity of the problems they faced, these people nonetheless had a very sophisticated understanding of what it would take to move the country to a free market economy. They weren't peasants from the potato farms. They were well-educated, urbane, and smart.

I had a feeling I would learn more on the second evening of the conference at an elaborate reception and dinner at the Kuskovo Estate to be hosted by Vladimir Potanin, who in addition to his role in MFK Renaissance was founder of the United Export-Import Bank, or Uneximbank.

People usually let their guard down at social events and will tell you privately what they would never say publicly. There was already some irrational exuberance about Russia bubbling in my brain, but I thought I'd wait and see what else there was to be learned. The gala, however, turned out to be more flash than fire, though there was, quite literally, a bit of fire.

The Kuskovo Estate in Moscow looked like a mini Hermitage, the grand and elegant winter palace of the tsars built in the mid-1700s and now one of the world's great museums. Statues of goddesses and angels abounded. Set on lovely Kuskovo Lake, the estate was to be used as a backdrop for a different kind of razzle-dazzle designed to ramp up our enthusiasm for Russia's potential as a place to park our collective personal and institutional money.

Potanin had a passion for jet-skiing, and to entertain us that evening he had flown in jet-ski champions from the States. As we stood on the banks of the lake, sipping champagne and eating caviar, the early summer sun extending the evening, these men dressed in wet suits rushed and roared and flipped about on their Ski-Doos, even jumping through rings of fire that had been set on the lake. There were rumors that Potanin had the skies above the estate seeded with some chemicals that would keep any rain at bay. Now that's serious money, I thought to myself.

After the show by the lake, attractive women hired by Renaissance escorted us to dinner. As QAQA and I chatted about the opulent surroundings, we were interrupted by one of Renaissance's well-tailored salesmen: "Excuse me. I would like to introduce 'Natasha Nazarkewicz.' She's an economics student." Natasha was stunningly beautiful, and QAQA was suddenly no longer interested in the virtues of the Kuskovo Estate. He started throwing out names like John Kenneth Galbraith and any other economist he could think of. I could have told him to save his breath. I looked around the estate and reasoned that Natasha was just one of many "economics" students dressed in "courtesan period costume." There were about forty-five others, and they all looked like fashion models.

Vladimir Potanin was not as rough around the edges as the other Russian megabillionaires. Unlike Mikhail Khodorkovsky (who started by importing computers), Alexander Smolensky (who started by selling materials to people building country cottages), and Vladimir Gusinsky (who sold copper bracelets on the street), he was a child of relative privilege, educated at the exclusive Moscow Institute for International Relations, which trained students for careers in the KGB or the Kremlin. His father had been a bureaucrat in the Soviet Foreign Trade Ministry (as was Vladimir at one time), and as such he had access to special food stores and foreign travel. During his years in the ministry, Potanin was essentially "a Soviet phosphate fertilizer salesman-bureaucrat," according to David E. Hoffman, author of *The Oligarchs: Wealth and Power in the New Russia*.

Just before the Soviet Union collapsed, Potanin had started a trade organization called Interros with money cadged from Soviet agencies trying to take a stab at capitalism. It was while running Interros that Potanin saw the need for a bank to finance import and export deals. In 1992, Potanin managed (how is not clear) to take hold of the assets, but not the debts, of a Soviet state-run bank, the International Bank for Economic Cooperation. According to Hoffman, almost overnight Potanin's bank was $300 million in the black. The following year he created Uneximbank and it, too, became an immediate success. In 1998, at the time of the MFK Renaissance investor conference, Potanin was still only in his thirties. His net worth was in the hundreds of millions of dollars, perhaps even more than $1 billion. (By the time he was in his mid-forties, in 2007, his net worth was estimated at approximately $4.3 billion.)

Like many who made fortunes in the new Russia, Potanin seemed to benefit from the hidden hand of state favor. And, like the others, he seemed to be able to make money out of thin air. The methods used by Potanin, Jordan, and others to gain control of state enterprises such as Sidanco, a state-owned oil company, were positively breathtaking in their hubris. Potanin "purchased" his 51 percent stake in Sidanco by loaning the Russian government $130 million of its own money—money that government entities had deposited in his banks in the first place. This so-called "loans for shares" scheme was Potanin's brainchild. Officially, these "sales" of state assets were accomplished by auctions, but only a select few—generally chosen by a top adviser to President Boris Yeltsin, who also just happened to be Yeltsin's daughter, Tatyana—were allowed to participate. Not long before our dinner at the Kuskovo Estate, Potanin had sold British Petroleum a 10 percent stake in Sidanco for $571 million! (Sidanco would later go bankrupt.) And Sidanco was only one of twenty former state-owned enterprises Potanin controlled.

I turned to Francis, who had joined me at the dinner table, and mused about the fantastic profits Potanin was generating. "I can't seem to get those kind of spreads," I said.

"You don't do so badly," he replied. "You've sold me paper [referring to Russian FTOs] at I-hate-to-think-what profit."

"Well," I said, "I can assure you, *not that kind of profit.*"

At that moment, on the stage at the front of the room, dancers from the Bolshoi Ballet appeared, twelve swanlike girls twirling about in white against the backdrop of a sign in block letters that read: MFK RENAISSANCE. I sat back. Waiters brought endless plates of food—caviar, champagne, Maine lobster—the dancers pirouetted, and lovely Russian "economic students" flitted about.

"Are these Russians totally insensitive?" asked Higginbottom, sitting down next to me. British, well educated, and refined, Higginbottom was tremendously energetic. He said he had asked the Renaissance personnel how much they had spent to put this trip together.

"What did they say?" I asked.

"They didn't."

"It's supposed to be elegant," I offered.

"It's a bit bizarre," he countered.

Arthur was right. There was something eerie about all this opulence. The ordinary Russian was having a very tough go of it in the new economy. Food and medical supplies were still in short supply. Prices were skyrocketing. Pensions were being lost. The sudden, wrenching transition from the womb of the state-run economy to the cold realities of capitalism wasn't going so well for the man or woman in the street. They were used to being taken care of and now they were owed back wages by the government.

It wasn't that I was suddenly becoming soft-hearted about the system that had done so well by me. I had been around these countries long enough to know that economic difficulties like those Russia were experiencing were often the dark days before the dawn and that, in time, life for ordinary Russians would improve. It was my job to be in those countries before they changed for the good. The terrible inequities were a prelude to change. And I made money on change.

"Next thing you know," Higginbottom said, "they'll bring out Nicholas and Alexandra."

"Maybe the royal couple would like to buy some Russian debt from me," I said, happy with my own joke.

Higginbottom patted me on the back. "Always working, Smith, always working."

Not always. When we returned to our hotel after the extravaganza at the estate, I suggested to Higginbottom that we have a drink elsewhere. I still like to see what's going on in a country, away from the prescribed banker agenda.

We went to a club near the hotel. Wallpapered and lit up in red, it looked like a bordello, which in fact it was, upstairs. The drinks cost twenty dollars each.

"Look," said Higginbottom. "I can't believe it."

"Can't believe what?"

"Those men are all wearing black shirts."

I don't usually pay that much attention to dress. Yes, they were wearing black shirts, black suede shoes, and black slacks.

"They're not fascists," I said. "That's what the mob wears here."

"Thank you, Bob. I feel much better."

Another menacing feature of the new Russia was the explosion of organized crime. From protection rackets to murder for hire, Russia had suddenly become a very dangerous place in the early 1990s. In 1998, it was still dangerous, both for Russians and foreigners. It was, for me, another risk factor to be calculated into the equation of whether Russia was indeed a good bet for investment.

The men in black unnerved Higginbottom, so I took him to the Cherry Casino nearby where there were, well, more men in black. The Cherry Casino was an over-the-top den of capitalist excess. We paid the cover charge—dollars only, of course—and went through the metal detector, which kept going off repeatedly when big men in shiny suits passed through, but no one stopped them. We may have been the only unarmed men in the place. The legendary tall, blonde, and long-legged Russian girls sat dourly at the tables, drinking tea.

"Look at them," Arthur said. "They don't smile. They're not having as good a time as the Argentineans or Brazilians when their countries were going down the toilet." Clearly, Arthur was less enamored of Russia's prospects than I was. Where I saw nothing but promise, he saw decay. I would, in short order, pay dearly for donning my rose-colored glasses.

With the tutorial portion of the investor conference and the elaborate party behind us, it was time for the real show: a four-day jaunt aboard a Yak-40 jet chartered to take the fixed-income investors in our group on a whirlwind tour of the vast economic promise of the new Russia, with stops at major industrial centers to meet the new captains of Russian industry. (The equity folks were ferried about on other planes to other locations.) I would later come to think of this as my Magical Mystery Tour of Russia.

The Soviet-made Yak-40 was the type of plane used in the old days to transport regional Communist Party bosses and important factory directors around the country. It was the ultimate status symbol in a country where the average worker labored in a "socialist paradise" and, theoretically at least, was the country's most important citizen. Our plane was quite old, roomy, and lumbering, and everyone, having claimed a seat, kept to it. The plane was the one place we could leave our things and be reasonably sure they wouldn't be stolen. The stewardesses looked nothing like the economics students we left behind in Moscow, and they smoked before, during, and after takeoff. They passed out bruised pears and warm grapes for little breaks and served nothing but a pathetic Chicken Kiev for meals.

Our first stop was a short one-hour hop to Lipetsk, home to one of Russia's largest steel mills. Lipetsk is about 300 miles southeast of Moscow, on the banks of the Voronezh River. As we drove through the town, we saw people sitting quietly on benches in the tree-lined square, vaguely curious as yet another busload of Westerners passed through. We obviously weren't the first economic tourists to hit town.

As we walked through the hot and noisy Novolipetska Steel Mill, Francis leaned over to me and said, "One of Blake's dark satanic mills, I see," referring to a poem by William Blake and the open ditches of hot lava in front of us that anyone could easily fall into. Not a place for investors in Gucci shoes.

The steel mill was as black as the scowls on the faces of the workers who watched us watching them, resentment etched into their faces. It was likely that, like most workers in Russia at the time, they weren't getting paid on time, if at all, whereas we were obviously well fed. I wanted to tell them to hold on; that eventually the pain of the transition to a market economy would work to their benefit. Had I tried, I probably would have been pitched into the lava trough.

The factory's general director was our guide and he prattled on about the machinery, the factory, its output, and surprisingly, how the factory operated in an environmentally responsible fashion.

"How do you mean?" asked "Jeff Dobbs" of "Turnbull Capital."

"I will show you," said the square-jawed, humorless director.

He walked us to the interior of the rectangular-shaped facility where there was a small pond in a courtyard of sorts. "See the swans?" he said. "They're alive."

Later we sat in an austere, musty auditorium that appeared not to have been touched since the days of the Bolshevik Revolution. We shifted uncomfortably on stiff wooden seats and asked the factory director about profits. Like many in Russia, he was a holdover from the Communist era. Eight years after the collapse of the Soviet Union, he still wasn't familiar with capitalist concepts.

"We produce," he said. "We have quotas for production."

"What about profits?"

He looked flustered.

"What about cost controls?"

Flustered.

"What about your costs?"

"We meet our production quotas," he said, firmly holding his ground.

Our next stop, four-and-a-half hours away by plane, was Norilsk on the Arctic Circle. We arrived at three in the morning. The sun shone brightly above. During summer, the sun barely sets in Norilsk.

In addition to his other holdings, Vladimir Potanin was part owner of the huge Norilsk Nickel Mine, which produces 20 percent of the world's nickel. He purchased his 38 percent stake for $250 million. As with Sidanco, the deal was very sweet. Much of the money Potanin used to make his bid had been deposited in his bank by the Russian government itself. By 2007, Norilsk had a market value of approximately $31.9 billion and annual profits in excess of $1 billion.

"This town looks like a war zone," I heard Higginbottom say behind me.

"Well, of course it does," said Francis. "It was an old prison town of about 100,000 people."

Then a woman stood up at the front of the bus and told us proudly in perfect English, "This is my hometown. But first I must tell you that I just spent two weeks with my sister in Wyoming. I did not like it because the potatoes weren't good. . . ." As she went on and on with other salient facts of her life, I fell asleep, as did the others on the bus, even in the bright Arctic sunlit night. It was, after all, three-thirty in the morning after a four-hour flight.

At the hotel we learned that the next day's meeting was set for 8:00 a.m. The younger crowd saw no point in going to bed and headed for a nightclub instead. I went to my Spartan bedroom, so typical of Russian hotels, where the plastic sheets are as thin as paper, the towels are the size of postage stamps, and the hot water is intermittent.

At seven-thirty the next morning we all gathered, in various stages of exhaustion, in the hotel lobby. Then a voice called out, "To the mines, mates!" It was QAQA. He always had a way with words.

After a breakfast at the hotel, which offered nothing anyone wanted to eat (unless you wanted *kasha,* a porridge made with wheat, buckwheat, oats, millet, rice, or potatoes, or some combination of them), we rallied ourselves to hear presentations on the running of a nickel mine. To our delight, we found out we wouldn't be taken inside one. Apparently the lift was too dangerous.

"You know," said Francis on the bus, "this town looks awful. And when you think that these were the people who were supposedly those most valued by the Communist regime. The workers. They were supposed to be given special consideration for working up here. You know, better pensions and so on. It doesn't look like they're getting them."

"This is no time to get sentimental," I said. "We're here to make money."

"And apparently not to get any sleep," he replied.

"I heard 'Sharon Brody' [another asset manager on our tour] on the phone through the wall in my room last night," said Arthur. "She's unloading her entire GKO position. Apparently she's not impressed with what she's seen so far."

"Foolish," I thought to myself. "This place can't miss."

Norilsk is the world's second largest city above the Arctic Circle, and probably the most polluted city anywhere on earth. So noxious is the discharge from Norilsk Nickel, there isn't a tree within about twenty-five miles of the smelter, and it is said that the soil is so contaminated that it has become economically feasible to mine it. Once a part of the Soviet Union's infamous Gulag, it was where countless Russians were sent as punishment for their crimes, political and otherwise, and what punishment it must have been. In December and January, the sun never shines, and snow cover lasts about 250 days a year. The winter cold cracks walls and foundations. The industry here was and is considered so vital (as were the intercontinental ballistic missile silos around Norilsk) that the city was closed to outsiders until the late 1990s. Foreigners and Russians alike needed special permission to visit, and it is today once again a closed city.

Four-and-a-half hours was a long way to travel to hear an unin-spiring talk by a factory manager and to visit a local museum, but we were soon on the road, or actually in the air, again.

The city of Krasnoyarsk was a two-hour flight. Here we were taken to a hotel where we were scheduled to meet the legendary General Alexander Lebed, who was now governor of the vast region, also known as Krasnoyarsk. Lebed had been a paratroop commander in the Soviet-Afghan War, national security adviser and secretary of the Security Council for Yeltsin, and reputedly the man who put an end to the ghastly war in Chechnya. His term as security adviser ended in October 1996, when Yeltsin fired him amid accusations that Lebed, who had designs on the Russian presidency, was building a private army in an attempt to seize power. He came to world atten-tion again shortly after 9/11 when he told 60 *Minutes* that Russia could not account for all of its "suitcase" nukes. (He would die in 2002 in a helicopter crash in Siberia, an incident that spawned many conspiracy theories.)

It was well known that Lebed hated Boris Jordan, though the source of the animosity wasn't clear, so it surprised us all when they walked into the meeting holding hands. This show of friendliness made us suspicious. After all, we read the newspapers. Lebed wanted money, we guessed, for Krasnoyarsk's hydroelectric business. When Jordan phoned him up to tell him that he was bringing investors, apparently Lebed said, "Tell them to bring their wallets."

On the day of his presentation Lebed tried to be on good behav-ior, but he was a bit of a loose cannon. He had hired an American spin-doctor and was trying to be careful about what he said, but the old Russian in him forced its way to the surface. It reminded me of the movie scene when Peter Sellers, playing the evil genius Dr. Strangelove, cannot stifle his Nazi salute.

"Russian privatization?" Lebed commented. "My grandfather fought for Russia and died. My father fought for Russia and died. Then, with privatization, I was given shares worth a bottle of vodka! That is all I have to say about that." (Obviously, he wasn't a huge fan of privatization or of the fortune Boris Jordan had made from vouchers. Perhaps this accounted for the antipathy the two men had for one another.)

A few people asked questions about investing in Krasnoyarsk, but most of us were paying little attention. We were too tired. Everyone had been out the night before. We couldn't wait to get back on the Yak so we could sleep.

Finally, we were driven back to the airport and to the plane. There was a stir. One of the investor analysts had met a girl of dubious provenance who seemingly had to get to Moscow. Here she stood with her luggage.

"You shouldn't be taking this girl to Moscow," said one of the women in our exhausted delegation.

"There are plenty of seats," replied the Russian girl's white knight.

We decided to convene a New England–style town meeting right there on the tarmac in Krasnoyarsk. The men voted in favor of giving the poor woman a lift back to Moscow. A spokeswoman for the women said, "There's no way that this prostitute is going to Moscow." A vote was taken, but since there were far more men than women in our group, we took off with one additional passenger. Once in the air, some people dozed, some read, and others lied about how much money they were making.

The last stop before returning to Moscow was Irkutsk. As we emerged from the plane and rode the bus into town, Francis said, "Irkutsk is very beautiful, isn't it? All these parks and statues."

"It's sort of like Paris," Higginbottom chimed in. "There's an intellectual bent. I think it's because the intellectuals were sent to prison up here."

As compensation for our grueling ordeal, we were allowed some R & R and were taken for a short cruise on spectacular Lake Baikal, the deepest lake in the world, just outside of the city. As always, the vodka flowed.

"It's beautiful, isn't it?" Francis observed once again as we sailed past the woods in the sun. Francis, being an aesthete, sees beauty everywhere. One of our Russian hosts, being pragmatic, replied, "Usually it's snow and ice. One month a year, this one, it's nice. But that's the month the mosquitoes are out. They're big as dogs. That's why we're on a lake. So we won't get eaten to death."

There was a metaphor here about the Russian economy. Some people, like me, had beautiful visions. The realists saw man-eating mosquitoes.

A week later I was back in Boston and practically took out Russian citizenship. I was so impressed. What a country! What resources! What potential! I bought Russian bank debt to add to my holdings in FTOs. I bought more Russian Eurobonds.

Saleh walked in, wondering if I was going to buy a *dacha* in the birch forests outside of Moscow. Saleh usually finds the deals we do, and then, as he puts it, he "reverse engineers" them. That means he understands the mechanics. I understand the people. He is usually more conservative than I am in business.

"Don't buy," he said. I didn't tell him it was too late. I was already in full swoon. "The market is falling. Never try to catch a falling knife!"

"I agree completely," I said, and went on buying. Some of my worst decisions have been made behind his back, but also some of my best. Between Turan and my own personal account, I now had about $20 million invested in Russia.

Anyway, why worry? The IMF had pumped the place up. People were still buying Russian bonds. "Julian Arthur" of "Tripoli Asset Management" had just published a rosy report about Russia and its economic promise. I later learned that Arthur was, at that very moment, selling the Russian positions he managed.

But it was starting to look like Russia's borrowing would never stop. Even as Goldman Sachs and Deutsche Bank were arranging the billions in Eurobond sales in the summer of 1998, a signal I took to be a bullish one, they were secretly loaning $500 million to Russia to be repaid from the proceeds of those sales. In July, Goldman underwrote $6.4 billion in Eurobonds to pay off the GKOs. Russia was sinking deeper and deeper into debt as the summer went on. When Russia got another $23 billion loan package from the IMF and several commercial banks, I said to Saleh, "You see. Nobody is going to let Russia fall."

On August 17, Saleh was on vacation in Nantucket. I was in the office, and as the news came on, I wondered where I was going to be sleeping that night. I was going to have one very angry wife. Russia was broke: They were devaluing the ruble and announced a ninety-day moratorium on all payments of their foreign obligations; it was, in essence, a default.

With the help of some of the world's leading investment banks, Russia had gotten drunk on debt, borrowing far more than it could repay to investors like me. Many of those investors were much smarter and larger than me, and yet they were also intoxicated on Russia's promise, despite the signs of distress that were hiding in plain sight. Tax collections were nil. The GKOs were nothing but a Ponzi scheme. Yeltsin's leadership was weak, as was his liver. The ruble collapsed. My Russia stake had gone, overnight, from about $20 million to roughly $5 million. Inflation in Russia soared to more than 100 percent. Some Russian firms started "asset stripping," a process in which the company's valuable assets, including foreign currency, are moved offshore, usually into entities created just to hold those assets, leaving creditors to fight over the crumbs. Others would default on their debts and then, after the crash, start buying those debts back, quietly and usually through an intermediary, at rock-bottom prices.

Author Paul Klebnikov succinctly described the fallout from Russia's default in *Godfather of the Kremlin: Boris Berezovksy and the Looting of Russia* (New York: Harcourt, 2000). To summarize: Overnight, foreign banks and investors lost an estimated $40 billion in the Russian debt market and $8 billion in the equities market, though some estimates were that combined losses exceeded $100 billion. Stock markets around the world fell 5 percent or 10 percent or more. Citibank, Chase, Bank of America, and Credit Suisse saw their profits for the year erased. Long-Term Capital Management, the giant hedge fund, collapsed, triggering fears of a global economic collapse. George Soros lost almost $1 billion when Potanin's telecom company, Svyazinvest, collapsed.

MFK Renaissance was a shadow of its former self, most of its capital now gone. Despite the huge hit I had taken I was in good company and, as the cliché goes, misery loves company. I was certainly miserable. Not everyone was unhappy, however. The firms that underwrote the bond deals made tens of millions of dollars.

I tried desperately and in vain to get hold of my contacts at Russian banks that had agreed to buy some of our FTOs to try and salvage myself, but the deals hadn't closed and now they never would. If Brazil had defaulted we'd feel some concern. The people I would be doing business with would answer the phone and say to me, "Robert, I can't pay you now. We'll figure this out. We'll have a samba. We'll get a couple of girls." A Nigerian would also answer the phone and tell me his uncle or his father just died and he could not complete the trade now, but maybe next week. But a Russian? He won't even answer the phone.

The money all of us put into Russia seemed to have disappeared over the Siberian fields. "Oh, God," I said, begging for sympathy from Sharon Brody of "DPK Capital Assets" in London. She had been on the MFK Renaissance trip and was the woman Higginbottom had overheard through the hotel walls unloading her GKOs by phone from Norilsk.

She looked down her nose at me over the telephone. "If you've been in the market for a long time and you see that nothing is clear, that corporate governance isn't transparent, that there isn't a legitimate tax system, and no rules or regulations to protect investors, you are not made to feel better by drinking lots of wine, eating good food, and flying in a private jet," she said.

I put my tail between my legs.

So there it was. Russia couldn't collect its taxes. The government debt was junk. The corporate debt was junk. Billions of dollars worth of syndicated loans from banks were reneged on. There was no cash in the system, so Russian companies were surviving through bartering. And I worried that I, too, might have to start surviving through bartering.

"Smith," Saleh said to me, "You violated the first rules of trading. If Wall Street is saying this is the best thing since sliced bread, the juice is all run out. You were being sold a bill of goods. Even ordinary Russians don't put any faith in their banks. Even they prefer the dollar over the ruble for savings."

He couldn't let it go. "The famous Russian writer Nikolay Karamzin said 200 years ago . . ."

"He can't be that famous," I said. "I've never heard of him."

"Smith, you only pay attention to spreads. Karamzin summed Russia up in one sentence: 'They all steal here.'"

I got his point.

What I had bought at forty or fifty cents on the dollar was now worth thirteen or fourteen cents. It was a huge hit, to my pocketbook and my ego. It didn't matter what the economists from Bear Stearns and Salomon were saying. We were hit. We were all hit. In fact, because of the default and devaluation of the ruble, more than $100 billion was wiped out—more damage, it seemed, than the Russians had caused during the Cold War. We'd been hit with an economic nuke.

I consoled myself by spending many nights drinking in New York at the Russian Samovar Restaurant on Fifty-Second Street and the Russian Vodka Room across the street. I bemoaned Russian business to the headwaiter, the cocktail waitress, and the maître d', any Russian I could talk to. I spoke movingly on Russian callousness, Russian thievery, Russian politicians, Russian businessmen (never Russian women), and Russian brains. They tolerated me as a lovable crank.

One night in September 1998, a few weeks after the Russian collapse, I was watching television at the Vodka Room. It was a smoky place then (before the citywide smoking ban went into effect), with an ancient piano player and a very authentic Russian sense of decadence about it. President Clinton had traveled to Moscow to show his support for Yeltsin, but it was hardly reassuring. On the very day of Russia's default, Clinton had been testifying before a federal grand jury about Monica Lewinsky. As for Yeltsin, well, he had just presided over the most spectacular economic meltdown of modern times. There, I thought, are two failures. I didn't feel much better about myself.

I even brought up the subject to a Russian cab driver in New York one day. He seemed to have the best grip on it of anyone.

"For years Russians had to survive through trickery. You think this changes?" I nodded in the backseat. "Anyway, wait," he said, "for more surprise."

In October, two months following Russia's meltdown, I went to Washington, D.C., for the annual joint meeting of the World Bank and the IMF. It's a huge affair attended by thousands of individuals and institutions and marked by lavish parties thrown by the likes of Merrill Lynch, Goldman Sachs, and the Bank of New York. The Bank of New York had recently been shaken by a major scandal involving the laundering of $7 billion out of Russia, some of which came from nefarious activities, and everyone but me and a few other brave souls was avoiding their hospitality. They had a tremendous banquet table set up laden with sushi, caviar, and all sorts of delicacies. I had it almost to myself and indulged.

During the visit to Washington, Gene Lawson, director of the

U.S.-Russia Business Council, of which I was a member, arranged for Saleh and me to meet with Victor Gerashenko, chairman of Russia's Central Bank. If anyone was capable of feeling my pain it was Gerashenko. He was calm and collected about the state of Russia's affairs.

"Don't worry," he said, "you will see. Russia will pay all of its Eurobonds." The price of Russian bonds had fallen so low that I figured what the heck, and I threw another $2.5 million of my own money in. At least I could lower the average cost of my investment and climb out of the hole sooner if Russia did indeed rebound. I was, as Saleh had said, still trying to catch a falling knife.

I have often made investment decisions based on a reading of politics, not economics. When Pervez Musharraf came to power in Pakistan in a military coup in 1999, Pakistan had only one small ($700 million) outstanding Eurobond issue. Nevertheless, the country was considered high risk by investors and had a poor international credit rating because of its political instability and weak economy. When Pakistan restructured the terms of its Eurobonds shortly after Musharraf took over, I was a buyer. This guy was going to want international approval and respectability, and he was going to want to encourage foreign investment if he had any hope of turning the country's economy around. He needed to establish Pakistan as a reliable debtor. There was no way he was going to default on the country's one Eurobond issue, and I was right.

Politics also figured heavily into my decision to leap headlong into Russia. The U.S. commitment to Russian democracy and capitalism was a centerpiece of Clinton's foreign policy. It didn't matter, or so I thought, what the economic fundamentals were: Russia would not be permitted to fail.

But I had misjudged the situation. The fall in oil prices, the failure to establish a legitimate, enforceable tax code and to collect taxes, the GKO pyramid scheme, the capital flight out of Russia, the Asian flu that decimated investor confidence in emerging markets—it was a perfect storm of economic bad news that no political commitments could overcome.

During my visit to Russia in June 1998, I had been shown a house of cards and thought it was the Trump Tower. As a consequence, I suffered my biggest losses in thirty years as trader in emerging-market debt.

In that failure, I realized that at the end of the day, a country has to rescue itself, because outside sources—the IMF, the World Bank, investment banks, and other nations—often have secondary motives that may not align with a country's national interest. For example, Russia was a bad borrower, but it was also the victim of bad lenders, some of whom had a thirst for short-term profits that outweighed any interest in Russia's long-term economic health. And there was a massive failure to do the kind of due diligence that normally accompanies even much smaller investments. When money is being stolen faster than wealth can be created, it's a recipe for economic disaster, and that's what was happening in Russia in 1998. Even so, everyone, including me, overlooked everything because, given the stakes the West had in Russia's success, it seemed unimaginable that it would ever fall so low that it would default.

Yet time would prove the Russian cabbie in New York—and Gerashenko—right. The Russians rallied. The government and the Central Bank seemed to get hold of financial discipline. Russians began producing goods themselves, since they couldn't afford to import anymore, and they became surprisingly resilient. The price of oil rose sharply between 1999 and 2000 and Russia paid off its debts. (Indeed, thanks largely to oil, Russia is now debt-free and has more than $350 billion in gold and foreign currency reserves, not to mention a stabilization fund worth more than $100 billion as of this writing.) Western-style accounting methods and other corporate reforms, undertaken so Russian companies could sell their shares on international stock markets such as the New York Stock Exchange, made Russian companies more transparent.

And it helped that Yeltsin, so unpredictable, so drunk so much of the time, left office to be replaced by Vladimir Putin. Though many people fear that Putin put Russia back on the road to authoritarianism, he did restore a sense of order, stability, and cold-blooded competence to the running of the country.

Putin laid down the law, sometimes literally, with the oligarchs: Pay your taxes and stay out of politics and I won't try and renationalize the companies you virtually stole from the state. (Those who bucked Putin paid a heavy price; most notably, billionaire oilman Mikhail Khodorkovsky, who had designs on the Russian presidency, is now in prison on what many believe are trumped-up tax evasion charges.) Gradually, the place started to operate a little more like a Western economy and a little less like the Old West. The country didn't fold. It made the biggest comeback I had ever seen and that, in fact, the world had ever seen.

"You see, Saleh," I said victoriously in 2002 when Russia had righted its economic ship, "I was right in believing in them." Not only had I held on to everything Russian I had bought and recouped my losses, I was even far ahead. I had taken the long view and held on to my Russian investments until they rebounded. It took a few years, but it happened. I managed to catch the falling knife and survived to tell the tale.

CHAPTER 7

IRAQ

Mission Not Accomplished

IN FEBRUARY 2004, less than a year after President George W. Bush, riding shotgun on a fighter jet, landed on the deck of the USS *Abraham Lincoln* and prematurely declared "mission accomplished" in Iraq, I flew into Baghdad in a private jet on a mission of my own.

I'd never been to Iraq, but it had been in my sights since the early 1990s, shortly after the First Gulf War. Iraq had racked up a mountain of debt, some owed to other governments, some to banks and other lenders, and some to trade suppliers, all incurred before the war, and huge sums to be paid as war reparations to Kuwait. In total, Iraq's indebtedness was in the neighborhood of $120 billion to $140 billion. Where there's debt there's money to be made trading it, but I'd never developed any business in Iraqi debt prior to my visit there. I went to Iraq, in part, to get a sense of the country in the aftermath of the Second Gulf War (not knowing at the time that it would devolve into a civil war or something close to it) and to size up the risks and possible rewards of trading Iraqi debt. I also went hoping to land the contract to reconcile Iraq's debts under the auspices of the Coalition Provisional Authority (CPA) that was running the country after the fall of Saddam.

When Saddam Hussein's regime fell in the Second Gulf War, all the cards in the Iraq deck were reshuffled. In the run-up to the war in 2003, Secretary of State Colin Powell famously cautioned President Bush about the so-called Pottery Barn rule: If you break it, you own it. The U.S. invasion did indeed break Iraq, and in 2003 the exercise of "nation building," once derided by candidate Bush, began. Among the countless challenges to rebuilding a new Iraqi state would be settling or restructuring the debts the country incurred during Saddam's brutal rule. To do that, you must first know who holds legitimate claims and how much they are owed. This is done through a process known as debt reconciliation, and it was no simple matter in post-Saddam Iraq.

If you think you have a long "to do" list, imagine what has to be done to rebuild a broken country, especially one with the ethnic divisions that are roiling Iraq. The history of the past several years has shown how severely the Bush administration blundered in Iraq, and how mind-boggling was its naïveté about what it would take to put Humpty Dumpty back together again. From training police and military to combating a deadly insurgency, to providing health care, water, and electricity and rebuilding infrastructure, writing a constitution, holding elections, and getting oil flowing again—these are just a handful of the countless formidable tasks that faced the CPA in the aftermath of Saddam's fall.

On such a daunting list, debt reconciliation stands out for its obscurity, but it is not unimportant. The long-term rebuilding of the devastated country would depend in part on the willingness of banks, brokerage houses, and trade suppliers to do business with Iraq and their confidence in its new financial institutions. Order had to be brought to the nation's finances and its creditworthiness established to the satisfaction of international markets and lenders. As part of that process, President Bush dispatched former Secretary of State James Baker to put pressure on Iraq's creditors to forgive as much as 80 percent of its debt so that Iraq could quickly regain its economic footing.

The rebuilding of Iraq made corporate sharks salivate. They could smell the money. Despite the physical dangers, which escalated dramatically after 2004, companies from Halliburton and Blackwater on down knew the U.S. government was going to throw countless billions of dollars at contractors lining up to do the work that needed to be done. There's always a cast of corporate characters who line up to profit from war, whether in Vietnam in the 1960s or Iraq in 2004 and wherever else the U.S. government has had billions of dollars to spend. (Prewar predictions from the Bush administration that the war and the reconstruction would be paid for largely from Iraqi oil revenues were wildly off the mark. Paul Wolfowitz, the deputy secretary of defense who made the administration's case on this point, was later made president of the World Bank before resigning under a cloud of impropriety.)

Amid the feeding frenzy, with many billions of dollars dispensed through no-bid, cost-plus contracts, there was one small piece of bait that was the immediate reason for my mission to Iraq: a request for proposals (RFP) to manage the Iraqi debt reconciliation process. Even as James Baker was seeking a dramatic write-down of the country's debt, the CPA needed someone to come in and figure out who was owed money by the previous government, when the debt was incurred, and how much was owed to each creditor, in addition to establishing an orderly system by which creditors could make their claims.

I learned of the Iraqi debt RFP from a contact at a private security firm with the improbable name of Custer Battles, founded by a former

U.S. Army officer and defense consultant, Scott Custer, and a former CIA officer, Republican operative, and unsuccessful congressional candidate, Mike Battles. I had been introduced to Custer Battles through one of our bankers at Citibank, to whom I had casually mentioned that I was interested in going to Iraq to sniff out some postwar opportunities in the market for Iraqi debt. Custer Battles had been awarded a $16.8 million contract by the CPA to provide security at the Baghdad airport and would later be charged with fraud for overcharging the U.S. government by millions of dollars using shell companies and false invoices.

But Custer Battles's problems were still months down the road when it tipped us off to the CPA's need for a contractor to handle Iraqi debt reconciliation. Debt reconciliation was, quite frankly, outside of our primary experience at Turan Corporation. We are a small bond-trading firm, well known for dealing in the sovereign debts of developing countries, but we had limited experience in debt reconciliation processes. When, for example, we bought Russian trade debts and Nigerian promissory notes, we did so on the condition that these obligations met (or would meet) the various registration and documentation requirements established by the authorities responsible for reconciling the debts of those countries. So, on a small scale with respect to debts we were buying, we were familiar with the process. But the notion that we could go into a broken country like Iraq and set up a system for reconciling its complex debts required a lot of chutzpah. Which is precisely why the idea appealed to me. I had learned long ago that in business, perception can be everything, and you can make a big impression if you simply think big and act boldly.

Back in 1973, when I was thirty-three, recently married, and living in Brazil, I made a friend named Michel Frank, a handsome playboy and a charming, fun-loving buddy who fell into bad habits and was eventually killed in Paris while dealing cocaine. His father, Egon Frank, a Swiss, had a spectacular apartment on Avenida Vieira Souto, the Fifth Avenue of Rio de Janeiro, and a beautiful house in Terezópolis. Egon thought I could become an example for his erstwhile and unemployed son (it didn't work out, obviously), so he took me under his wing.

Egon knew I was casting about for a way to establish myself in Brazil. Deltec Bank, where I had been working, had ceased operations there and I was unemployed. One day he said to me, "A friend of mine, a very rich entrepreneur from Sydney, has just arrived in Brazil with his wife and parents. They're living at the Othon Palace Hotel in Copacabana. They're looking for an apartment here in Rio. They want to go into business and be active in the community. You speak Portuguese, you know Brazil, and he has capital and knows how to set up a business. I want to introduce you."

Thomas Barton was a small, pudgy man in glasses. He spoke a quiet, impeccable English. His father, Alexander, was a tall, elegant Hungarian, very distinguished and very well spoken. Over lunch with our wives one day, shortly after we'd met, Thomas charmed us with his deep interest in my background, my education, and my experiences with USAID and Deltec Bank. He also had convincing visions of making millions in real estate in Brazil, with my involvement. I knew he had made a fortune in Australia already, so it was hard to resist his offer. "Real estate is always a profitable business," said Thomas. "The Brazilians have a Government Housing Bank that finances the purchase of houses. The middle class is surging in Brazil and people want to buy homes. We can tap into that. Why don't you put in half, I'll put in half, and we'll form a corporation and get into the real estate business."

Exactly why Thomas needed a partner was unclear, and I hardly had much start-up capital to contribute to the enterprise, but after a series of discussions we agreed to go into the business together.

"There's just one thing," said Thomas, "I want my wife, Gail, to be your partner, and I want her name to appear on the books and records." I didn't think much of it at the time; I figured Thomas had some tax or financial reason for wanting Gail to be my nominal partner.

I had never been to business school and had just one, maybe two undergraduate economics classes under my belt. My USAID experience taught me nothing about real estate. My only business model was with my father and his small-time collections law practice. I figured Thomas and I would start small and grow our business over time.

I was wrong. In the ensuing months, Thomas would give me the only business education I ever had, one I took to calling my Harvard Business School education, the one that would, more than thirty years later, leave me with no qualms about boarding a private jet bound for Baghdad to show up unannounced at CPA headquarters to press my case for taking control of Iraq's debt reconciliation.

Despite my hubris, I do know what I don't know, and I knew that to win the Iraq debt reconciliation bid my little bond-trading outfit, Turan, would need a partner with some name recognition and gravitas, hopefully someone with actual experience reconciling sovereign debt. Over the years, my business partner Saleh Daher and I had had many dealings with BDO Stoy Hayward, one of the largest and most respected accounting firms in the world. It had been among the firms tasked with settling creditor claims against the Bank of Credit and Commerce International (BCCI) when, in 1991, BBCI imploded spectacularly amid charges of money laundering and fraud. A report by the United States Committee on Foreign Relations summarized BCCI's wrongdoing this way:

> BCCI's criminality included fraud by BCCI and BCCI customers involving billions of dollars; money laundering in Europe, Africa, Asia, and the Americas; BCCI's bribery of officials in most of those locations; support of terrorism, arms trafficking, and the sale

of nuclear technologies; management of prostitution; the commission and facilitation of income tax evasion, smuggling, and illegal immigration; illicit purchases of banks and real estate; and a panoply of financial crimes limited only by the imagination of its officers and customers.

In short, BDO Stoy Hayward had experience in the trenches. If I could persuade the firm to be our bid partner, I knew it had other credentials that would appeal to the CPA, primarily the fact that it was a British-based firm affiliated with BDO International, with offices in 105 countries. The CPA was eager to make Iraq reconstruction more than an American affair, provided you came from a country that was part of the mighty "coalition of the willing" (a coalition of the United States, Britain, Australia, Italy, and such international powers as the tiny Pacific island nation of Palau) that had been cobbled together by the Bush administration to go to war in Iraq. Our Iraq debt reconciliation team was to be an inspirational example of transatlantic cooperation—a coalition of willing accountants. BDO Stoy Hayward also had specific experience in Iraq, having been the principal accountancy consultants to the United Nations Compensation Commission, which was set up to handle claims against Iraq arising from its invasion and occupation of Kuwait in 1990–1991.

Joining with BDO Stoy Hayward was a marriage of convenience in another way, too. My real interest in Iraq was to get into the business of trading Iraqi debt, and the key to that business, as it was in El Salvador, Guatemala, and everywhere else I had been, was to get a list of the debt holders—the potential sellers. Such a list is, as I have said before, the holy grail of my business. Give me a list of the potential sellers and I'm halfway home to some riches from the ruins. Because of BDO Stoy Hayward's work for the United Nations, my partner, Saleh, and I knew the firm had to have a list of Iraqi debt holders, or at least know where to find one. For its part, BDO Stoy Hayward was interested in expanding its business of advising governments and institutions on their sovereign debt issues, and we had experience to share about the real world of trading sovereign debt. We had something to learn from each other and we both knew it. Indeed, I didn't really want to be in the business of Iraqi debt reconciliation at all; it was simply the road to the list.

We had only a month to put together our bid and submit it to the U.S. Treasury Department. In consultation with the Iraqi Ministry of Finance and the Iraq Central Bank, the Treasury Department and the CPA would ultimately decide who would get the contract, once the bids had been vetted by the Department of Defense. It was a contract we figured might be worth upwards of $10 million.

Gervase MacGregor and Peter Daniel, both in their forties, are forensic accountants in the London offices of BDO Stoy Hayward. For one week in early 2004, shortly before our trip to Iraq, they worked in our small offices on Federal Street in Boston as we cobbled together our proposal. We looked like four college seniors cramming for finals. There was paper everywhere, empty pizza boxes were piled in the hallway, and we looked as though we hadn't slept in days, which we hadn't.

Gervase and Peter, who would join Saleh and me on our trip to Baghdad to sell ourselves to the CPA, have very different temperaments. Peter has a wife and five children, a quiet family man with a touch of the aristocrat. Educated in England's finer prep schools, Peter has what one might describe as proper British reserve. Gervase is a divorced workaholic, a self-made man from a working-class background. He can't sit still, work is his life, and everywhere he goes he carries an international pocket airline guide that he consults frequently. Gervase is a man in constant motion.

In preparing our bid, "DABV01-04-R-0001: Reconciliation Services for Iraqi External Sovereign Debt," I kept in mind the first lesson I learned from watching Thomas Barton in action: Think big.

No sooner had Thomas Barton and I—or more precisely, Thomas's wife, Gail, and I—agreed to form a real estate company in Brazil together in 1974, than Thomas had plans to rent the entire fifth floor of an office building on the Praca Demétrio Ribeiro. "We're going to hire five or ten brokers right away," he said, "and we'll get some impressive furniture and office equipment and we'll look like an important entity."

"Thomas," I protested. "I have limited money and the company has limited funds. We can't afford it."

"Don't worry," he said. "I have a plan." Thomas always had a plan.

We walked over to meet the rental agent for the office space, the palm trees offering little shade from the blazing sun. "Thomas," I asked, "what brought you to Brazil?" We'd never really discussed it before. "Australia is such a thriving place. I took R & R in Australia when I was in Vietnam, and it seemed a place full of opportunity."

"The government is rather restrictive there," Thomas replied. "We don't have personal freedoms." He didn't seem eager to discuss the matter.

This struck me as odd. Australia is a democratic country with an American-style frontier spirit. Whoever heard of Aussies complaining about a lack of personal freedom? That night I related the conversation by phone to my mother-in-law who, over many years, proved to have an abundance of common sense and good intuition about people.

"Something doesn't smell quite right," I said. "Maybe it has something to do with taxes," she replied. Brazilians always think it's something to do with taxes, and I didn't give the matter any further thought.

A few days later I visited Thomas at a luxurious penthouse apartment facing Copacabana beach that he and Gail had recently rented. I was envious. I was sleeping at my wife's apartment with her three brothers in the next room. Thomas came from money. I didn't. But his apartment gave me pause. When it came to our business he would be spending his money *and* mine, and he obviously liked to live in style.

It took a while to contact all corners of the expansive, lethargic Brazilian bureaucracy and get all the permissions needed to set up a properly constituted Brazilian company, and the building inspectors needed their whiskey money before we could occupy the rental offices. But once all the bureaucratic details had been attended to, it was time to make some money.

To furnish our offices we went to Mesbla, the Brazilian equivalent of Sears and Roebuck. Thomas picked out everything he wanted and then got the salesman to find his manager, and that manager to find his manager, until finally we had the manager of the entire store standing with us in the furniture department. Thomas asked countless questions, with me serving as his interpreter. "What's selling? What isn't? How is the Brazilian economy faring in your view, and what do you see as sales trends in your store? Where are you from? Do you have a family here in Rio?" For the life of me I couldn't figure out the point of all these questions, but when Thomas suggested he could pay for the furniture in dollars, he was able to negotiate an additional discount of 30 percent. The questions were all designed to soften up the target. Thomas knew that if you could connect with people and find some common ground, new possibilities usually presented themselves.

Once the furniture had been ordered, Thomas called the local Xerox office and negotiated a one-month trial of a business copier, telling the sales representative that we had large needs for copiers but wanted to test several machines before making a commitment. When the month was up he'd stall for time, saying the purchasing manager was on vacation. In the meantime, he'd work out another one-month trial with another vendor, and so on.

It was Thomas who taught me that to get big you had to think and act big from the get-go. You had to be willing to bluff and puff out your chest a bit, like a bird in a mating ritual. It was from Thomas that I learned to put the names of several business entities on the door of my office to give the impression of a large, going concern. Let other people make assumptions about you and, if they seem to serve your purposes, don't do anything to disabuse them of their assumptions.

Our first business venture was to broker small apartments, *conjugados* they were called, on the beach in Rio to up-and-coming Brazilian yuppies. We called our company *Citadella Emprendimentoros*, or Citadel Investments. Real estate was a hedge against Brazil's rampant inflation, so the market was hot. Advertising was key, and Thomas had a plan for economizing on advertising, too.

"Look, Bob," Thomas said one morning, "we have a very limited advertising budget. We have to write ads that have impact and stand out. I will go down to the newspaper today, the *Journal de Brazil*. That's where we'll advertise. I need you to translate."

At the *Journal de Brazil*, Thomas asked to speak with the advertising manager. "Tell this gentleman exactly what I'm saying," said Thomas. "Tell him I'm very sorry I don't speak your language. I'm taking lessons two hours a day. I love your culture. Where do you come from, by the way?" Then, a little chat, through me, ensued about the advertising manager's hometown. "We're a very big, foreign multinational real estate company that is about to launch an experimental office in your fine country. We would like to use your newspaper, one of a few, to judge the response to our ads. We're going to start with a small budget, but our senior vice president is coming and we will increase that budget as soon as we know which papers draw."

The *Journal* extended us ninety days of credit for our daily ads. The next step was to find an ad agency to help plan the campaign. Again, Thomas played the same cards. We went to three different agencies and told them we were soliciting ideas for an expensive advertising campaign. We asked them to submit ideas and based on that we would decide which agency to use. Then we hired a young kid who could draw and used all the ideas that had been thrown at us by the competing agencies.

"People," Thomas said, "will let their imaginations carry them to extremes. If you look big, people will assume there is a huge international company behind you. You don't have to affirm or deny their assumptions. Because you worked for USAID, which is part of the U.S. government, some people will always think you were in the CIA. You don't have to disabuse them of the notion if it might help you in business." (Even today, some of my friends believe I worked for the CIA, though I have tried to disabuse them of the notion.)

As Saleh, Gervase MacGregor, Peter Daniel, and I prepared our bid for the Iraq business in 2004, I kept in mind the lessons I had learned from Barton thirty years before, and another spoken by a renowned philosopher, Woody Allen, who once said, "80 percent of success is just showing up."

Saleh will tell you that the real reason for our trip to Iraq was to give me a chance to relive my glory days, an act of derring-do, in which I would head off to whatever corner of the world seemed most distressed at the moment. Iraq appealed to my sense of adventure, and the physical risks only heightened the appeal. But I also believed in Woody Allen's dictum. If we had *cojones* big enough to show up in Baghdad unannounced to press our case for the debt reconciliation contract, I was sure this would make a big impression on the decision makers. And, unlike the other bidders, who we were sure would be proposing to set up shop in Qatar or the United Arab Emirates, we proposed to operate right out of Baghdad. We wanted to show we had the right stuff to work in a tough environment. All we had to do was find the decision makers, connect with them on some personal level, and impress them with our nerve. I was very confident we could win the contract.

When I told my wife, Salua, I wanted to go to Baghdad, she didn't voice any apprehension. "Go," she said, "you love that stuff." Maybe she was thinking about my life insurance policy.

So, in early February of 2004, Saleh and I made plans to meet Gervase and Peter in Beirut to travel on to Baghdad. "You'll be the only Jew in Baghdad," Saleh teased. Though that wasn't really true, I did feel rather exposed going to Baghdad, despite the U.S. military occupation, where antipathy toward Israel and Jews runs high. Though most people would probably be hospitable, the constant drumbeat of anti-Semitism in much of the Islamic world made me nervous about being a Jew in Baghdad.

Beirut was at peace and thriving. Painstaking years of economic recovery following the country's virtual destruction in the 1980s were paying off. This was the old Beirut we knew and loved, a beautiful seaside city filled with life, art, and history. In little more than two years, in the summer of 2006, Beirut and Lebanon would see all of this progress reversed in a few short weeks as war raged between Israel and Hezbollah, but for now, in 2004, Beirut was basking in the fruits of peace.

Custer Battles was to take care of us, and our security, starting in Beirut. After spending the night at Beirut's Intercontinental Phoenician Hotel, we met Gervase and Peter at the airport the next morning and boarded a jet chartered by Custer Battles for the two-hour flight to Baghdad. Gervase, normally voluble and excited, was oddly quiet. Peter seemed ill at ease. The murderous insurgency that was beginning to grip Iraq hadn't taken full flight in Baghdad yet, but still, this was no business trip to Chicago.

Peter and Gervase didn't know Mike Battles as we did, and Mike's agent in Beirut had been a bit opaque. When Peter asked him where we'd be staying in Baghdad, he didn't know; in fact, he knew very little about what plans had been made for us, adding to Peter and Gervase's apprehension.

After passing over the snow-covered mountains of Lebanon, the landscape below quickly turned to an endless expanse of brown desert. We could see the confluence of the Tigris and Euphrates rivers that marked Baghdad, and the plane began a steep, corkscrew descent to the airport to avoid missile fire. Numerous relief and other flights in and out of Baghdad had been fired upon recently, and the pilot was taking no chances.

The moment we stepped onto the tarmac, private security guards employed by Custer Battles surrounded us. Hank, their top security agent in Iraq, welcomed us. He was a U.S. Army veteran with the body of a weight lifter, wraparound sunglasses, and a southern charm and confidence that lifted Peter and Gervase's spirits a bit. We were given heavy-duty flak jackets capable, we were told, of stopping an AK-47 round. We put them on immediately and were taken to a small room in the virtually abandoned airport terminal building for a short briefing that can be summed up in a few words: We will envelop you like a cocoon wherever you go; listen to everything we have to say and do everything we tell you to do without hesitation. We were impressed. There was no dissent.

Our security detail comprised four men, led by an imposing veteran, an African-American from New York City named L. T. Like many working security details in Iraq, L. T. was a former infantryman. When his tour of duty in Iraq ended, he went to work for many times his military salary for a private contractor. Two of the men in the detail were Gurkhas, Nepalese descendants of eighth-century warriors renowned for their ferocity in combat and their quiet, steely calm. The Gurkhas are highly trained killers and known to be remorseless. They were polite but emotionally removed throughout our trip, and I had the sense that they would gladly kill us if someone came along and made them a better offer than Custer Battles. The entire detail carried high-powered automatic rifles (a lightweight M4 for L. T., an AK-47 for Eric, his subordinate from Texas, and British-made L1A1s for the Gurkhas) and communicated through wireless microphones and earpieces. These boys had some big toys. It was all very impressive, if unsettling. Peter called us "storm troopers of the accounting profession."

Baghdad International Airport was like something out of *The Twilight Zone.* Formerly known as "Saddam International Airport," the letters on the outside of the main terminal spelling "Saddam" had been removed, but their ghostly shadows remained on the facade. The sign now read simply, "International Airport." Once busy ticket counters were completely abandoned. The flight arrival and departure board showed flights that had come and gone months ago.

If the airport was eerily quiet and frozen in time, the ride from the airport to the Green Zone, the secure area where the CPA was housed, jolted us back to the grim reality of Iraq. It was like a Disney thrill ride with weapons. We piled into two black SUVs with tinted glass all around and screeched out of the airport at high speed onto the highway linking the airport to Baghdad. The road would later earn the ignominious nickname the "highway of death," because of the frequent shootings that made passage perilous.

"Is the car armored?" I asked L. T. "No," he replied calmly. "We want to be able to smash the windows from the inside with our rifle butts if we have to, and breaking the glass on an armored car is impossible." That's reassuring, I thought, and turned to look out the window.

The weather was surprisingly cold, and all around the scene was one of brown and dust. As we sped down the road at eighty miles per hour, I counted only a dozen cars on the main highway to the city. Passing under overpasses worried me. It would have been a relatively simple matter to drop a grenade and bring an abrupt end to our Iraq mission.

At those speeds, the Green Zone was only about twenty long minutes away. When it came into view, I felt like yelling, "Land ahoy." A sense of relief settled over us. We'd only been in Iraq an hour, but already we had a chilling sense of just how dangerous a place it could be.

"Look," said Thomas, once we had everything in place to start our real estate business in Rio. "Before we learn how to use the government's money to finance housing, let's do some simple brokerage. We can sell these studio apartments on the beach that go for about $50,000. There are hundreds of them. The currency is devaluing so quickly and people have nowhere else to invest because there are so many foreign exchange controls. They can buy these apartments to keep their money at value."

It seemed like a good idea to me. But no sooner had we set up shop and started to sell a few apartments than things fell apart. One morning I got a call from my mother-in-law, who lived some 1,500 miles north of Rio in Maranhão. "Turn on the television," she said.

The arrest of Thomas Barton and his father, Alexander, by Brazilian police was all over the news. Wanted for major securities fraud in Australia, Interpol had been pursuing them for months. I was devastated. Thomas's comment a few months earlier about lack of freedom in Australia suddenly made sense. And now I knew why Gail was my nominal partner. I thought I was ruined. I'd never done anything illegal in my life. I had been a banker, a lawyer, a U.S. government official, and now I was involved with an international fugitive. My sense of self-esteem didn't improve when I found out that Egon Frank, who introduced me to the Bartons, knew of their legal problems.

"Yes, it's a pity," said Egon when I went to him in desperation.

"But why did you put us in business together?" I practically cried. "My reputation will be in ruins."

"I thought they could start over here," said Egon. "If they had got Brazilian citizenship they would be safe here because Brazil doesn't have an extradition treaty with Australia. I thought everything would work out."

"Well, now I'm in a mess," I said. I returned to the office and sat at the beautiful desk Thomas had purchased for us. I tried to reassure our employees who, to my surprise, seemed to take the news as business as usual.

The next week I got a call from Thomas. Amazingly, he had been released on bail. He gave me an address on the Barra de Tijuca, outside of the city, and begged me to come. Thomas was in one of several small, cheap motels on the Barra called *motels de rotivadade* ("motels of rotation") where married men would go with their girlfriends and rent a room by the hour. There were mirrors on the wall and a Jacuzzi, and the plaster was falling down. The bedsheets, I noticed, were made of plastic. I couldn't believe that my promising real estate business had come to this.

"Bob, this a total misunderstanding, but I won't be able to be active in the business. I want you to buy me out and I think $5,000 is a fair price." It was quite unlike Thomas: He always taught me that in a negotiation you should never be the first to state a price. By waiting the other guy out, you let him establish the floor. It may be higher than you expect. If it's lower, you've lost nothing. Since we had each invested about $30,000 at that point, it *was* a fair price, and I was in no mood to negotiate anyway. I simply wanted to untangle myself from Thomas. The corporation was transferred to my name.

In the end, despite the fear, the anger, and the anxiety, working with Thomas was the best business education I ever had. I learned that trust should not be dispensed too easily, that you can travel a long way on a good bluff, and that business is largely about shaping perception. But it was too late to put those lessons into practice in Brazil. I was now an American in business for myself in a foreign country, and a small business at that, with no competitive advantage. I could only put my ads in the paper and hope for the best. I bought and sold perhaps two apartments in the next sixty days and made a total commission of about $10,000. But I was able to salvage some riches from the ruins of my Brazilian real estate business when I sold, at a decent profit, the lease, the phones, and the furnishings to an engineering firm building the new subway in Rio.

I still ask myself: Why didn't I check on my smooth-talking business partner with the Australian embassy? Why didn't I do any due diligence? Because, as Thomas himself said to me, people's imaginations will let them believe what they want to believe, and I wanted to believe in Thomas. He was the man who could help me stay in

Brazil and make a success of myself there, and so I overlooked obvious clues.

In Baghdad, three decades later, I would employ some of the lessons Thomas had taught me to try and wrangle the Iraqi debt reconciliation business. I was sure we could make a winning impression by showing up, ingratiating ourselves with the decision makers, and comporting ourselves with confidence and a little bit of bravado. I was wrong.

The Coalition Provisional Authority occupied one of Saddam's former palaces in the heavily fortified Green Zone. The palace itself was surrounded by military checkpoints and you could only be admitted if someone working inside had authorized your visit. In our case, no one had because no one knew we were coming. We simply showed up and relied on our escorts from Custer Battles, well known around the Green Zone, to talk us past the checkpoints and into the palace.

The palace itself was garishly ornate. The décor was something that someone with Albert Speer's ego and Tony Soprano's sense of taste would have chosen, and indeed, Saddam was something of a cross between a sadistic fascist and a mob boss. Walking down the hallways, with their ornate marble inlays, we noticed cables for Internet, phones, and computers secured with duct tape running everywhere. It was jarring to see American G.I.s using the fourteen stall bathrooms with gold fixtures and eating in Saddam's formal dining room, and just as striking when you realized how young these kids were for the awesome responsibilities they are asked to undertake. Eighteen-year-olds manning checkpoints. Nineteen-year-olds driving armored personnel carriers, the lives of several comrades in their hands. And twenty-year-olds in charge of small regiments on dangerous patrols in the city.

It was an odd scene inside, almost like a small town hall with signs marking the rooms occupied by different departments within the CPA: Water and Irrigation, Prisons, Secondary Schools, Banking—you name it and there was a little department for it. Inside many of these rooms were just a handful of young staffers sitting at metal desks with computers on them. As Thomas E. Ricks points out in his book *Fiasco: The American Military Adventure in Iraq*, many of these young staffers had absolutely no qualifications for the jobs they were supposed to perform, but they had been activists in the Republican Party. It was hard to imagine that you could run a country as complex as Iraq from inside a heavily secured fortress, with a few desks, a few computers, and a bunch of twentysomethings. I had the sense that by marking each little department with a sign, the CPA was trying to create the illusion of control and order where none existed. The CPA, too, was operating on Bartonesque principles.

I had only one name—one possible connection here—that of Andrew Tullock, a former banker with Bank of America serving a six-month stint with the Treasury Department in Baghdad. I knew Tullock's daughter, a conference organizer with Merrill Lynch who handled big events, such as the firm's participation in the annual meeting of the IMF/World Bank.

We found a room with a sign that said Treasury Department and walked in, fresh from our flight into Baghdad. A handful of people sitting shoulder to shoulder at their desks and staring at computer screens looked up at us with all the enthusiasm of a seventeen-year-old kid behind a McDonald's counter. "Can we help you?" someone piped up after they'd given us a wary once-over. We introduced ourselves and said we'd come to follow up on our bid for the debt reconciliation contract. There was only one person in the room old enough to be Andrew Tullock and he stared at us in disbelief, as if to say, "What in the world are you doing here?"

After a few moments of awkward chitchat, one of the younger staffers noticed that Saleh was wearing a ring bearing the seal of his alma mater, M.I.T., and allowed that he had graduated from M.I.T. as well. It wasn't much, but at least we weren't staring at one another in silence anymore. We asked a few perfunctory questions about their work and their experience living in the Green Zone, then tried gracefully to exit so that we could get something to eat and regroup. We thought that by showing up we'd make a big splash. Instead, we'd laid an egg.

After lunch in the Halliburton-run cafeteria, we decided to try to speak with the Department of Defense contract officer. Maybe Treasury wasn't involved yet, maybe that explained the blank stares. It was our impression that all contracts for work in Iraq were vetted by DOD, so we decided to go down the hall. The DOD contract officer, too, was surprised to see us. She was young, in her thirties, and though surprised to have us in her midst she gave little ground.

"What are you doing here?" she asked. It was becoming a common refrain. We stated our business.

"We have a PowerPoint presentation we'd like to present to you and the Ministry of Finance. We want to know what we have to do to win this bid. We came all this way to prove we're serious."

She was curt and dismissive. "I'm not allowed to discuss your bid with you." There was no room to maneuver. We'd come halfway across the world to a war zone and all we'd managed to do within a couple of hours of our arrival was to hit a wall. I had the distinct impression that the bid process was a formality and that the successful bidder had already been selected.

We'd been told by the representative of Custer Battles just before boarding our plane in Beirut that we'd be staying at the Hyatt during our stay in Baghdad. During the flight we puzzled over this choice, wondering how a hotel chain owned by a Jewish family, the Pritzkers, operated in Iraq. Unfortunately, we'd misunderstood. He meant *the Al-Hayat Hotel*. After a dash in the SUVs from the Green Zone through Baghdad's chaotic traffic we arrived at this four-story hotel surrounded by a ten-foot concrete barrier (known as a Bremer Wall, after CPA Chief L. Paul Bremer) with a single Iraqi guard armed with an AK-47. L. T. told us to run from the car to the front door and to keep our heads down as we did. There was no doorman in a blue uniform to let us in.

The hotel was dark and dirty, and the empty swimming pool was filled with rubbish and algae. There was only one other guest, an Egyptian pipe salesman. But the Al-Hayat had the distinct advantage, according to L. T., of only having been attacked once by rocket-propelled grenades. And they were able to get us rooms together toward the back, which meant the safer side of the building. The guys from Custer Battles took rooms on either side of ours, providing a safety buffer between us and any adjoining rooms where God knows what could be going on. After getting settled in our rooms, we all met downstairs in the dilapidated restaurant and ordered the only thing on the menu: chicken and rice, some inedible bread, and for desert, ice cream. It was the worst hotel meal I've ever been served, bar none. There was nothing left to do but head back to the room, watch some Arabic TV, and shower, though even that proved impossible since neither the electricity nor the water was working when we got back upstairs. So far, Baghdad was proving rather rustic.

Helicopters flew overhead and gunfire and small explosions punctuated the night. It was difficult to sleep, and I was beginning to think the whole trip, impetuous as it was, reflected poorly on my business judgment. After all, we'd traveled this far and all we'd gotten for our troubles was a lousy chicken dinner.

The following day we returned to the Green Zone, once again speeding through Baghdad's chaotic streets. Suddenly, we came to an abrupt halt. U.S. soldiers had located a suspected improvised explosive device, or IED, near an overpass. IEDs would become more and more sophisticated, more and more common, and ever more lethal as the insurgency took hold. Luckily for us, we were in Bagdad in the relative calm before the storm. Nevertheless, we remained stopped for close to a half-hour as the military carefully defused the device and it was safe to continue.

Hurtling through the streets of Baghdad, we were very conspicuous. The SUVs were brutish among the smaller cars Iraqis drive, and our drivers were very aggressive. Perhaps I'm paranoid, but I sensed that people on the streets were looking at us, clearly foreigners, with hostility as we sped by. It would be hard to blame them. We'd liberated them from the indescribable cruelties of Saddam, but we'd broken the country, too, and it was unclear how we were going to put it together again. People were wary. Storefronts were filled with "white goods," refrigerators, washing machines, and the like, a sign of life in the economy, but the oil wasn't flowing, water and electricity were scarce, and the security situation was dicey and about to get much, much worse. I could hardly blame Iraqis for their wariness.

Even in 2004, before the deadly insurgency had really taken hold, a casual observer could have told you that Iraq was mission impossible. Iraq is the vortex of a religious conflict between the Sunnis and the Shia that goes back more than a thousand years, to say nothing of the Kurds, ethnically distinct and, to a large extent, self-governing, who control the northern part of the country. And, to make matters even worse, we were, and are, the infidels on their sacred soil. That Iraq would become a quagmire was entirely predictable, and many wise people outside the Bush administration predicted it.

We arrived back in the Green Zone after clearing what seemed like a dozen military checkpoints. Andrew Tullock, it turned out, had nothing to do with the Iraqi debt reconciliation project. He was there to assist foreign banks in setting up operations in Iraq. But he kindly invited us to a farewell party for a treasury official who was finishing up his tour of duty and returning home. He said he could introduce us to some of his colleagues there.

The poolside party on the grounds of Saddam's former palace was a desultory beer and peanuts affair, and we looked and felt like the unwanted relatives at a bad bar mitzvah. Those we managed to engage in conversation were enthusiastic about their mission and optimistic they'd be able to help Iraq become a functioning country again. Things had not yet spiraled out of control. We'd be asked about our business in Iraq, but no one gave any hint that they could or would be of any help to us. We'd played the best card we had, but it was a two of clubs.

That night, back in the hotel, I tried to figure out where we'd gone wrong and what had possessed me to throw myself into such an ill-fated venture. Here I was, sixty-four years old and already wealthy beyond my parents' wildest imagination and, indeed, my own. I had nothing to prove, I didn't need another conquest, and yet here I was, in another war zone, trying to hustle some business.

I was, at one time in my life, a heavy smoker, and to me the craving for adventure, to be on the move, to see history as it unfolds, is as strong as the craving a smoker has for nicotine. Adventure comes in many forms. Some people surf thirty-foot waves, some climb sheer ice faces with picks and axes, and others jump out of airplanes. For me, being on the periphery of dramatic events, especially when there's an opportunity to make money, is my adventure. Living by my wits in an unpredictable environment is a thrill I seek over and over. In that sense I am still running from the predictability of my middle-class upbringing where each day is pretty much like the next. That is why I came to Iraq. This craving to be in the game, so to speak, is never satisfied, and I expect I'll be chasing the thrill until I'm too old to move or think. It would have been nice to get the contract in Iraq, but in the end that was secondary. Chasing the business was the fun part; the work itself would have been dull by comparison.

There was little we could accomplish with more time in Baghdad, so just seventy-two hours after we'd arrived in a private jet taking evasive action to avoid possible missile fire, we were escorted by our

Custer Battles security detail back to the airport. There we received an unpleasant surprise. The private jet that was supposed to fly us out had been grounded by a mechanical problem. We had no choice but to pay $700 each for one-way tickets to Amman, Jordan, a short hop on a Royal Jordanian Airlines Bombardier Q400 Turbo-Prop. The price was extortionate, but who were we to argue? It was either that or try and hop on a cargo plane to Qatar or Kuwait or, even worse, try and get out of Iraq by car. The whole scene reminded me of my USAID days in Vietnam, when I had flown to the Cambodian border with a Vietnamese colonel to count food stocks being stored in USAID warehouses and the Air America plane (operated by the CIA) that was supposed to come for us didn't arrive on time. I remember the extreme anxiety of the prospect of being abandoned as night fell in some godforsaken, dangerous corner of Vietnam. (The plane, as noted, eventually did arrive, a couple of hours late.)

In Amman, we checked into an oasis known as the Four Seasons and tried to wash away the dust of Baghdad and the bitter taste of knowing we'd never get the Iraqi debt reconciliation contract. We had been, as Peter Daniel put it, "on a fruitless mission to see people who didn't want to see us." The contract hadn't been awarded yet, but we knew the die had been cast. And we later learned that trying to lobby the decision makers on a bid like this was verboten. The debt reconciliation contract eventually was awarded to Ernst & Young, one of the biggest accounting firms in the world.

From a business point of view, the trip had been a bust. From a personal point of view, I loved it. And Saleh and I did get what we had sought from the beginning: that list of Iraqi debt holders. After we returned from our joint trip to Baghdad and had bonded in the crucible of shared mortal danger, Peter and Gervase enlightened us. Few knew, except BDO Stoy Hayward, that though there was no list per se, if you waded through the thousands of publicly available documents posted on the U.N. Compensation Commission's website, you could create a list of the debt holders. The information was in something of a raw form, but there it was. Nevertheless, by the time we got our hands on it, it was of little use.

The debt reduction plan that Secretary Baker worked out with Iraq's creditors made what we do, trade in a secondary market of smaller amounts of Iraqi debt, virtually nonexistent. To help rebuild Iraq, it was essential that the country be given a way out from under its crushing debt burden, so Baker persuaded Iraq's major creditors—the countries and large institutions that were owed billions of dollars—to take an 80 percent write-down of their claims, or, as we say in the business, an 80 percent haircut. Once a scheme like this gains momentum and the major players are on board, the little guys, those with claims in the tens of millions or less, have little choice but to join the party. The writing is on the wall: Either you agree to the new terms and participate in the debt-restructuring program, or you risk being left out in the cold altogether.

Once the 80 percent haircut was in place, the question was, on what terms would Iraq repay the 20 percent of the debt that remained? To help figure out how to repay the remaining trade supplier, commercial, and bank debt ("commercial" debt), the Iraq Central Bank (ICB) retained Citigroup as its adviser and, in particular, a certified financial genius with the unlikely name of Nazareth Festek-jian. It was Festekjian's scheme that really left little room for a player like Turan.

Festekjian advised the ICB to buy back—that is, pay—all of the smaller debts (now reduced by 80 percent) that are usually our bread and butter. Rather than have to sort out countless small claims and issue bonds to the claimants, the ICB would settle those "small" debts, those claims of less than $35 million, with immediate cash payments and develop a long-term plan to clear up its larger debts.

To repay its larger commercial debts, Iraq issued $2.79 billion in bonds to the debtors, payable over twenty-two years with a coupon of 5.8 percent. (As of this writing, in June 2008, the yield to maturity on these bonds is approximately 11 percent. The yield on a bond fluctuates based on how much someone is willing to pay for the bond.

The lower the purchase price, the higher the yield and, the higher the yield, the higher the risk. Recently, the price of an Iraqi bond has been fluctuating between sixty to seventy cents on the dollar.) Many hedge funds are buying these Iraqi bonds, and Saleh and I are brokering some of them and holding a modest amount for our own accounts.

At first blush, it might seem that the risks in a country as driven by ethnic strife and chaos as Iraq, a country embroiled in a war whose outcome is uncertain, to say the least, would drive the price of its bonds much lower and the yields much higher. Why? Because the risks, on the surface, seem so great. While a yield of more than 10 percent is certainly an excellent return, one might expect it to be higher.

But there are reasons the market is not assigning the level of risk to Iraq that one might expect. Some of them have to do with the terms of the bonds themselves—the terms of Iraq's debt restructuring, to put it another way—and some have to do with the *realpolitik* of Iraq itself.

As for the bonds themselves, they are Iraq's *only* outstanding external debt issue. To move forward, Iraq has to prove it can be a good economic citizen or else no one will lend or invest in Iraq. Thus, repayment is a high priority for the government And everyone knows that Iraq, with its enormous oil reserves, has a way to generate cash. Iraq is both willing to pay and it has the ability to pay the interest and principal on its bonds. Even with the war, Iraq exports enough oil to have a positive balance of payments and, at this writing, it has approximately $79 billion in hard currency reserves.

Furthermore, the bonds pay 5.87 percent interest with repayment of principal deferred toward the end of the term of the bond issue. Though the amount of interest paid will increase each year, interest payments on the $2.79 billion bond issue amount to approximately $160 million a year. A country with $25 billion in reserves isn't going to default on $160 million in interest payments on its only outstanding bond issue.

Yet another reason Iraqi bonds are priced reasonably is the perception that they come with an implied guarantee from the United States, just as El Salvador bonds did in the 1980s. The United States has a strong interest in seeing Iraq succeed, an interest that will continue regardless of how many troops we have in Iraq or what their role is. The belief among investors is that if Iraq can't pay, the United States will, or provide the money needed to prevent a default. In short, despite the mess that is Iraq, Iraqi bonds have an attractive yield for what appears to be low to moderate risk.

Even a partitioning of Iraq into three political subdivisions, Shiite, Sunni, and Kurdish, a plan advanced by some politicians, would not likely derail Iraqi bonds. If a confederation of some kind emerged, the central government would likely assume the debt. If the country splintered into three independent states, as Yugoslavia did, for example, each new state would likely assume some portion of the debt.

What *could* derail repayment of Iraq's current debt? A complete descent into chaos and anarchy, the total collapse of the Iraqi government and the Iraqi state—an event that would likely severely restrict or halt Iraq's oil exports—would certainly send the price of Iraqi bonds plummeting as investors assigned a much higher level of risk to them.

Though the trip to Baghdad got us enamored of the possibilities of doing business in Iraqi debt, we lost perspective. Having risked our lives to travel to Baghdad (leaving two very nervous wives at home), and knowing that Iraqi debt has all the elements of the business we are good at, we continued to bang our heads against the wall, even when we should have known that Festekjian's buyback plan had cut out the type of business we specialize in. Thomas Barton wasn't familiar with baseball, but he often told me, though in different words, that you aren't going to hit a home run every time you swing the bat. But at least we swung the bat.

I saw Barton again, nearly twenty years after our ill-fated partnership, in 1994 in Australia. His extradition, with his father, from Brazil followed years of work to track them down and bring them back to face multiple charges of massive securities fraud. According to one Sydney solicitor, people with money in the early 1970s had been falling over themselves to give it to the Bartons.

The self-confident Barton, who had given me my business education in Brazil in the early 1970s, was not the same man I knew in Brazil. Though he had worn out the Australian legal system and managed to gain acquittals on every charge brought against him, he looked bedraggled, tired, and distracted. As we shared a dinner at a seafood restaurant next to the beach in Bondi, it was clear to me that he still had a taste for the thrill of the chase. A gold trading firm he'd established in 1979, cleverly named *Bargold,* had gone belly-up, but now he had a firm trading stock futures called First Financial Strategies. As another Hungarian-born Australian financier, Sir Paul Strasser, once said to the *Sydney Morning Herald,* "If you and I walked to a traffic light, and it was red, we'd wait until it turned green before we crossed the road. Barton would get there and start working out ways of getting to the other side." I like to think the description fits me, too.

Though he seemed down, I wasn't too worried about Barton. I knew he could operate in Upper Volta if he wanted to. He had the persistence to carry on. When I first met Barton in Brazil, I was naïve, without self-esteem, and I desperately wanted to stay in Brazil and avoid the sedentary life my parents had in mind for me. I learned from this great salesman, this con man, how to persevere, invent, sell, endure. He showed me the power of advertising, which I used to great effect in El Salvador and Guatemala. He taught me the importance of connecting with people on a personal level—asking about their interests, their families, their health—to advance a business agenda, not in a cynical way, but in a genuine way. Most of all, he showed me how to negotiate. The lessons I learned at his elbow, in department stores and the offices of newspaper advertising executives and ad agencies, have been parlayed into the fortune Thomas dangled before my eyes at our first lunch together, even if it materialized in unforeseen ways. The skills he taught me helped me make a lot of money over the years.

But, from Thomas I also learned that things don't always break your way, and to thrive you have to be a survivor. You have to take your knocks and get up to fight again another day. In Iraq in 2004, we got knocked down, or rather, we fell down, flat on our faces from a business point of view. But my wife Salua was right: I *love* this stuff.

CHAPTER 8

AMERICAN TWILIGHT

IN 2004, MY WIFE, SALUA, and I traveled to Mozambique as part of a small delegation organized by Citigroup and the United Nations Development Programme (UNDP). The trip had a name, "A Journey to Africa: Getting Engaged with Your Philanthropy," and a purpose, which was to introduce affluent customers of Citigroup Private Bank to various philanthropic opportunities in one of the world's poorest countries.

We were invited to see firsthand many remarkable and innovative programs, and we met many resourceful and committed people working to create a better future for their country. We saw education centers offering young people courses in civic education and sexual and reproductive health, and training in the arts. We traveled to a farming cooperative and a child-run radio network (where I was interviewed in Portuguese, the national language, which I speak fluently). In short, we saw people taking control of their lives and working for the common good. I was most impressed with a tea plantation we visited near the Zimbabwe border. It was run by a minister

who infused the operation with God and discipline, and many of the
workers were refugees from Zimbabwe. They not only worked on the
plantation, they were taught to read and write, too, and perhaps most
important, they shared in the profits. Everyone had an economic
stake and that, I believe, is the crux of the development dilemma:
finding a way to give people a financial stake in the fruits of their
labors.

As mentioned early in this book, I have tried to give back to the
various communities of which I have been a part, whether my alma
maters, Roxbury Latin School and Bowdoin College, or the Massachusetts General Hospital, where Salua and I started a foundation
to fund mental health research, or the synagogue in my mother's
hometown of Bath, Maine. But on the trip to Mozambique, I realized
that all of my travels had made me part of a far larger community. At
the risk of sounding Pollyannaish, having made my fortune globe-
trotting from Brazil to Vietnam, El Salvador to Iraq, and many other
places in between, I had truly become a global citizen during the
most intensive period of globalization in human history. And in Mozambique, I saw the world that had made me rich in a new light.

During the years when I was searching for riches among the ruins,
wherever I traveled I was always looking for opportunities to make
money. Not that I was indifferent to the suffering I saw around me,
whether it was the violence of the civil war that touched so many
Salvadorans, the war-weary Vietnamese, or the impoverished street
urchins of Lagos, Nigeria. I was well aware of the deprivation, but at
the same time I was disconnected from it. I was scrambling to make
a success of myself, driven perhaps by the distinction of having graduated last in my class at Roxbury Latin and the need to prove myself
to a mother and father I seemed to forever disappoint. I was, in a
sense, in a glass house as I traveled through the developing world,

staying in Western hotels (though even some of these, as in Lagos, were severely lacking) and meeting with each country's movers and shakers: the bankers, the ministers, and the diplomats. I was not, as I was in Mozambique, looking squarely into the eyes of hungry children, young mothers dying of AIDS, and thirty-year-old men who looked twice their age.

The annual per capita income in Mozambique when I visited in 2004 was approximately $200, less than my monthly electric bill. More than half the adult population was, and remains, illiterate. Nearly 200 of every 1,000 children born in Mozambique die in infancy, and more than a million of the country's 18 million citizens are infected with HIV/AIDS. You can read about the devastation wreaked by HIV/AIDS, but until you have visited a clinic or hospital in a country like Mozambique, all underfunded and understaffed, you simply cannot grasp the magnitude of the suffering. The average life expectancy in Mozambique is 42.1 years, the second lowest in the world. Yet, despite the obvious hardships, the country is filled with the sounds of laughter, and Mozambicans greet you with warmth and a ready, genuine smile. Amid the ruins they may not have found riches, but they have found hope.

During our trip in 2004, I saw the developing world, where I had made my fortune, from an entirely new perspective. Yes, the debts of these countries could be bought and sold, but beneath this mountain of debt were people struggling to make a future for themselves. And making a market for these debts played a modest role in easing the crushing debt burdens carried by their governments. Once I bought and sold their unloved bonds and promissory notes, it gave those instruments a quasi-liquidity that encouraged future transactions and established a benchmark by which the international financial community could gauge their worth. Furthermore, many of the bonds and promissory notes I sold were converted, in debt/equity swaps, into local businesses that provided local jobs and helped grow local economies. By creating markets for a country's debt where none existed, I was, in a small way, making it easier and safer for foreign investment

to flow into developing countries. But, still, what I did was far removed from changing lives on the street or in the villages, and my
motives were personal and financial, not philanthropic.

I am not going to tell you that my life radically changed, or that
I gave up all my worldly possessions to live among the earth's poor
after my trip to Mozambique. I am not Mother Teresa. But I left the
country with a more layered and nuanced understanding of the world
in which I had worked for so many years. And I also began to think
a lot about how perspective can be hard to come by when you are
especially close to something. I had traveled repeatedly to the developing world, including many African countries, Nigeria, Zambia,
Tanzania, and Angola among them, but I was so focused on my business that there was much I missed. Mozambique showed me what I
had failed to see.

Mozambique also started me thinking about another country I
thought I knew well: the United States. What, I wondered, might I
see if my perspective was altered, as it had been in Mozambique?
What if I could see my own country through the lens that I used to
assess my business prospects in El Salvador, Nigeria, or Guatemala?

As readers well know by now, I often arrived in cities such as
San Salvador, Lagos, or Guatemala City on reconnaissance missions,
paying visits to banks, businessmen, and diplomats while trying to
get the lay of the financial and economic landscape. My education
about a country—my diagnosis of its economic condition—began at
the airport and continued in the cab as I picked the brains of the
driver about local conditions while scanning the view for more clues
about the state of the economy. The cleaner and more orderly the
streets, for example, the more prosperous the country. Hordes of
money changers trying to buy dollars on the black market signaled
a country in distress. Currency controls—efforts by governments to

restrict money flowing out of the country (always counterproductive)—was a sure sign of economic desperation. This wasn't economic science; it was economic impressionism, but it was always helpful.

What if, metaphorically speaking, I flew into Kennedy Airport from abroad, took a cab to Manhattan, and starting making my usual rounds? What would I see? What would I learn? Would I see a country in which I'd want to invest?

As I write this book in mid-2008, the U.S. economy is in turmoil. The subprime lending disaster, falling home prices, the credit crunch, huge write-downs by major financial institutions, low consumer confidence, the soaring price of oil, a volatile stock market, massive budget and trade deficits, a falling dollar, rising unemployment, huge indebtedness, and a looming recession—all have combined to make these the most uncertain, even frightening economic times since the Great Depression.

Kennedy Airport would certainly be a major step up from many of the airports I have flown into over the years. It reflects the nation's affluence and shining modernity. But there's a reasonable chance that the U.S. carrier I flew with is just climbing out of, or about to go into, bankruptcy, or it is about to merge with another airline to survive. At customs, I can count on reasonably fast and efficient service, without being shaken down for a small bribe or "commission" (as would happen in many other parts of the world), another indicator of a country's economic health.

But some of the luster might begin to dissipate during the cab ride. Though I wouldn't have to worry about being driven onto a side road and robbed (as in Russia) or threatened by an unruly mob (as in Nigeria), the cab would probably be a gas-guzzling older model Ford or Chevrolet made by a company hemorrhaging cash and being beaten badly in the marketplace by Japanese or Korean competitors.

Whether driven by an American or one of the legions of immigrants who make up New York's cadre of cabbies, I would no doubt hear from them that times were tough. Gas prices? Unaffordable.

House? Maybe skirting foreclosure. Income? Working two jobs to make ends meet.

The bridges into Manhattan? Crumbling with no funds for repairs. The Manhattan skyline, the towers of capitalism, would still look impressive, but are their foundations, again metaphorically speaking, strong? If we walked around some of the towers near Wall Street, we would see some rot because, disturbingly, the United States, the world's foremost military power and, until recently, the undisputed greatest economic power, is exhibiting economic symptoms that once characterized only the world's poorest countries.

I always used to describe a country's economic condition in medical terms. A country staying afloat on IMF and World Bank loans, for example, was a country on life support. A country that had defaulted on its debts and was trying to renegotiate them was a country in cardiac arrest and in need of resuscitation. A country on the verge of default was in critical condition. Today, I would describe the United States as ailing and on the verge of hospitalization. If we continue to pile up debt as we have for the past eight years, and if the dollar continues to fall, and if oil (priced at more than $135 a barrel as I write) continues to climb, this country, economically speaking, could become seriously and even chronically ill.

Though the United States is beginning to exhibit symptoms I once associated only with developing-world countries, I don't want to overstate the analogy because there are many significant reasons why the United States is not, and will never be, a "third world" country, and I'll come to them momentarily. But it is worth considering the parallels, because we Americans, so close to the situation, don't have perspective on just how far our great country has fallen in recent years. As I did in Mozambique, it is worthwhile shifting perspective.

One of El Salvador's biggest exports, both in the 1980s and today, is people. Countless Salvadorans (and migrants from many other developing-world countries) come to the States, legally or illegally, to earn money to send home. Those remittances are a big part of the global economy and keep many national economies afloat. So far, Americans aren't flocking overseas to work, but we are sending something similar abroad: jobs. We are exporting jobs and then buying— that is, importing—the goods and services those jobs produce. In the process we are not only running up huge trade deficits (simply put, the difference between the value of our exports and our imports), but we are running up huge debt, both personal debt and the national debt.

The United States is now the world's largest debtor nation. We owe more than $9 trillion to lenders, much of that to foreign countries that are financing our debt through the purchase of various U.S. Treasury securities. In early 2008, Japan, the largest holder, owned more than $586 billion in such securities; China, the second largest holder, owned nearly $487 billion.* It isn't just that we are borrowing to pay for imports ranging from oil to dolls to barbecue grills; we're borrowing to pay for the war in Iraq, too. Individual Americans are, on average, deeply in debt, and so are their local, state, and federal governments. Indeed, our national debt has grown so large that every American citizen now owes, metaphorically speaking, approximately $40,000.

One of the characteristics I always associated with developing-world countries was a staggering amount of debt. And it's not just that we are deeply in debt. When it comes to buying goods manufactured in China, for example, goods once made by American hands in America, we are borrowing money from the Chinese *to pay the Chi-*

---

*The gross domestic product (GDP) of the United States is about $13 trillion. This kind of debt-to-GDP ratio is the kind of dismal economic news that would have the IMF and creditors screaming for better fiscal management if the country were Nicaragua, Zambia, or any of dozens of developing-world countries.

nese. Twenty or thirty years ago, this situation would have been un-thinkable.

Walk the aisles of a Wal-Mart or a Home Depot and look at where goods are manufactured. A strong manufacturing base is one important indicator of a first-world nation, but America's manufacturing base has been dwindling for decades. We are, in a sense, a victim of our own success. Our affluence made it very expensive to produce goods at home as the costs of wages, health care, and energy rose, making it cheaper, for example, to buy steel from India or Brazil than from Pittsburgh.

The U.S. trade deficit is now running in the neighborhood of $70 billion per month, or more than $2 billion a day. That means we send $70 billion more overseas each month to buy goods and services than we collect for the goods and services we produce at home and sell abroad.

As I write, the value of the dollar against major foreign currencies has plummeted by as much as 40 percent and is weaker than it has been in more than thirty years. For the first time since 1976, an American dollar is worth less than a Canadian dollar. Why currencies rise and fall is a complex issue that could fill several textbooks. Suffice it to say that it is the market's way of rendering a verdict about the underlying strength of an economy, and that verdict, in the global information and digital age, is rendered minute by minute by traders at computer screens all over the world.

As the dollar loses value, American assets become cheaper for foreigners to buy. As an article in *Newsweek* succinctly put it, "Big American banks like Citibank used to fund Third World governments—now those governments are buying Citibank on the cheap." When a country like El Salvador, Nigeria, or Iraq gets deeply into debt, there isn't necessarily a rush to buy up its banks, factories, and real estate because they are politically unstable, often dangerous places to be. But when those assets become relatively cheap and are located in a country that boasts political stability and highly functional legal, tax, and financial systems, the rush is on.

The falling dollar has other potentially devastating consequences. For decades the dollar has been the world's reserve currency of choice. When foreign countries put money in the bank to pay their international obligations, it is primarily dollars they are banking. The dollar was appealing because its value typically held steady, and the dollar held steady because people, and countries, had faith in the long-term growth of the U.S. economy.

The dollar is still the world's de facto international currency. Major international commodities such as oil and gold are priced in dollars. But when the value of the dollar begins to fall, not only does your purchasing power and mine take a hit, but countries like China, with huge stockpiles of dollars, take a hit, too. Suddenly, buying all those U.S. Treasury notes, the interest on which is paid in dollars, is less appealing—unless, of course, the interest rate goes up to compensate. And when the interest rate goes up, it requires more and more dollars to finance our trade deficits, our budget deficits, and our wars, all of which are being run on borrowed money.

Our trade imbalance and enormous foreign debt owe much, of course, to our thirst for oil. The United States imports about 9 million barrels of oil every day. And where does the money go? To Hugo Chavez in Venezuela, and the Saudis, and the Russians, regimes that don't necessarily have our best interests at heart.

One prominent characteristic of the developing-world countries in which I did business was their dependence on bigger powers. These were countries that could barely survive without the goods and services (and foreign assistance) provided by wealthier nations to whom they became deeply indebted, economically and politically. Disturbingly, the United States increasingly finds itself dependent on friends and foes alike, not only for the oil on which our entire economy is based, but even for basics such as barbecue grills. In this country, which invented barbecue, many of the backyard grills we now buy are made in China. When this country can't even make its own barbecue grills at a competitive price, you know you have a problem.

And it isn't just our dependence on outside sources for energy and goods. Venerable U.S. banks and financial institutions like Citigroup and Merrill Lynch have been in need of bailouts or large cash infusions to cover huge losses, and increasingly that money is coming in the form of investments by so-called sovereign wealth funds, investment pools owned by foreign governments looking to do better than the returns they are getting from our treasury notes.

Another characteristic of countries in the developing world is a gross disparity in the wealth of the masses and the wealth of a privileged few. In the United States, the wealth and income gap has risen steadily for the past half century. We see it not only in executive pay, which has risen to obscene levels in many cases, but in the concentration of wealth in the hands of the top one percent of the population. The middle class, where one could expect to live a life of relative comfort—an important indicator of a strong country with a strong economy—is dwindling, and those holding on are increasingly squeezed.

There will always be, of course, pockets of poverty even in rich nations; pockets that bear a resemblance to the way millions of people live in some of the world's poorest countries. But that poverty is often invisible to most people. This is certainly true in the United States. The inner city of Newark and the remote mountains of West Virginia are places few of us ever travel. But then Hurricane Katrina threw back the curtain on a racial and economic divide that we often whisper about but rarely confront. Poverty in the United States is remarkably resilient. In the developing world, when natural disaster strikes, it is almost always the poorest who suffer the most because they are often the most exposed. Their housing is worse, they have few resources to help them cope, they have no means of escape, and their infrastructure is poor. When monsoons strike the Bay of Bengal, millions of Bangladeshis living at sea level find their world inundated by water. In New Orleans, it was no different, and the poor paid the biggest price. The infrastructure (the levee system) that was supposed to save them proved to be their ruin.

Most Americans were shocked by the images of Katrina's aftermath, especially the scenes of thousands of refugees, mainly black and marginalized in our capitalist system, living in the squalor of the Louisiana Superdome. They couldn't believe that what they were seeing was happening in America, not in some third-world country.

If a modern infrastructure—bridges, levees, the electric grid, the highway system, and so on—is a sign of a first-world country, and if a dilapidated one is a typical characteristic of a third-world country, then the United States is slipping slowly down the scale. According to the federal government, for example, some 77,000 bridges in the United States need urgent repairs that would cost billions of dollars if the country is to prevent another deadly bridge collapse such as the one that occurred in Minneapolis in 2007. Yes, our water is mostly safe to drink, our food supply mostly safe (though it seems even that is called into question more frequently these days), and we have a remarkably developed and robust infrastructure. But the cracks are showing, and given our already-massive debt, where is the money going to come from to make the future investments needed to keep our basic infrastructure robust? (Of course, it's all about choices. A fair share of the massive borrowing and deficit spending we are doing is funding the Iraq War. As always, every dollar spent on guns is a dollar that isn't available to be spent on butter.)

In many developing-world countries, military spending and war (civil or other) account for a substantial proportion of the foreign debt that keeps people in poverty and squeezes out investments in health, education, and social development. In 2006, according to the widely respected Stockholm International Peace Research Institute, global military spending reached $1.204 trillion, of which the U.S. share was a staggering 46 percent. It is all the more staggering when you consider that the next four highest spenders on the military were the United Kingdom, France, Japan, and China, each of which was responsible for just 4 percent to 5 percent of that $1.2 trillion total. *Russia wasn't even in the top five.*

There are some people who argue that U.S. military spending since 2001, including the wars in Afghanistan and Iraq, is a leading cause of our economic woes today, while others point out that military spending, at about 4 percent of GDP, is affordable. Indeed, U.S. military spending has been high in good economic times, too. I will leave it to the economists and academics to slug this one out, but just as many of the developing-world countries I visited were heavily militarized or at war, and devoting precious resources to preparing for or fighting wars, so, too, is the United States spending a huge proportion of its wealth for the same purpose. And, most worrisome, we are borrowing to do it.* This doesn't mean there is no war worth fighting, but it does mean one should be wary of wars of choice built on false premises.

In short, looking at my own country today with the same critical eye with which I have examined developing-world countries for their long-term economic potential, I see distressing signs that we have slipped down the scale that has developing-world nations at one end and its most advanced at the other. Make no mistake. The United States is a long way from becoming a third- or even a second-world country. I am simply saying that our preeminence at the high end of the scale can no longer be taken for granted. Budget deficits, trade deficits, astronomical foreign debt (again, owed not to friendly bankers but to creditor nations whose interests are not our own), loss of our manufacturing base, the export of millions of jobs, an aging infrastructure, a rapidly weakening dollar, the collapse of the housing market, oil dependence, and massive borrowing—all give me pause.

---

*According to former U.S. Comptroller General David Walker, it is Medicare spending, not military spending, that threatens to swamp the economic ship of state within the next thirty years or so. Current commitments made to American workers, the aging baby boom generation, and health care costs that are rising at twice the rate of inflation—all contribute to a looming crisis that no politician wants to touch. In fact, all health care spending in the United States is a world-high 15.4 percent of GDP.

Yet, would I invest here? You bet I would. I am an economic optimist first and foremost. I made millions of dollars betting that even countries at the bottom of the development barrel would someday crawl out from under their debt and make good on their promises to pay. I believed in El Salvador when it was at war with itself. I believed in impoverished, militarized Guatemala and in Turkey when it was the "sick man" of Europe. I believed—oh, did I ever believe—in Russia when it was about to veer off a cliff, when it fell off the cliff, and when it managed to get back on its feet. I believed in Nigeria in its darkest days of corruption and crushing foreign debt. I believe, with less conviction, in Iraq today, but I would still buy its bonds because, like AIG, Iraq is too "big" (that is, too important) to the United States, to be allowed to fail.* If I believed in those countries, where the rule of law was often the rule of one man, where markets and financial institutions were virtually unregulated and nontransparent, where tax and securities laws were practically nonexistent and currencies often worthless outside their country of origin, then I am certainly going to be bullish on the United States.

Notwithstanding all of its economic woes and symptoms I once associated with the economies of the developing world, the United States is still a country where riches can be made in what appear, increasingly, to be ruins. At the end of the day, the United States remains differentiated from many of the countries where I did business, and those differences inspire long-term confidence. I have already alluded to many of those differences, but let's go through them one by one.

First, the United States is a politically stable democracy where the rule of law prevails and property rights are respected. In developing-world countries, investors are at the mercy of many forces outside

---

*I am speaking only of Iraq's debt, not the war effort, which is, in my view, almost certain to fail because of our failure to understand the consequences of our actions, a lack of strategic vision, and a fundamental misjudgment about the nature of the conflict we were entering.

of their control. In politically unstable countries, where a military coup may be the most common means of changing governments, investors cannot take anything for granted. Property may be nationalized and appropriated without compensation. There is often no legal recourse when deals go bad. By contrast, our highly developed, highly regulated, and transparent markets, our auditing and accounting standards (notwithstanding some spectacular failures such as Enron and WorldCom), and our legal system provide reassurance and predictability that is typically absent in developing-world countries.* It may not work perfectly, and people get hurt, but shareholder class-action suits, criminal penalties, and regulatory oversight by government agencies help ensure a modicum of recourse and stability.

Indeed, our system is self-correcting to a large extent. Failures, whether they be in auditing and reporting or inadequate controls over financial products (subprime mortgage loans, for example), tend to result, through our political process, in reforms. While these failures can mean plenty of economic pain and misery in the short run, the response to them augurs well over the long haul. Will there be future breakdowns that rock the foundations of our economy? Almost certainly. But our fallible legal, regulatory, and financial systems nevertheless keep us from operating as Russia did, for example, where the early days of capitalism were a chaotic mess.

A highly literate, educated, and relatively cohesive population, a first-rate higher education system, and a highly productive, innovative workforce also differentiate the United States from many of the developing-world countries where I have worked. We may argue over everything from gay rights to guns, stem-cell research, and abortion,

---

*Whether our markets are regulated enough is a question that repeatedly arises, especially when crises such as the subprime lending debacle arise. Whether our markets, our financial institutions, and our corporations are underregulated or overregulated is a question that will be debated ad infinitum. My point here is that by comparison, markets, financial institutions, and corporations in the United States operate in a framework that provides relative predictability and stability when compared with the developing world.

but we aren't, as so many developing-world countries are, divided by tribalism (Nigeria) or religion (Iraq, where there is even division among two sects, Shia and Sunni, *of the same religion*). We are not, as the Salvadorans were, fighting a civil war over our political differences. In short, we aren't killing one another over economics or politics.* We can lay claim to more distinguished institutions of higher learning than any country on the planet (foreign students come here in droves to study at them), and American workers continue to lead the world in technological innovation across many disciplines.

Lastly, while millions of people still flock to our shores in search of a better economic future, the line of Americans queued up to leave the country to escape economic hard times is virtually nonexistent. That tells you a lot right there.

In short, the United States, for all its economic problems, is and will remain a stable and relatively predictable place to invest, create a business, and thrive. And notwithstanding the challenges to American economic preeminence, the United States, with only 5 percent of the world's population, remains in absolute terms and by a wide margin the global leader in industrial output, manufacturing output, and services output. Our GDP is more than 25 percent of the world's total. The United States also ranks first in global competitiveness as measured by 259 criteria, including openness of the economy, development of financial markets, infrastructure, technology, and political and judicial institutions. It also ranks first in innovation, a measure that includes adoption of new technology and interaction between business and science. Eight of the eleven largest businesses in the world are U.S. companies, as are three of the five largest banks. And our stock market capitalization is nearly five times as high as the

---

*We are, unfortunately, killing one another in staggering numbers, thanks, in part, to the ready availability of guns, but we don't have warring factions in this country that are trying to settle their differences by force of arms. We slug it out on the talk shows and in the newspapers.

second largest stock market in the world, which is Japan's.* In short, the positive side of the ledger still looks pretty good.

No serious person today would refute the inevitability of the process we call globalization. It is a phenomenon that can be managed, but not controlled or stopped, and on balance, it has been good for the United States and good for the developing world, too. If I ever needed proof of the inevitability of globalization, it came during a 'round the world trip I took in early 2008. I had decided that for three weeks I would try to take a break from keeping up with the world news—no easy feat for me because I am a complete news junkie. But even in Timbuktu, in the African country of Mali, I was unable to honor my self-imposed moratorium, for even there, in a city whose name has come to be synonymous with remote desolation, I could watch CNN and the BBC via satellite on the television set in my hotel room. Even the baggage handler at the airport was carrying a cell phone. People can take to the streets to protest globalization, but they may as well be protesting the fact that the sun rises in the east.

Having spent much of the past thirty years wandering the streets of countries that have been brought into the global economy, I see globalization as a positive force in the world, even though global economic interdependence has its price. You can see it in the way financial crises tend to spread like viruses across borders.

In my view, the biggest challenge we face in a global economy is one we face in our own country, and it is something I alluded to earlier: the growing gap between rich and poor. Here at home, the vast middle class is shrinking while a handful of hedge fund managers

---

*The various rankings are based on data in *The Economist Pocket World in Figures*, 2008 edition (London: Profile Books).

are taking home paychecks as high as $3.7 billion—*in a single year.* (That is an actual figure in the case of John Paulson of Paulson & Co.) While enormous wealth has always been concentrated in the hands of a relative few in America (as was true in Central America in the twentieth century as well, and one of the major reasons many of those countries found themselves at war), the problem is getting much worse, and it *is* a problem, as even some of those at the very top, such as Warren Buffett, will tell you. Indeed, in 2005, then chairman of the Federal Reserve Alan Greenspan succinctly described the problem this way with respect to the United States: "The income gap between the rich and the rest of the U.S. population has become so wide, and is growing so fast, that it might eventually threaten the stability of democratic capitalism itself."

As countries such as Nigeria and Russia realize their oil wealth, tens of millions of their own citizens continue to live in poverty. Worldwide, as in Mozambique, billions of people live lives of deprivation most Americans cannot even begin to imagine. I don't pretend to have an answer for these problems, but as someone who has traveled the world as both an economic mercenary and a concerned citizen, I see this as perhaps the greatest moral and economic challenge facing the world today.

Looking back over four decades that have taken me from the jungles of Vietnam to the chaos of post-Saddam Iraq, it is clear that the riches I found among the ruins were not simply the kind of riches I can count by looking at my bank statement. When I was a young collections lawyer and miserable in my work, my life, as far as I was concerned, lay in ruins. My prospects were dim. I thought I would continue to labor under my father's wing until he retired, at which time I would take over his law practice and spend the rest of my life sending out my demand letters and opening envelopes containing the payments of small debts. It was this prospect that first led me to Vietnam, just as my experience in collections first took me to Turkey.

You now know the rest of the story, too. From something I hated I found, as my wife said, something I loved. I didn't realize it when I began this book, but the real riches I pulled from the ruins weren't the spreads on my bond deals. The riches came from a lifetime of unforgettable experiences in some of the most exotic and remote corners of the world—riches that I pulled from the ruins of my own young life. Don't get me wrong. I loved the thrill of the deal, and I loved making money. But I have always believed that it's not how much money you make, but how you make your money that matters most. And making money while indulging a life's passion is the best of all possible worlds.

ACKNOWLEDGMENTS

NO BOOK IS A SOLO ENDEAVOR, and I am deeply grateful to many people who helped to make this one possible.

I started ruminating over the possibility of writing a book about my adventures in business almost a decade ago. Frequently, I sought and received sage counsel from Robert Lenzner, John Spooner, and Frank Partnoy, all accomplished business writers and learned men. My profound appreciation to all of them.

Saleh Daher and I have been business partners for more than twenty years. Saleh has often tamed my more impulsive instincts and I am richer, literally, for it. It has always been a joy to come to work with Saleh, and he made many valuable contributions to this book. He corrected my sometimes-faulty memories and helped resurrect others.

Other colleagues at Turan Corporation also helped in myriad ways. My assistant, Karen Waldron, keeps me organized (an uphill battle at times), and Beth Kalafa and Robert Towler held down the fort while I was immersed in writing this book.

A number of other people read chapters and sections of the manuscript and provided valuable insight. I am indebted to Alan J. Cushner, Joshua Goldstein, James R. Hammond, Frederick Z. Jasperson, Kent A. Lucken, Jeffrey P. Ross, Alan Trustman, and Jeffrey Waxman. If I have overlooked anyone, my sincere apologies.

I am most grateful as well to a number of people who helped me reconstruct events from many years ago: Peter Bartlett, Laurence Bergreen, Keith Berman, Paul Caseiras, Adam Cleary, Catherine Cullen, Carl C. Cundiff, Peter Daniel, Fulvio V. Dobrich, Lorenz Fischer-Zernin, Valerie Friedman, Hans Humes, Lynn Kessler, Peter Lazaro, Gervase MacGregor, Peter Marber, Ricardo Angel Matesanz, Bob McCarthy, Robert S. Minton, Stefan Pinter, Sophie Pompea, Frank T. Riess, Albino Roman, Theodore R. Sayers, Martin W. Schubert, Victor Segal, Faruk Seyrek, James F. Summers, Richard S. Weinert, and Arthur Winn. If I have inadvertently omitted anyone, I trust they will forgive my oversight.

Two writers collaborated with me on this book. Gay Walley helped get this book off the ground by taking my ramblings and giving them some structure. She was also an indefatigable interviewer who spoke at length with dozens of people in my business and others with whom I had worked over the years. In short, Gay did yeoman's work gathering much of the raw material that formed the basis of this book.

Despite Gay's efforts, the book languished in my lap for a long while. A couple of years later, I met a distant cousin, Peter Zheutlin. Peter was working on a book about a common ancestor of ours, Annie "Londonderry" Kopchovsky, who, in 1894, left her husband and three small children in Boston to bicycle around the world, becoming the first woman ever to attempt the feat. Peter called me at the suggestion of his mother, my second cousin Baila, to see if I knew anything about Annie's story. Alas, like his mother, I had never even heard of Annie. But, Peter and I met and eventually decided to work together to resurrect my dream of writing my own book. Peter has often commented on the similarities between our ancestor and me: both of us sought our fortune while traveling the globe. Peter had no background in business or economics, which turned out to be a blessing in disguise. He made sure this book would be accessible to the lay reader and kept it from getting bogged down in the esoterica of international finance, which is my niche. I am grateful to both Gay Walley and Peter Zheutlin for their invaluable contributions.

My agent, Joelle Delbourgo, represented me with enthusiasm and skill. She is a consummate professional, and I am deeply appreciative of her efforts.

My editor at AMACOM, Bob Nirkind, was always enthusiastic and encouraging, and his careful editing and thoughtful suggestions always improved the manuscript. Karen Brogno, my copyeditor, also did a fine job polishing the text. Thanks, too, to Jim Bessent, associate editor at AMACOM, for all of his help moving the book through the production process.

Finally, I have been blessed with a wonderful, supportive family that not only tolerated my globe-trotting, but encouraged it, understanding that it brought me great joy in living. My wife, Salua, my daughter, Fiona, and my son, Edward, mean the world to me. I am deeply, deeply grateful for their love and support in all things.

INDEX

Robert P. Smith is the founder and managing director of Turan Corporation, a Boston-based investment firm that pioneered the trading of obligations of developing countries. Mr. Smith has served on the boards of various educational and non-profit organizations including the Caribbean/Latin American Action Committee and the Massachusetts Trade Advisory Board. As an officer with the Agency for International Development, U.S. Department of State in the late 1960s and early 1970s, Mr. Smith was stationed in Vietnam, the Dominican Republic, El Salvador, and Brazil. Mr. Smith is a graduate of Bowdoin College and Boston University School of Law. He lives in Boston and New York City with his wife, Salua.

Peter Zheutlin is a freelance journalist and author whose work appears regularly in the *Boston Globe* and the *Christian Science Monitor*. Mr. Zheutlin has also written for the *New York Times*, *AARP Magazine*, and numerous other publications. He is the author of *Around the World on Two Wheels: Annie Londonderry's Extraordinary Ride* (Citadel Press, 2007) and the co-author, with Thomas B. Graboys, M.D., of *Life in the Balance: A Physician's Memoir of Life, Love and Loss with Parkinson's Disease and Dementia* (Union Square Press, 2008).